Quick Fixes

The Jacobin series features short interrogations of politics, economics, and culture from a socialist perspective, as an avenue to radical political practice. The books offer critical analysis and engagement with the history and ideas of the Left in an accessible format.

The series is a collaboration between Verso Books and Jacobin magazine, which is published quarterly in print and online at jacobinmag.com.

Other titles in this series available from Verso Books:
Class War by Megan Erickson
Building the Commune by George Ciccariello-Maher
People's Republic of Walmart by Leigh Phillips and Michal Rozworski
Red State Revolt by Eric Blanc
Capital City by Samuel Stein
Without Apology by Jenny Brown
All-American Nativism by Daniel Denvir
A Planet to Win by Kate Aronoff, Alyssa Battistoni, Daniel Aldana
    Cohen, and Thea Riofrancos
Toward Freedom by Touré F. Reed
Yesterday's Man by Branko Marcetic
The Panthers Can't Save Us Now by Cedric Johnson

Quick Fixes

Drugs in America from Prohibition to the 21st-Century Binge

Benjamin Y. Fong

VERSO

London • New York

First published by Verso 2023

Excerpt from "Sam Stone"
Words and music by John Prine
© 1971 (Renewed) COTILLION MUSIC INC.
All Rights Administered by WC MUSIC CORP. All Rights Reserved.
Used by Permission of ALFRED MUSIC.

1 3 5 7 9 10 8 6 4 2

Verso
UK: 6 Meard Street, London W1F 0EG
US: 388 Atlantic Avenue, Brooklyn, NY 11217
versobooks.com

Verso is the imprint of New Left Books

ISBN-13: 978-1-80429-017-0
ISBN-13: 978-1-80429-019-4 (UK EBK)
ISBN-13: 978-1-80429-020-0 (US EBK)

British Library Cataloguing in Publication Data
A catalogue record for this book is available from the British Library

Library of Congress Cataloging-in-Publication Data

Names: Fong, Benjamin Y., author.
Title: Quick fixes : drugs in America from Prohibition to the 21st-century
binge / Benjamin Y. Fong.
Description: London ; New York : Verso, 2023. | Series: The Jacobin series
| Includes bibliographical references.
Identifiers: LCCN 2022058907 (print) | LCCN 2022058908 (ebook) | ISBN
9781804290170 (hardback) | ISBN 9781804290200 (ebook)
Subjects: LCSH: Drug abuse—United States—History. | Drugs of
abuse—United States—History. | Psychotropic drugs—United
States—History.
Classification: LCC HV5825 .F65 2023 (print) | LCC HV5825 (ebook) | DDC
362.290973—dc23/eng/20230313
LC record available at https://lccn.loc.gov/2022058907
LC ebook record available at https://lccn.loc.gov/2022058908

Typeset in Sabon by MJ & N Gavan, Truro, Cornwall
Printed and bound by CPI Group (UK) Ltd, Croydon, CR0 4YY

Sweet songs never last too long on broken radios.

— John Prine, "Sam Stone"

Contents

Introduction   1

1. Coffee, or the Serene Delight   23
2. Cigarettes, or Knowledge Is Not Power   37
3. Alcohol, or Commodity Fetishism   57
4. Opiates, or Civilizing the Orient   77
5. Amphetamines, or Inappropriate Perseverance   97
6. Psychotropics, or Diagnostic Creeps and Rational Paranoids   113
7. Psychedelics, or the Dialectic of Control   133
    Addendum on Peyote   149
    Addendum on Dissociative Anesthetics   153
8. Cocaine, or Hyperreality   157
9. Marijuana, or Profit Wins in the End   177

Conclusion   193

Appendices
    A: Psychoactive Drug Use Trends in the United States   204
    B: Timeline of Drug Discovery   209
    C: Key Dates in Psychoactive Drug History   211

Acknowledgments   219
Notes   221

Introduction

American drug use today is truly world historical. At 4 percent of the earth's population, Americans consume 80 percent of its opioids, including 99 percent of its hydrocodone, and 83 percent of its attention deficit hyperactivity disorder (ADHD) medications.[1] One in three Americans suffers from anxiety, depression, or both (globally, that number is about one in twenty), and one in six is on a psychiatric medication.[2] The $500 billion per year we spend on pharmaceuticals is complemented by another $150 billion per year on illegal drugs.[3] By any measure, we are a uniquely *drugged* society. When the sun sets on the land of the free, the owl of Minerva will simply fall off its branch in an intoxicated haze.

During the twenty-first century, every metric of American drug consumption has gone through the roof. The opioid crisis is the most familiar part of this trend, but marijuana, antidepressant, antipsychotic, amphetamine, and benzodiazepine use have all shot up as well. The most tragic development has been the escalation of drug overdoses, primarily responsible for the precipitous rise in American deaths of despair.[4] While the scale of drug use in modern America is novel, the United States has had a torrid love affair with drugs for well over a century. Global cocaine consumption in the '80s was driven by Americans, who, according to one report, spent over $60 billion on almost 400 tons of cocaine in 1988 alone.[5] The story of psychedelics is inextricably bound to that of the American counterculture in the '60s. Amphetamine, barbiturate, and benzodiazepine use was fully normalized in postwar America. And the late nineteenth- to early twentieth-century American

"Commuter Drugstore," from the New Yorker, August 11, 1956. © 1956 Charles Addams. © renewed 1985 by Charles Addams. With permission from Tee and Charles Addams Foundation.

"patent medicine" industry was enormous, with an estimated 50,000 proprietary nostrums (often containing alcohol, opium, cocaine, cannabis, chloral hydrate, and other psychoactive substances) on the market at the turn of the century.[6] "Of all the nations of the world," early drug policy architect Hamilton Wright told the *New York Times Magazine* in 1911, "the United States consumes most habit-forming drugs per capita."[7]

What's curious about the American appetite for drugs is that it's attended by an equally unique *fearmongering* about drugs. Not only the success but the very goals of the American moral reform movements in the late nineteenth and early twentieth centuries attest to a distinctive enthusiasm. The very idea of total *prohibition* would have struck most people in the early nineteenth century as absurd, more of a pipe dream than a nightmare.[8] Not only did Americans make it happen in dramatic and blundering fashion, but they also led the early twentieth-century efforts to suppress the opium and cocaine trades.[9] Though contradictory, selectively enforced, racially biased, socially destructive, and a failure on its own terms, this project of punitive prohibition continues on to the present, in the lingering and ever shameful War on Drugs.

The historian Richard Davenport-Hines best lays out the stakes of modern drug history: "All the most important problems in drug history since the 1860s could be resolved by a clear answer to one question: what is so distinctive about the United States?"[10]

The Underlying Narrative

The individual chapters of this book follow a certain explanatory arc, but they can also be read in any order as standalone pieces.[11] Each provides a unique historical lens through which it is possible to catch glimpses of the character of American society. Many chapters start outside US national borders to chart the evolution of meanings, trends, and technologies that the United States has absorbed and sharpened. And many others follow the links in the networks of production and distribution that supply the United States with its mountain of medications. This is an inevitably global journey, but it's centered in the dynamics of American capitalism.

While each psychoactive drug or class of drugs has its own story to tell, the book is also held together by an underlying narrative connecting drug attitudes and consumption patterns to different historical modes of capitalist society. Not every detail fits neatly into the story, but it is a helpful enough preliminary answer to Davenport-Hines's guiding question. The narrative is broken into four parts.

The first begins in the late nineteenth century, when the temperance cause really took off as a national movement. For much of the nineteenth century, a wide variety of drugs that would later gain very different connotations—opium, tobacco, alcohol—were all culturally acceptable and widely available.[12] In addition, the drug and alcohol "traffic" at the time was enormously profitable for a wide range of planters, merchants, traders, and investors, and a key source of state revenue.[13] So why the eventual move to prohibition?

Simply put, with industrialization and urbanization, poor and working-class drug and alcohol use became more escapist, more visible, and more dangerous. An intoxicated workforce in an increasingly mechanized world was simply unacceptable to a modern, capitalist sensibility.[14] This period produced the first major narcotics regulation, the Harrison Narcotics Tax Act in 1914; Prohibition from 1920 to 1933; and most of the connotations associated with "drug fiends" and the criminal underworld they inhabit. Industrial capitalism unleashed a new kind of evil, but given the peculiar dominance of the American ruling class and the corresponding appearance of the *immutability* of capitalism, reformers naturally invested in moral rather than structural changes to American society.

The second phase in the narrative roughly corresponds to the so-called "Fordist-Keynesian" period, a time of stable economic growth shared in by the working class.[15] The era's new ethos of consumerism broke the temperance cause for good, ushering in a long period of sanctioned drug use. Amphetamines, barbiturates, benzodiazepines, cigarettes, alcohol, and a variety of other uppers and downers were all acceptable substances at this time, and they were all used for the purpose of conforming to the new Fordist paradigm.

The end of World War II also saw the United States become the global hegemon, the undisputed center of international capitalism. This pursuit of world dominance led America to become both home to the largest pharmaceutical industry in the world and involved in either tacitly approving or actively supporting some of the major international illegal drug production and distribution operations, including those in the Golden Triangle and the Golden Crescent. *We Sell Drugs* is the blunt title of a book by historian Suzanna Reiss about the seizure of control over international drug flows in the postwar period.[16]

The third phase begins with the neoliberal reorganization of the '70s, which opened a new era of class war, one component of which was the War on Drugs. Nixon's war is known for taking aim at illegal substances, but legal ones were no less in his crosshairs.[17] He wrote of the harm done to "several million American college students [who] have at least experimented with marijuana, hashish, LSD, amphetamines, or barbiturates."[18] The Controlled Substances Act of 1970 thus created a drug scheduling system, still with us today, that curbed the availability of *both* legal and illegal drugs.

The biological revolution in psychiatry, victorious with the publication of the third iteration of the *Diagnostic and Statistical Manual of Mental Disorders* in 1980, effectively cut against these control efforts. It established a new diagnostic paradigm, within which drugs were the answer to every question in the expanding field of mental health. The stage was set for the appearance of blockbuster SSRIs like Prozac and Zoloft, as well as the return of amphetamines and benzodiazepines in the '90s. Legal drugs suffered only temporarily in the War on Drugs.

The same is true of illegal drugs, though not of their users. In 1973, a new enforcement agency, the Drug Enforcement Administration, was created in order to stamp out Nixon's "enemy number one." Their initial actions did in fact lower the marijuana and heroin supply, but in doing so, they opened a space for Andean cocaine to begin flooding the United States. Cocaine represents the neoliberal era quite well: an ephemeral jolt of irrational confidence, it was powdered candy for the upper and professional classes, and an "epidemic" for poor and black Americans. Those most suffering from the rollback of the welfare state and the "informalization" of labor were now subject to the predations of a growing system of incarceration.

In political scientist Cedric Johnson's rendering, having "abandoned the use of state power to guarantee the most basic material needs and protection from market volatility," the ruling elite needed some new means of "managing a huge and growing surplus population," "often confined to the ghetto-ized zones of the inner city, blighted inner-ring suburbs, and depopulated Rust Belt towns."[19] Rather than beefing up the welfare state, they turned instead to cheaper, punitive measures, justified in part by the scourge of dangerous drugs and associated violence.[20] Meanwhile, the rest of the population saw increasing inequality, a decline in overall living standards, the decimation of the power of organized labor, and growing atomization and social chaos—a climate generally welcoming of pharmacological relief.

The fourth phase of the story is the one we are currently living through. It is characterized simply by the breakdown of neoliberalism; no subject of history seems to be guiding us toward a new regime. It's appropriately a moment where older categories are breaking down. Drugs have become medicines (ketamine), and medicines have become drugs (fentanyl). The legal drugs have become disreputable (tobacco), and the illegal ones reputable (psychedelics).[21] Uncoincidentally, as I've already covered, it is also a moment of *fabulous* drug use.

In one sense, this is a cyclical story: crackdown with industrialization, normalization with the postwar compromise, crackdown with neoliberalism, normalization with the breakdown of neoliberalism.[22] For some drugs, like amphetamines and marijuana, consumption levels closely track these cycles (see appendix A). But it's also a more linear tale of ascent and decline.

Part of the promise of Prohibition was that it would deliver widespread prosperity by teaching profligate immigrants and racial minorities how to behave. It was the last gasp of a direct paternalism that would be eliminated for good in the new consumer society. The New Deal coalition actually delivered the material prosperity that was promised by temperance reformers, and while this was in part thanks to the high point of working-class insurgency in the 1930s, the postwar compromise was also predicated on breaking the back of left-wing political organization and trade unionism.[23] Thus, while the period was affluent, it did not create a space for the pursuit of freedom from alienating work conditions. Indeed, the spike in drug consumption was above all about *adaptation*—to a vicious office environment, to "a mechanical monster whose body fills whole factories," or to an isolating domestic cell.[24]

This remained the case in the neoliberal period, but the jobs got worse and more precarious. Unions and mass membership organizations, once vehicles of both popular political pressure and communal fellowship, have drastically declined in size and influence, giving way to a soulless nonprofit advocacy universe and a fragmented civil society of isolated individuals (all "bowling alone," to use political scientist Robert Putnam's evocative phrase).[25] And now, in addition to this hollowed-out civic universe, mountains of debt, and mindless, low-paying jobs, Americans also have to cope with the looming threat of climate disaster, political stasis and confusion, and deep social division.

To point to the postwar period and the present one as times when drug use was "normalized" can thus only be something of a cruel joke. Postwar polydrug use reflected a fundamental belief, however coerced and driven by an underlying anxiety, that America was *worth it*. Today it paints a portrait of the country as a giant palliative care unit.[26]

Orienting Claims

"Everywhere and at all times, men and women have sought, and duly found, the means of taking a holiday from the reality of their generally dull and often acutely unpleasant existence," wrote Aldous Huxley.[27] Opium, coca, tobacco, and cannabis have always been tied to human settlement and cultivation.[28] Throughout history, drugs have been used for a variety of purposes. Sometimes these are explicitly ritualistic, as in Indigenous uses of ayahuasca in South America, cannabis in India, and psilocybe mushrooms and peyote in Mexico. But they're often more mundanely social, as with khat in East Africa and the Arabian Peninsula, kava in the Pacific Islands, betel nut in Asia, and coca in South America.[29]

Life is hard; bodily existence wearisome. A few laughs, energy and relief, mind-blowing transcendence—these are genuine miracles, and capitalism certainly didn't create their allure. "Man, being reasonable, must get drunk," wrote Lord Byron.[30] But the fact that drugs are pleasurable and desired cannot alone explain either the intense, racialized phobias around drugs, or the extent, regularity, and kinds of use that exist in modern America.[31] For this, we need to understand the particular conditions that structure and spur drug use and abuse, as well as their popular perceptions. What follows are five orienting claims in that direction.

1. Work structures "normal" drug use into a dosing regimen.

In a capitalist society, work tends to have particular characteristics that make people peculiarly susceptible to chemical charms. The profit motive dictates that we work regular, long hours and at an ever-quicker pace, leaving us exhausted and desperate for pick-me-ups. And the brevity of our leisure hours, used to wash away the stresses and frustrations of the working day, requires fast-acting but temporary relief. To cope with the demands of work, we rely on a steady cycle of uppers and downers—a dosing regimen often considered to be "normal."

Thus, though we often think psychoactive drug use is about sociability or mind expansion or simple *fun*, much of the time we are taking drugs for more boring reasons: either to be better at (or, at least, tolerate) work, or to quickly and temporarily unwind after work to prepare for the next day of work. In both cases, drug use is about helping "patch up the organism with a congeries of pharmacological bandages," to quote historian Theodore Roszak.[32] The enormous market for caffeine, antidepressants, amphetamines, and now (for a certain class of people) microdosed psychedelics is there to get us up for the day. In addition to waking us up enough to complete the tasks before us, stimulants also provide more oblique job security in an age when, for many people, selling one's personality is as important as actually doing one's job. Stimulants offer the requisite "pep" in an environment that demands we all "sparkle." An old ad for a dextroamphetamine targeted patients for whom "the seemingly endless, daily routine of living is approached with apathy, inertia, and lack of interest."[33] No truths about capitalist society are as raw as they are in pharmaceutical ads.

Alcohol, cigarettes, opiates, cannabis, and benzodiazepines, on the other hand, are there to give us a relatively short break from work, or to alleviate the pain and misery of work. As the writer Fitz Hugh Ludlow, known as the Hasheesh Eater, wrote at the onset of American industrialization: "The terrible demands, especially in this country, made on modern brains by our feverish competitive life, constitute hourly temptations to some form of sweet, deadly sedative."[34] It just so happens that those temptations, at least in their approved usage, are well delimited, like the twenty-two-minute sitcom or the three-minute pop song—meant to abide by the constraining limits of "free time." Opiates are a somewhat liminal drug here, in that they have always chafed against the descriptor "recreational," but their liminality proves the rule: since the late nineteenth century, they have been feared primarily because they *interrupt* hard work rather than merely providing reprieve from it.

The role of the accepted uppers and downers in acclimating us to a demanding work environment is nothing new. Coffee has long been prized as a promoter of mental efficiency, and cannabis and coca have been important aids to agricultural work.[35] Opium kept the Chinese coolie on the labor treadmill, and alcohol emptied the pockets of industrial workers at night so that they would dutifully return to their stations in the morning, heads pounding.[36] Psychoactive drugs offer a potentially infinite exploration of human experience, but the demands of work reduce them to tools of arousal maintenance.

There is a flip side to this argument. Since work structures "normal" drug use into a dosing regimen, it also frames "abnormal" drug use as that which transcends regimented consumption, and in so doing threatens rather than aids one's ability to abide by the demanding rhythms of work. There is a well-established inverse correlation between illegal drug use and stable employment, and no doubt there are many cases where drugs ruin the lives of "good kids" from the middle and upper classes, who would otherwise be destined for decent-paying office jobs.[37] But this view of the corrupting influence of drugs more often than not gets things exactly backward: the absence and precarity of work, the resulting insecurity,

The clock in the house of Coke Ennyday, the protagonist of the 1916 silent short film The Mystery of the Leaping Fish, *dir. John Emerson (Culver City: Triangle Film Corporation, 1916).*

impoverishment, and humiliation, and the punitive measures of dealing with what social scientists somewhat cruelly call the "surplus population"—people who are, from a strictly economic perspective, *unnecessary*—are themselves *causes* of increased drug use and abuse. In addiction specialist Gabor Maté's view,

> If I had to design a system that was intended to keep people addicted, I'd design exactly the system that we have right now ... The more you stress people, the more they're going to use. The more you de-stress people, the less they're going to use. So to create a system where you ostracize and marginalize and criminalize people, and force them to live in poverty with disease, you are basically guaranteeing they will stay at it.[38]

2. Psychopharmacology is the science of treating atomization.

Both reinforced by and reinforcing the misery of the labor market is the pervasive loneliness and atomization in American society. This has been especially pronounced in the last fifty years, during which the associational landscape has been gutted. But even before America's civic universe collapsed, the cultural life of the postwar era was aggressively individualistic and atomizing. The doldrums of consumer domesticity and the caginess of what the sociologist C. Wright Mills called "the competitive personality" certainly don't speak to anything resembling "community."[39]

Atomization is a form of isolation, but it's also a form of disempowerment: it's evident in the pervasive belief (true in a certain way) that we are all left to our own devices to face the vagaries of a hostile world—that civilization-ending war, grotesque inequality, the security state, the mass displacements of climate change, and the cruelty of corporate-dominated politics are there to bandy us about like playthings. Atomization thus translates to fear—fear about things over which we lack control, a fear that stops our thinking in its tracks, that immobilizes us and makes us paranoid. If work is the primary conscious reason we turn to drugs today, atomization is the *un*conscious reason.

Naturally, "mental health" has been the arena within which Americans have most readily attempted to both depict and manage their atomization. At the end of the nineteenth century, when the need to make sense of growing mental instability and exhaustion emerged in the United States, psychological theorizing was actually pretty honest about the fact that it was *social* factors (ruthless competition, the sundering of traditional communities, the amorality of industrialized society) that were the root cause of what became known as "neurasthenia"—a disorder that William James thought best to call "Americanitis."

12

In the postwar period, the designation "neurasthenia" disappeared, giving way to a new discourse on American "anxiety" that bore many of the same features. Once again, it was common to think that American society lay at the root, and that anxiety was an unfortunate, if tolerable, side effect of the onward march of freedom. It was only in the '80s that the biological revolution in psychiatry took hold, obscuring the role of the social causes of Americanitis (now predominantly labeled "depression") and tracing the roots of all mental illness to brains and genes. (See chapter 6 for more on this history.)

In all three periods, drugs, both licit and illicit, have served capably as aids for what ails us. About half of people with severe mental health disorders today are also affected by substance abuse, and that's not counting the consumption of psychotropic medications.[40] The government administration devoted to mental health also covers substance abuse, in recognition that you can't really understand mental health without also looking at psychoactive drugs.[41]

Against the present psychiatric consensus, the mental illnesses that drive both medication and self-medication with psychoactive substances are not *simply* disorders of the brain; they are also, as both the theorizing and advertising of the postwar era acknowledged, illnesses of *society*, mercilessly preyed upon by large pharmaceutical companies. It is an uncomfortable thought, but capitalist society does not simply sit like a carapace upon individual subjects, waiting to be thrown off with the right political organizing; it rather penetrates to the deepest levels of our psyches, where its influence can be found in our pleasures, our frustrations, and our neurotic and psychotic behaviors.[42]

Personal trauma and conflict undoubtedly play their part in creating the conditions under which pharmacological relief is so desired, but as the Frankfurt School philosophers first emphasized, individual development and relations mediated through the institution of the family in a capitalist society will necessarily be stunted—by the lack of parental authority and autonomy, by a dearth of care and time, by moral expectations laid out in a competitive framework. Herbert Marcuse once said that capitalism is not responsible for your problems with your girlfriend.[43] He was right that we are not excused from our personal failings, but wrong that social structure cannot be mined from the psychic depths.[44]

3. Drug producers are typical capitalist organizations.

Drug producers, both legal and illegal ones, are often taken to be special kinds of organizations, particularly seedy and unethical, but they are in reality very typical capitalist organizations. The hatred and fear of the drug trade is a veiled hatred and fear of capitalism itself, made more palatable by the incorrect notion that we're dealing with an *abnormal* instance of the dominance of profit-making over our lives rather than merely a particularly visible one. Drug discourse is thus one of the prominent ways in which Americans unwittingly express their fears about society in general.

Let's start with Big Pharma, which is often singled out as an especially corrupt industry. While its average profit rate does far exceed that of most industries, pharmaceutical corporations are simply organizations that make drugs for profit. To ensure that this profit is regular and sizable, they do what all corporations do:

- Lobby (and sometimes bribe) politicians to remove or relax all regulations on their products
- Artificially stimulate demand through advertising that stretches the bounds of the ethically fathomable
- Suppress or counter any negative press, often by molding or marshaling expert opinion
- Maintain exclusive patents or other advantages over the competition

THE PITIABLE ARMY

Evening Herald and Express, *February 21, 1934. Cartoon by Jimmy Hatlo. From Richard J. Bonnie and Charles H. Whitebread II,* The Marihuana Conviction: A History of Marihuana Prohibition in the United States *(Charlottesville: University Press of Virginia, 1974), 99.*

- Justify the externalities of their business as the cost of dynamic entrepreneurship
- Seek markets where demand is reliable and scalable

It's true that these very typical practices, when marshaled to sell powerful molecules ingested by people, have pernicious effects, effects that seem unconscionable and smell of corruption. Lax regulations lead to serious illness, the combination of egregious advertising and expert "thought leaders" creates legitimate public paranoia, and pharma's focus on chronic illnesses (illnesses that require a steady stream of medication) accelerates the medicalization of social problems. But again, there's nothing exceptional at root here: pharmaceutical corporations are first and foremost corporations, and as capitalist corporations they will engage in these practices as a matter of course. Remove the Sacklers and Shkrelis of today, and without changing the basic structure of drug profiteering, new models of "capital personified" would rise tomorrow to take their place.

Illegal drug operations are also businesses like any other, and indeed, for many people who write about drugs, they are *ideal* market actors. In anthropologist Philippe Bourgois's characterization,

> Like most other people in the United States, drug dealers and street criminals are scrambling to obtain their piece of the pie as fast as possible. In fact, in their pursuit of success they are even following the minute details of the classical Yankee model for upward mobility. They are aggressively pursuing careers as private entrepreneurs; they take risks, work hard, and pray for good luck. They are the ultimate rugged individualists braving an unpredictable frontier where fortune, fame, and destruction are all just around the corner, and where the enemy is ruthlessly hunted down and shot.[45]

Journalist Sam Quinones echoes Bourgois: "Heroin was never about the romantic subversion of societal norms. It was instead about the squarest of American things: business—dull, cold commerce … Dealers could … organize heroin distribution almost according to principles taught in business schools."[46] The notorious cocaine trafficker Pablo Escobar's great invention was *apuntada*, an insurance scheme that protected investments in cocaine shipments—real glamorous stuff.[47]

The obvious counter to this line of familiarization is, in brief, *violence*: as opposed to the subtler malice of the pharmaceutical industry, illicit drug producers and distributors are practically synonymous in the popular imagination with unthinkable acts of brutality—Escobar's own cartel being the most extreme and ready-to-hand example. Hardly capitalism as usual? To some extent, this association has been overemphasized by American culture's pornography of violence: roughly one-fifth of incarcerated people in the United States are in for *non*violent drug offenses, and most of the time the drug trade is built on trust.[48] But it's undeniable that the illegal drug trade can indeed be a gruesome affair. What's curious about drug violence, however, is that it obeys a market logic. To again quote Bourgois,

> Regular displays of violence are essential for preventing rip-offs by colleagues, customers, and professional holdup artists. Indeed, upward mobility in the underground economy of the street-dealing world requires a systematic and effective use of violence against one's colleagues, one's neighbors, and, to a certain extent, against oneself. Behavior that appears irrationally violent, "barbaric," and ultimately self-destructive to the outsider, can be reinterpreted according to the logic of the underground economy as judicious public relations and long-term investment in one's "human capital development."[49]

In brief, the violence of illicit drug production and distribution is not an otherworldly evil but simply one feature of what profit-making behavior looks like in the perversely regulated, underground economy.

It's a mistake, however, to see the great accumulation of profit in the black market in neoclassical economic terms—rugged individuals making their way in a free (though illegal) market.[50] The illegal drug trade does not operate by the providence of the invisible hand: as we will see, very large and very powerful government agencies, from the East India Company to the CIA, have intimately shaped global drug production, distribution, and consumption. And the pursuit of the great profits in the *legal* drug market, admittedly often made by illegal (or at least wildly unethical) means, have artificially inflated demand for illegal drugs.

But in this, the illegal drug trade *does* adequately reflect the nature of capitalist activity in the twentieth and twenty-first centuries, which is not a story of agile entrepreneurialism but one of corporatization, bureaucratization, and elite management. Even in the drug world, there are few "little men of business" in C. Wright Mills's sense, but mostly little servants of large and corrupt public-private partnerships: "As individuals, they are only insecure and tortured creatures, being pushed by forces or swallowed by movement that they do not understand."[51]

4. The difference between licit and illicit drugs is a class distinction.

According to the official mythology, illicit or unapproved drugs are *dangerous*, while licit or approved ones are *safe*. It's difficult to imagine the kind of person who believes this.

The actual rule governing the boundaries of the presently allowable is rather: drugs that are taken by a respectable class of people are licit (in the sense of "acceptable"), and drugs that are taken by an unrespectable class of people are illicit ("unacceptable").[52] The law might lag considerably behind changing configurations of respectability, but the legal-illegal divide is largely predicated on the culturally licit-illicit one.

In the late nineteenth century, Chinese immigrants using opium were disgusting dope fiends, while morphine habitués in what historian David Herzberg calls the "doctor-visiting classes" were "'pitiable' victims with an 'earnest longing to be free.'"[53] Morphine is, of course, a derivative of opium: same drug, opposed social judgments. According to Herzberg, this basic logic repeats itself in the mid-twentieth-century distinction between opiate "addiction" and sedative "habituation" (innocent housewives being the victims of the latter). At work here is a longstanding schizoid distinction between white market medicines and black market drugs, with all the racialized connotations therein.[54]

In the '70s and early '80s, cocaine was technically illegal but culturally licit, in the same way that microdosed LSD is today, and for the same reason: because it was used by the professional classes.[55] It's possible that cocaine could have been decriminalized at this time—a district court judge in Massachusetts ruled in 1977 that cocaine was "an acceptable recreational drug," and Carter's drug czar Peter Bourne claimed that cocaine "is probably the most benign of illicit drugs currently in widespread use."[56] But by the mid-1980s, the profile of the drug had changed; it was now associated with the rather more disreputable figure of the poor, black, inner-city addict, and instead of being decriminalized, the drug became a pretext for decades of police warfare.

Again, even at physiologically harmful and socially disruptive levels, drugs are only deemed illicit if they are taken by disreputable people. This is obvious in one way, and yet cultural attitudes toward licit and illicit drugs are typically not seen for what they are: class judgments. These judgments are very often racialized in immediately legible ways for the contemporary observer—marijuana and Mexicans, opium and the Chinese, cocaine and black Americans—but they can also be an all-"white" affair, as in the cases of alcohol and the Irish and Germans at the beginning of the twentieth century and of cigarettes and opiates and the "white working class" today.

There are, however, various forms of institutional resistance that sometimes prevent the licit and the legal from becoming one and the same. The distinction between legal and illegal drugs is institutionally upheld by the differing purviews of two instruments of American state bureaucracy: the Food and Drug Administration (FDA) and the Drug Enforcement Administration (DEA). Drugs controlled by the DEA are invariably subject to the romance and paranoia of the illicit. Drugs produced by large corporations with powerful lobbying operations and then regulated by the FDA, on the other hand, are immune to the same moral panic propagandizing.[57] But class judgments can still be made within these confines: cigarettes might never be made illegal, but that won't prevent confident condemnations of smokers as an underclass.

In 1967, the philosopher Alasdair MacIntyre signed a letter calling for the legalization of marijuana. Responding to the anger elicited by the letter, MacIntyre suggested that what made the pharmacological Calvinists hate "cannabis is not the belief that the effects of taking it are harmful, but rather a horrifying suspicion that here is a source of pure pleasure which is available for those who have not *earned it*, who do not *deserve it.*"[58] Although drug "menaces" are built up into unqualified evils for the sake of ratings and political gain, and though the ravages of physical dependency and long-term use are real, it is this basic capitalist antipathy to *undeserved pleasure* that undergirds the category of "illicit drugs."

5. Drug policy is not about drugs.

In 1994, Richard Nixon's aide on domestic affairs, John Ehrlichman, admitted to journalist Dan Baum:

> The Nixon campaign in 1968, and the Nixon White House after that, had two enemies: the antiwar left and black people. You understand what I'm saying? We knew we couldn't make it illegal to be either against the war or blacks, but by getting the public to associate the hippies with marijuana and blacks with heroin, and then criminalizing both heavily, we could disrupt those communities. We could arrest their leaders, raid their homes, break up their meetings, and vilify them night after night on the evening news. Did we know we were lying about the drugs? Of course we did.[59]

In a sense, he was telling the world what it kind of already knew: that drug policy is pretty clearly not about drugs. Which is to say, when people aim to control or regulate drugs, they are actually aiming to control or regulate other things about society. The "drug menace" is ideological cover for the continuing offenses of Big Pharma, the demonization of already oppressed racial groups, the rollback of the welfare state, the enhancement of security apparatuses, and the erosion of civil liberties.[60] It has been one or all of these things since the beginning of the twentieth century, and only secondarily, if at all, sensible policy based on the benefits and dangers that psychoactive drugs pose.[61]

On both sides of the political spectrum, we nonetheless continue to believe that drugs are essentially what's at stake in drug policy. Conservatives can recognize that the War on Drugs is irrational at times, and plainly destructive, but justify this as the cost of eliminating a real danger to society. Liberals tend axiomatically to point to the social costs, but somehow return again and again either to drug demystification ("Everything you know about drugs is wrong!") or obvious policy countermeasures. The first is bound by the idealistic belief that if we just knew the *truth* about drugs, if we just had all the right *information*, drug paranoia would evaporate at the source. The second suffers from a *post hoc, ergo propter hoc* fallacy: since drug policy has been a leading edge of the growth of the security state, reversing irrational drug policy will in turn address the problems of brutal policing and mass incarceration.

If only it were that easy. The story of the swelling of the prison population since the '80s is one of racism, of perverse incentives, and of the defeat of the left, but at root it is one of economic contraction and the retrenchment of the welfare state. Since drugs have served so prominently as a pretext for hyperincarceration, it's natural that reformers have mostly focused on attempting to repeal civil forfeiture and mandatory minimum laws, legalizing marijuana, and so on.[62] Removing the irrational accretions of a century of prohibition would undoubtedly do some good, but the problem of economic expendability would remain. If we legalized heroin and cocaine today, without providing the kinds of jobs and social protections needed for basic livability in twenty-first-century America, something else would step in to provide the same justificatory function as illicit drugs tomorrow. Drug laws, no less than drugs, tend to treat not causes, but symptoms.

Drugs naturally point beyond themselves: to the problems in our lives and to our ways of dealing with them; to greedy and exploitative organizations and institutions; and to a society of growing dysfunction, fear, and misery. The "problem" of drugs is never really about drugs, and so it's always a mistake to linger too intently on either the substances themselves or the rules of their engagement.

A final word: the chapters here are not arguments for or against. Both drug demonization and drug enthusiasm can be misguided and harmful, and besides, drugs themselves are thoroughly contradictory. Smoking is both sublime and a true disaster. Psychedelics are about both freedom and control. Heroin gets you to the peak and the nadir of human experience. The good and the bad of drug use in America are thoroughly interwoven, and oftentimes the good can only be made sense of with reference to the bad. What the social theorist Theodor Adorno said of the culture industry applies here as well:

> People are not only, as the saying goes, falling for the swindle; if it guarantees them even the most fleeting gratification they desire a deception which is nonetheless transparent to them. They force their eyes shut and voice approval, in a kind of self-loathing, for what is meted out to them, knowing fully the purpose for which it is manufactured. Without admitting it they sense that their lives would be completely intolerable as soon as they no longer clung to satisfactions which are none at all.[63]

Why do people take drugs? Because they like their experience at least a little bit better on drugs than not. If we accept that explanation, all the interesting follow-up questions have to do not with drugs, but with *experience*.

1

Coffee, or the Serene Delight

Within a single generation of the disappearance of Coffee from
the face of the earth, gaiety, geniality, and cheer began to wane!
Another important result was that sluggishness, inertness, and
mental dullness threatened civilization's progress until various
drugs were used to combat their ingress! All this was due to the
removal of Coffee from the diet of Man—truly a remarkable
substance!

—Philip J. Bartel in "The Elixir of Progress" from
1935, imagining a future society in which coffee
is forgotten after being prohibited by "the United
Socialistic States of North and South America"

In the seventeenth century, the average English family consumed
approximately three liters of beer per person per day, children
included, and beer brewing was a regular part of domestic
duties.[1] To convey a sense of the pervasiveness of beer in the
seventeenth and eighteenth centuries, the historian Wolfgang
Schivelbusch recounts "that breakfast as a rule consisted of
beer soup," a mixture of beer, eggs, and butter responsible for
the portly figures of Jordaens and Rubens.[2] Such was daily life
in the Western world before coffee.

With increasing transoceanic commerce, coffee began to
appear in Europe in the late sixteenth century, and since it
had been drunk mostly by Muslims for two centuries prior,
it arrived in the West as an exotic and somewhat frightening curiosity—the "wine of Islam."[3] This changed around the
middle of the seventeenth century, when it became widely
appreciated for one powerful (if mostly fantasized) property:

the ability to make one sober.[4] In the humoral perspective, alcohol made one "wet," with all that that implied. Coffee, by contrast, made one "dry," and the anti-erotic element did not go unnoticed by the emergent bourgeoisie, who appreciated the cold industriousness that the desiccating elements of coffee promoted.[5]

Ever since, the ruling class has borne unwavering praise for coffee, something that can be said of no other psychoactive substance. Coffee is a pleasure uniquely suited to the capitalist world, achieving "chemically and pharmacologically what rationalism and the Protestant ethic sought to fulfill spiritually and ideologically."[6] It brought us out of beer-soaked unreason and into the blinding light of modernity.

Today, well past the heroic phase of bourgeois entrepreneurialism, coffee is the most widely used drug in existence (followed by alcohol, and then tobacco), and it trails only crude oil as the most traded commodity in the world.[7] It is humanity's great maintenance medication, helping us wake up to meet the day, unmeetable as those days may sometimes be. What the *Boston Transcript* aptly noted in 1923 (during Prohibition, admittedly) still resonates today: "In a sad world, and especially in a country like ours ... the function of coffee in bringing serene delight is an important one."[8]

Dialectic of Enlightenment

Like the bourgeoisie, coffee entered history roasting in the fires of revolution. Everywhere it was consumed, it sped up the clearing away of the old structures. In England, Charles II tried to close the coffeehouses on account of the seditious speech they fomented but failed on account of pressure from the coffee dealers.[9] After trying and realizing it was too difficult to ban coffee altogether, Frederick the Great issued coffee-roasting licenses exclusive to the nobility and clergy so as to keep it from the hostile commoners.[10] The Boston Tea Party was planned in a coffeehouse.[11] In 1789, Camille Desmoulins led a mob from a café and took the Bastille two days later. According to William H. Ukers, "Wherever [coffee] has been introduced it has spelled revolution."[12]

Depictions of the seventeenth- and eighteenth-century British coffeehouse bear some common features: a few dozen men (and only men) socializing, drinking very weak coffee (commonly brewed with water from the Thames), and enjoying the other new exotica associated with what the historian David Court-wright calls "the psychoactive revolution"—chocolate, tobacco, tea.[13] But they also present a split image. On the one hand, the coffeehouses were thought to be dangerous and chaotic places. As centers of a new information culture, where both licensed and unlicensed print publications were shared and discussed, these "penny universities" were brimming with fake news, heated debate, and rebellious scheming.[14] But other accounts present the coffeehouse as an essentially "sober and serene" environment, a place for polite conversation that attracted "effeminate fops" and "pretty fellows"—coffeehouse habitués who inflamed a rather different cultural anxiety.[15]

This freedom from the uncivil debauchery of the tavern also made the coffeehouse an ideal center of commerce. Lloyd's of London actually began as a coffeehouse. Its transformation into one of the largest financial institutions in the world began with the sale of insurance, including the insurance of slave ships.[16] The coffeehouse thus housed the contradictory imperatives of modernity under one roof: at some tables, the consumption of coffee fueled raucous conversation testing a new emancipatory horizon; at others, deals were made to organize the trade in human oppression.

Saint-Domingue (Haiti) was a key target of early coffee colonialism. By the late eighteenth century, it was one of the world's largest coffee exporters (making about 60 percent of the world's coffee) and slave importers (absorbing 40,000 African slaves per year, more than the United States at the time).[17] The cruelty of slavery in Haiti was unparalleled: in North America, Haiti was invoked as a bogeyman, a hell to which masters would threaten to send their disobedient slaves.[18] According to one account at the time, the monstrously high mortality rate among slaves "in Saint-Domingue was due not to sickness but to the tyranny of the owners."[19]

After the plantations were razed in the Haitian slave revolt of 1793, the center of coffee production moved to Ceylon (Sri Lanka), first under the Dutch and then under the British. The colonial coffee estates of Ceylon were the largest producers of coffee in the world until "coffee rust," a fungal disease lethal to coffee plants, appeared in the late nineteenth century, wiping out crops not only in Ceylon but also in India, Java, Sumatra, and Malaysia.[20] Tea consumption had risen by leaps and bounds in England beginning in 1700, thanks to the monopoly of the East India Company, and coffee rust sealed the transition of the world's greatest coffee fanatics in the early eighteenth century to tea in the nineteenth.[21]

Just as Haiti's decline made room for the expansion of production in Ceylon, so too did the quick uprooting of coffee in Ceylon allow for the rise of a new coffee powerhouse. Brazil had gotten into the coffee game on the heels of its break from colonial rule in 1822, after which its coffee production took off—along with its slave imports. "Brazil is coffee and coffee is the Negro," explained Brazilian senator Silveira Martins in 1880.[22] It proved to be one of those stark assertions whose certainty belied imminent change: Brazil banned slave importation in 1888, making it the last country to do so in the western hemisphere.

Keen to find replacement workers for their plantations, the coffee barons of São Paulo convinced the government to subsidize the immigration of poor Europeans, mostly Italians, and it was under this new *colonos* system of labor that coffee production really exploded. In pursuing the riches of coffee monoculture, Brazil unloaded 16.3 million bags of coffee on the world in 1901, while neglecting the cultivation of more basic subsistence crops.[23] With 130 pounds of beans in each bag, that was enough to make forty-eight cups of coffee for every single human being on the planet at the time. In historian Heinrich Jacob's telling, "One who speaks of coffee in Brazil ... is compelled to use words and images that in other respects seem only appropriate to the taming of natural forces."[24]

Marx wrote that capitalist production develops "only by sapping the original sources of wealth—the soil and the labourer."[25] Wherever coffee production has become an intensive national focus (as with Vietnam in the '90s), environmental devastation has followed. By the 1920s, Brazilian forests were being cleared at a clip of more than 1,100 square miles per year, largely to provide more space to grow coffee.[26] You can still see this happening today in vast tracts of what was once the Amazon: an endless flat plain of coffee plants, where indentured workers drag the last few harvests out of a dying soil.

Burning

By the turn of the century, Brazil was experiencing one of those problems unimaginable in precapitalist ages: too many investors wanted in on the coffee market, too much land had been cleared, and soon the country was buried in beans. In 1906, the government began taking out loans to buy and stockpile coffee to keep prices artificially high, a process known as "valorization." After years of valorizing Brazilian coffee, the São Paulo Coffee Institute finally went bankrupt on October 11, 1929, sending coffee prices plummeting in New York—the world's largest coffee exchange center. Given the global importance of coffee in international commerce, it was a canary in the coal mine: a little more than two weeks later, the stock market crashed, bringing on the Great Depression.[27]

In 1930, with 26 million bags of coffee in storage (1 million more than had been globally consumed the previous year) and coffee prices in freefall, Brazil initiated a program that would be an enduring and marvelous display of capitalism's irrationality. In order to "revert to the time-honored law of supply and demand," they began burning their coffee.[28] In the first year alone, 7 million bags were burned; in 1937, they burned 17 million bags at a time when annual *global* consumption was only 26 million bags.[29]

In addition to being irrational and destructive, capitalist overproduction also gave us consumer goods that no one asked for. Invented just before the First World War, soluble coffee was much cherished among soldiers, but being rather dreadful in comparison to the real thing, its market evaporated at war's end. It was at the behest of the Brazilian government that Nestlé created Nescafé, the world's first mass-marketed instant coffee, in 1938. Determined to make a better tasting product, Nestlé invented a new technique of powderizing coffee, just in time for another wartime instant-coffee boom. This time it had staying power, increasing its share of the coffee market throughout the Fordist period until reaching a peak of 34 percent of all coffee consumed in the United States in 1978 (today it accounts for 19 percent of coffee sales). According to Nina Luttinger and Gregory Dicum, instant coffee "was part of the same wave that included prefab houses, TV dinners, nylon stockings, and plastic of all kinds; it remains the Spam of hot drinks."[30]

But even with coffee bean bonfires and the creation of crap secondary markets, the Brazilian coffee glut remained a problem. In the '30s, Colombia began eating into Brazil's export market and benefited enormously from the inflated prices of the Brazilian valorization scheme. When efforts to convince Colombia to adopt similar methods failed, Brazil dumped their reserves on the market in 1937 in frustration, instantly collapsing coffee prices again.[31]

Cartelization

Rescue came from none other than the United States. Despite America's reputation for free-trade fanaticism, the US was a willing participant in a new system to keep prices stable and high. The reasons were, unsurprisingly, political. The first agreement, signed in 1940, was intended to keep countries like Brazil on the right side during WWII. The second accord—the International Coffee Agreement (ICA), signed in 1962—was an explicit instrument of Cold War anti-Communism.[32] Speaking in support of the ICA, Hubert Humphrey claimed that raising coffee prices was

> a matter of life or death, a matter of Castroism versus freedom
> ... Castroism will spread like the plague through Latin America
> unless something is done about the prices of the raw materials
> produced there; and those prices can be stabilized on an inter-
> national basis.[33]

The Colombian senator Enrique Escovar put it in even starker terms: "Pay us good prices for our coffee or—God help us all—the masses will become one great Marxist revolutionary army that will sweep us all into the sea."[34]

Luckily for the ruling class, the US had the clout to fix global coffee prices. America was the first mass market for coffee: already by 1923 it was consuming half the world's coffee, and during WWII it was importing roughly $4 billion (about $66 billion in today's dollars) worth of the stuff, which, remarkably, accounted for almost 10 percent of *all* national imports.[35] Coffee roasting was big business, and the ICA, which set coffee export quotas that prevented smaller buyers from entering the market, only helped it get bigger. According to the small American roasters who had survived the conglomerations of the '50s,

> The monstrous International Coffee Cartel set up with the
> support of our Government, contrary to our Trust Busting laws,

is having the only effect it can have. The big are getting bigger and the small have the hangman's noose around the neck tightened daily.[36]

Large regional roasters were absorbed by even larger corporations. General Foods bought Maxwell House, Nestlé bought Hills Brothers and Chase & Sanborn, and Procter & Gamble bought Folgers. As the big got bigger, the coffee unsurprisingly got worse, thanks in large part to their willingness to increase the proportion of robusta over arabica beans in their blends. Robusta is cheap but harsh and bitter. Arabica is harder to grow but clearly superior in taste. High-end cafés almost exclusively brew arabicas; the major supermarket blends often include some robusta but also a good amount of arabica to make it palatable.

To make up for the increasing inferiority of their product, the coffee giants invested more and more in advertising. They even teamed up in 1952 to form the Pan-American Coffee Bureau, which notably invented the phrase "coffee break" and then spent much of the bureau's $2 million annual budget spreading the good word on radio and television.[37]

Undoubtedly the most disturbing feature of the new corporate coffee advertising world was the explicit misogyny. Coffee had been a flashpoint in the war of the sexes from the moment it first arrived in Europe. In England in 1674, a broadside entitled "The Women's Petition against Coffee" claimed that coffee "has so *Eunucht* our Husbands ... that they are become as *Impotent* as Age, and as unfruitful as those *Desarts* whence that unhappy berry is said to be brought."[38] They warned that coffee drinkers would soon be "Cuckol'd by Dildo's," referencing the increasing popularity of the French dildo among English ladies.[39] The men replied soon after that

> Coffee Collects and settles the Spirits, makes the erection more
> Vigorous, the Ejaculation more full, adds a spiritualescency to
> the Sperme, and renders it more firm and suitable to the Gusto

Advertisements for Chock Full o'Nuts and Chase & Sanborn. "Men! Don't let it come to this!" (1962), Luttinger and Dicum, The Coffee Book, 144. "If your husband ever finds out," Life magazine, August 11, 1952, 103. Reprinted with permission.

of the womb, and proportionate to the ardours and expectation too, of the female Paramour.[40]

What these struggles really concerned, though, was not so much coffee itself as sexual segregation: the coffeehouses of the time, like most centers of business, generally excluded women.[41]

Coffee was still a man's drink in the mid-twentieth century, but the site of consumption had moved from the coffeehouse to the breakfast table. If you go by the advertising of the time, this was decidedly not to the benefit of women. The small print of Chock Full o'Nuts's "Men! Don't let it come to this!" ad reproduced here reads: "A man's home is his castle! You have a right to good coffee in your home, and your wife has a duty to serve it. Don't be the victim of womanly penny-pinching!" Chase & Sanborn were even more direct in their "If your husband ever finds out" campaign. Years later, Alecia Swasy discovered that Procter & Gamble were very consciously pushing the limits of just "how ugly and aggressive [they] could get in the ads," having conducted research that demonstrated that "women 'would accept as reasonable all sorts of abuse' in ads because many of them heard it at home."[42]

Deindustrialization

US coffee consumption peaked at 46.4 gallons per person in 1946.[43] Coffee was the moral lubricant of the Fordist machine, keeping workers efficiently plodding through rote tasks. In the kind of unwitting critique borne only of unreserved enthusiasm, Margaret Meagher, author of *To Think of Coffee* in 1942, aptly named the function of coffee, then and today: "Coffee has ... expand[ed] humanity's working-day from twelve to a potential twenty-four hours. The tempo, the complexity, the

Ad from the Joint Coffee Trade Publicity Committee in Tea and Coffee Trade Journal 40, no. 2 (February 1921): 205.

tension of modern life, call for something that can perform the miracle of stimulating brain activity, without evil, habit-forming after-effects."[44]

The postwar era was the high point of America's productive capacity and stimulant consumption. With deindustrialization, overall coffee consumption tapered, and a new market in "specialty coffee" appeared, uncannily presaging the psychic horrors of the postmodern age. In their otherwise excellent *The Coffee Book*, Nina Luttinger and Gregory Dicum describe the "relative decommodification of coffee" in the specialty roaster industry and an attention to "origin, quality, processing, and cultivation methods as relevant qualities of the bean."[45] The truth is that the specialty roasters, at first with the ignorance of craft devotees and later with full knowledge, *commodified* these other aspects of coffee. They were selling a completely different product than the coffee giants, and the relative autonomy of the specialty coffee market from the regular coffee market bears this out.[46]

Benoit Daviron and Stefano Ponte call this the "symbolic production of coffee"—the production of qualities that "cannot be measured by human senses or complex technological devices" and which are "based on reputation and often embedded in trademarks, geographical indications and sustainability labels."[47] Unsurprisingly, absurdity reigns in this particular simulation. In 1996, it was discovered that Central American beans were being routed through Hawaii so that their producers could brand them as Hawaiian Kona coffee, even though professional cuppers recognized the imitation coffee as better than Kona itself.[48] One of the most expensive coffees today is the Kopi Luwak, which has been eaten by the Asian palm civet and retrieved from its feces. Predictably these animals are now captured, caged, and force-fed coffee beans (one could imagine a cruel meal pairing of Kopi Luwak and foie gras).[49] And of course almost every specialty roaster is in a cutthroat competition with the others for the ability to say that they can simultaneously lift Indigenous peoples out of poverty and save the planet—if only you buy their beans.

Sadly, the emotional pull of this advertising gimmick was made more genuine by vast transformations in the global trade in coffee. Despite the Reagan administration's obsession with the Nicaraguan Sandinistas (and their nationalized coffee enterprise, ENCAFE), the Cold War fears that had animated the ICA slowly abated in the '80s, and with them the willingness of the United States to pay artificially inflated coffee prices.[50] The ICA finally collapsed in 1989, and the price of coffee dropped by nearly 75 percent in the next five years.[51] The "coffee crisis" that followed was a massive disaster in all producing countries: dispossessed farmers turned to violence, to the guerrillas, or else to coca and opium poppy cultivation.[52] The Rwandan genocide of 1994 was preceded by the value decline of coffee, which had accounted for 80 percent of the country's exports.[53] Letting the ICA lapse was the functional equivalent of the United States halving its world aid budget.[54]

Withdrawal

In 1980, "caffeinism" was added to the *Diagnostic and Statistical Manual of Mental Disorders* (alongside "ego-dystonic homosexuality"), capping years of silly alarmism about coffee's supposed health effects, but was soon removed. The truth is that coffee is an addictive but largely harmless diuretic, but throughout the history of capitalism, its relative harmlessness has been employed in the service of the endurance of harm. As Luttinger and Dicum argue, "Coffee has always been the perfect complement to dehumanizing industrialization," and no less has it been the perfect complement to dehumanizing *de*industrialization.[55]

Coffee keeps us awake, it keeps us alert, it renders to our habits a machinelike efficiency. It helps us acclimate to the imperatives of American society, while also providing some reprieve from its atomization. Howard Schultz, the CEO that oversaw the rapid expansion of Starbucks, sees coffee shops as fulfilling the need for a "third space," a term he borrows from sociologist Ray Oldenburg.[56] A "third space" is one that is neither work nor home, a public space sought as an escape from both alienation and isolation. Coffeehouses have always offered "the diversion of company" in a "nursery of temperance," to quote the seventeenth-century author of *Coffeehouses Vindicated*, but in the unforgiving environment of neoliberal society, they are pillars of social reproduction in providing spaces for us to be alone together.[57]

Today, global climate change has begun to threaten the production of this wonder drug. On our current trajectory, the amount of land suitable for coffee cultivation will be halved in thirty years and *eliminated* in sixty.[58] It is hard to imagine a world without coffee—especially for the 20 million rural families who currently depend on coffee cultivation for their livelihood.[59] But then so too is it difficult to fathom the other myriad effects of social and environmental erosion, most of which promise to be much more devastating than caffeine withdrawal.

2

Cigarettes, or Knowledge Is Not Power

I can do nothing unless I take into myself at moments this culture
of nothingness.

—Antonin Artaud

Cigarettes are different from most other commodities in two
important ways. First, they cause cancer—though that's only
half the story. The use of the word "cause" in this last sentence
was made possible by the development of meta-analysis in
statistics and epidemiology that the scientific pursuit of the
carcinogenic effects of cigarette smoking spurred.[1] To say that
cigarettes "cause" cancer is like saying that Jesus "preached
Christianity," or that Freud "analyzed" his patients. What cigarettes caused is a specific understanding of *causation*.[2]

Second, thanks to the waves of litigation that followed this
discovery, we happen to know more about the inner work-
ings of the corporations that produce cigarettes than we do
about any other capitalist industry.[3] Critics are fond of calling
the tobacco giants "rogue" corporations, but there's nothing
surprising or out of the ordinary about their methods or their
excesses. Again, we just happen to know more about them.

You might object: "But didn't the tobacco companies *lie*?
They marketed to kids! They paid scientists to create fake con-
troversies!" All this is true, but it's no less than any corporation
responsible to its shareholders would do. The massive global
public health crisis that tobacco companies are responsible
for is a result of the lethal force of their product ("The only
consumer product that kills when used as directed," as historian Robert N. Proctor says) combined with the very typical

practices of capitalist firms, which include an indifference to "incidental" considerations unless they hamper or bolster profits.[4]

The cigarette thus provides a privileged window into the world of profit-making, not unlike that of Jim Mouth's face while breaking his own world record for most cigarettes smoked at the same time. Its tale is at once revolting and unbelievable, but the true horror lies in the generalizability of its lessons: this is not the story of an exception but of a rule. Eyes bulging to absorb every last bit of death the culture has to offer, we are all, in some way, Jim Mouth.

Innovations

Tobacco came to Europe in the seventeenth century, around the same time as coffee, tea, chocolate, and other new exotica— "the first objects within capitalism that conveyed with their use

Jim Mouth smoking 155 cigarettes in 1993. Carlos Schiebeck/AFP via Getty Images.

the complex idea that one could *become* different by *consuming* differently," according to anthropologist Sidney Mintz.[5] The preferred vehicle of tobacco consumption then was the pipe, which would be supplanted in the early nineteenth century by the cigar, in turn overcome by the cigarette in the later nineteenth.[6]

Two technical developments paved the way for the dominance of the cigarette: First, the invention of "flue curing," or drying tobacco at higher temperatures, which produced a golden yellow leaf with much milder smoke.[7] Before flue curing, tobacco was air dried, and its smoke was typically too harsh to be inhaled. After flue curing, tobacco smoke *had to be* inhaled to get the same nicotine satisfaction, and inhalation is the difference between a recreational activity and slowly killing yourself.[8] As historians Gary Cross and Proctor explain,

> The shift from air-cured to flue-cured tobacco was something like the shift from opium to heroin or from eating to injecting drugs by means of a hypodermic needle: a new form of "consumption" based on a new and intensified form of packaged delivery.[9]

Curiously, it was making tobacco more mild that allowed it to become more lethal.

The second innovation was the mechanization of cigarette production: before the 1880s, cigarettes were all rolled by hand, typically at a rate of five a minute. In 1881, inventor James Albert Bonsack created a machine that could churn out 20,000 cigarettes in ten hours, which he quickly sold on an exclusive contract to the American Tobacco Company.[10] With this technological superiority, ATC dominated global production until 1911, when it was broken up into four companies by the exercise of the Sherman Antitrust Act. These four firms—ATC, Liggett & Myers, R. J. Reynolds, P. Lorillard—along with Philip Morris, formed the oligopoly that would oversee the twentieth-century boom in cigarette smoking.[11]

They would be aided in their efforts by the First World War. Not only did wartime seriousness mute the comparatively more trivial concerns of anti-tobacco advocates (still not yet armed with scientific proof of negative health impacts), but cigarettes were an easily "realizable desire" at a time when desires were not easily realized.[12] They also diverted soldiers from what one contemporary called "bad liquor and worse women."[13] General John J. Pershing, commander of the Allied Forces in France, half joked, "You asked me what we need to win this war. I answer tobacco as much as bullets!"[14] Previous allies of the anti-cigarette cause, like the YMCA and the Red Cross, became major distributors of cigarettes during the war. A YMCA fundraiser in Texas asked residents to "put a nail in the Kaiser's Coffin" with their donations, effectively revaluing the old pejorative term for the cigarette, "the coffin nail."[15]

Correspondent Henry L. Wales, of the International News Service, with his face and hands bandaged as a result of a bad accident, receiving a cigarette from Miss Winifred Bryce, 294 Henry Street, Brooklyn, NY, of the American Red Cross Evacuation Hospitals #6 & #7. Souilly, France, October 13, 1918, loc.gov.

Soldiers returning home after the war further found their new habit perfectly suited to routinized labor time. Whatever you think of them, cigars are an *experience*, not something you fit in between shifts. Cigarettes, by contrast, are an anywhere, anytime pleasure, something that can be done *now* to break up the monotony of the day. In 1925, the *New York Times* editorialized, "Short, snappy, easily attempted, easily completed or just as easily discarded before completion—the cigarette is a symbol of a machine age in which the ultimate cogs and wheels and levers are human nerves."[16]

Advertising

If flue curing and mechanization created the product, and the rhythms of capitalist society created the consumer, it was the nascent advertising industry that connected the two. Advertising was not simply used to sell cigarettes: thanks to unprecedented spending and a willingness to push the boundaries of propriety and truth alike, the tobacco industry *created* modern advertising.

What is most remarkable about the "allure" meticulously crafted by cigarette advertising in the crucial interwar period was its shapelessness.[17] Cigarettes were masculine if you wanted to be manly, feminine if you wanted to be womanly, practically medicine if you wanted to be healthy, or a mysterious danger if you wanted to rebel. Perhaps the most enduring association forged at this time was the link between smoking and eroticism: film heroes and heroines, elegantly lighting up, surrounded by lovely blooms of smoke, created the undeniable attraction of a dangerous beginning. Never would they end up stinking and greedily sucking on a dying stub. In the unconscious, as Freud said, there is no time.

The industry was particularly interested in breaking the traditional taboo on women smoking, and their publicity henchmen employed two appalling measures for this purpose. The first was to reinforce the association of the cigarette with the cause of women's empowerment. In 1912, the Women's Political Union had distributed cigarettes with the motto "Votes for Women" printed on them, arguing that they were a "temporary substitute for the ballot."[18] Capitalizing on this sentiment, public relations progenitor Edward Bernays (Freud's nephew) had debutantes march proudly in the 1929 New York City Easter parade, lighting up their Lucky Strikes as "torches of freedom."[19] By the late '30s, women smokers were seen as "bringing about a new democracy of the road," and surveys showed that most women at college were smokers.[20]

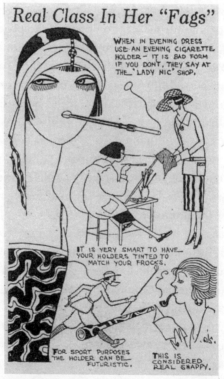

Sacramento Star, *June 21, 1922. From Tate, Cigarette Wars.*

The second and, of course, contradictory tactic was to raise women's anxieties about their bodies. In 1928, Lucky Strike landed Amelia Earhart in an ad with the tagline: "For a slender figure—Reach for a Lucky instead of a sweet."[21] In addition to offending the National Confectioners Association, the campaign also drew fire from critics who claimed that they were marketing to children, which, of course, they absolutely were. Tobacco companies knew early on that lifelong smokers typically begin smoking before the age of eighteen, and while they couldn't ever officially market to what the industry called "replacement smokers," they have crossed about every line there is to cross (see Joe Camel).[22]

The success of cigarette advertising was astounding: In 1950, 90 percent of tobacco was consumed in the form of cigarettes, up from 5 percent in 1904.[23] By the late '50s, Americans were purchasing more than 15,000 cigarettes per second.[24] The cigarette was sociable even though it stunk; it represented autonomy even though it created dependence. As one critic asked in 1930, "Has there been in all history so colossal a standardizing process—such a vast demonstration of the sheep-like qualities of the human race as in the spread of the tobacco habit?"[25]

To say that the cigarette epidemic was perfectly "engineered" would, however, not be quite right, for even its creators were surprised by the dramatic cultural shift they were able to enact. It's true that they had a receptive audience, as Americans fell "in love with smoking at a time when their collective life was low on other consolations," in historian Richard Kluger's characterization.[26] But new sociological and psychological tactics were in play, tactics now cynically accepted as the norm in the media world but which were baffling and terrifying at the time. Advertisers themselves—"blind probers through a jungle of irrational impulses," in their own self-conception—"were concerned that extravagant claims, paid testimonials, and aggressive competitiveness" were threatening the legitimacy

Silva Thins are thin and rich.

Advertisement for Silva Thins. American Tobacco Company, "Cigarettes are like women. The best ones are thin and rich," 1970, Richard W. Pollay Cigarette Ads Collection, industrydocuments.ucsf.edu.

of advertising itself and hoped to create internal norms to rein in certain excesses.[27]

Controversy

By 1950, damning studies about the link between smoking and lung cancer had been published, and doctors were quitting the habit in droves.[28] Without of course publicly recognizing the problem, the industry took the threat seriously. Filtered cigarettes were a novelty in the '40s, but they became commonplace in the '50s, and with radical promises attached.[29] Lorillard director of research Harris B. Parmele claimed in 1954 that "the air you breathe through a Kent cigarette is several times cleaner than the air you normally breathe in an average American city."[30] As one might suspect, filters don't actually reduce the harms of smoking: as Proctor illustrates, adding filters to cigarettes is like "running your Jack Daniels through a series of fine-mesh screens before you chug it down."[31]

Tobacco advertisers also had to change up their strategy, and their new methods would soon snuff out even the smallest twinge of moral feeling. At this point they knew that the products they sold were killing their customers; the task was now to *appear* to be taking the risk seriously, while persistently upholding the position of "more research needed."[32] In 1953, Hill & Knowlton (which would much later do PR work in the War on Drugs, and then the Iraq War) released their "Frank Statement to Cigarette Smokers," accepting "an interest in people's health as a basic responsibility, paramount to every other consideration in our business" and announcing the formation of the Tobacco Industry Research Committee (TIRC) to study the problem.[33]

The TIRC was, of course, not a research committee at all, and its director, C. C. Little, was an industry shill. But under the close guidance of Hill & Knowlton, it succeeded in keeping cigarette sales rising through the '50s and '60s through the dissemination of "scientific" counterinformation. According to historian Allan Brandt,

> Hill & Knowlton had served its tobacco clients with commitment and fidelity, and with great success. But the firm had also taken its clients across a critical moral barrier ... By making science fair game in the battle of public relations, the tobacco industry set a destructive precedent that would affect future debate on subjects ranging from global warming to intelligent design. And by insinuating itself so significantly in the practice of journalism, Hill & Knowlton would compromise the legitimacy and authority of the very instruments upon which they depended.[34]

As the evidence mounted, thanks to advances in the field of epidemiology, the line stayed the same.[35] We don't yet know;

maybe we'll *never* know, and besides, what even is "knowledge," anyway? "Doubt is our product," a Brown & Williamson VP emphasized in 1969.[36] But keeping up this agnosticism was more than a marketing strategy: by the '60s, industry lawyers saw no other choice than to maintain this position or else incur legal risk. So Big Tobacco found itself in quite a pickle when the Federal Trade Commission, on the heels of a scathing surgeon general's report in 1964, demanded warning labels on all cigarette packages.[37]

Once again, the tobacco industry found a way to turn these developments to its advantage. Seeing the inevitability of some warning label, they decided that all was not lost—as long as they got to craft the message. When the Federal Cigarette Labeling and Advertising Act was passed in 1965, it only required an ambiguous warning to appear on all labels: "Caution: Cigarette Smoking May Be Hazardous to Your Health."[38] This was more than just a successful watering down of a known fact: by including a warning label on their product, a label that saddled them with no culpability, the tobacco industry created the cornerstone of a powerful legal argument.

Individual Responsibility

In 1983, attorney Marc Edell filed a complaint against four major tobacco companies on behalf of Rose Cipollone. Cipollone had been a smoker since the age of sixteen, and she would die of lung cancer less than a year into her suit at the age of fifty-nine. When the jury finally rendered a verdict on June 3, 1988, they awarded $400,000 to Cipollone's husband Antonio, marking the first successful judgment against Big Tobacco.

But the jury also ruled that Rose Cipollone was primarily responsible for her own death, and that the tobacco companies were not guilty of fraud and conspiracy.[39] Edell had tried to demonstrate that Cipollone was *addicted* to cigarettes, but Americans weren't yet ready to burden smokers with a heavily stigmatized term like "addict." Statistically, heroin users are more likely to kick their habit than smokers.[40] But Cipollone was no addict, said the industry lawyers; she knew very well the risks involved in smoking, and thus she was ultimately responsible for her own death. She smoked for over forty years: What did she expect?

This "assumption of risk" defense, used in all similar suits, was an ingenious one. The industry, of course, could not come out and admit that cigarettes were actually dangerous. Instead, they "contended that the 'controversy' regarding smoking and health was well-known and highly publicized; as a result, plaintiffs were well-informed of any 'alleged' risks."[41] As an R. J. Reynolds executive wrote, "We believe the general public has long been aware of the contention that smoking may be injurious to health."[42] The introduction of federally mandated warning labels on all cigarette packs had, in fact, shored up this defense. While deterring few smokers, these labels allowed industry lawyers to point to the package itself: Who but a willful risk taker would look at this product and actually use it?

It's worth meditating on the nature of this legal argument, which structures much of contemporary reality. "No one knows for sure that X is dangerous. There is a debate about the harmfulness of X, but it's important to remember that there are two sides to every debate, and we ought to consider both to be fair. That being said, since knowledge of the *possible* harms of X is widespread, any individual who engages in X must be held responsible for any harms that X causes." This is not just an argument about smoking, and not just a peek into the *ur*logic of gaslighting. It is also an argument about the general responsibility of individuals for social ills.

Defeat in Victory

At the outset of the '80s, the tobacco companies were apex predators of the American economy. Industry attorney Matthew Myers proudly proclaimed that "there had never been a piece of antismoking legislation passed that the industry didn't want."[43] Without restraint and at the peak of its powers, Big Tobacco began to feed: R. J. Reynolds merged with Nabisco in 1985. That same year, Philip Morris acquired General Foods, then did the same with Kraft Foods in 1988. Tobacco companies had long advertised their products as appetite suppressants; they were now in charge of some of the largest diversified food corporations in the world.

But the industry's defenses were beginning to buckle. Disappointing as the outcome of the *Cipollone* case was, Edell at least scored one lasting victory: he had gotten his hands on some 300,000 internal tobacco industry documents, which the judge admitted into the public record, to the loud protest of the defense attorneys.[44] These documents were the first breach of the industry's defenses. They would be further weakened in 1990, when paralegal Merrell Williams released what would come to be known as the "cigarette papers," some 4,000 pages of damning evidence on tobacco giant Brown & Williamson.[45] Unsurprisingly, these documents demonstrated a radical discrepancy between industry statements and industry activity.

To many critics, the end of Big Tobacco seemed to be assured by the flood of damning information being made public, but the limits of the impact of this knowledge soon became clear in two stunning failures of corporate journalism. In 1994, ABC's broadcast news magazine *Day One* released a story about how cigarette companies artificially "spike" their product with extra nicotine to keep people addicted, and they were promptly sued by Philip Morris. Despite the seeming likelihood of exoneration, ABC settled its suit and issued a public apology.[46] The Walt Disney Company was on the verge of buying ABC, and they wanted the suit gone before the deal went through.[47]

Around the same time that ABC was settling, *60 Minutes* was preparing to run its interview with Jeffrey Wigand, an industry whistleblower whose travails would later be depicted in the film *The Insider*. With the *Day One* suit fresh in their minds, and in the final stages of a $5.4 billion merger with Westinghouse, CBS executives chose to kill the story.[48] Thus were two of the most important public health stories of the twentieth century squashed under the weight of giant corporations growing even bigger.

Having reached the limits of individual litigation and main-stream media reporting, anti-tobacco forces finally turned to mass litigation, where tobacco lawyers couldn't pin the blame on reckless individuals as easily. Particularly effective were the battles of state attorneys general to recover Medicaid costs for tobacco-related diseases. Mississippi was the first to file such a suit in 1994. In an appeal to the rights of the taxpayers, a member of the team that filed the suit aptly noted, "The State of Mississippi has never smoked a cigarette."[49] Similar suits soon followed from Minnesota, West Virginia, Florida, and Massachusetts, and in 1997 tobacco executives agreed to a proposed "global settlement," which would reimburse states to the tune of $368.5 billion.

Celebrations over the global settlement proved prema-ture, as its enactment required congressional legislation. John McCain's aggressive attempt to make good on the global settlement was tanked by the millions the industry spent on lobbying and advertising.[50] The watered-down Master Settle-ment Agreement, functionally a new excise tax on cigarettes that inadvertently made states dependent on tobacco revenue, was finally passed in November 1998.[51] As Richard Scruggs, a key player in the genesis of the global settlement, noted, "The perverse result of what we did was essentially put the states in bed with the tobacco companies."[52] With remarkable tenacity

Duane Hanson, Supermarket Shopper. *© 2022 Estate of Duane Hanson / Licensed by VAGA at Artists Rights Society (ARS), NY. Photograph by Carl Brunn.*

and skill, the tobacco companies have turned every threat into an advantage.

Losers

Cigarette consumption reached a high in the United States in the '70s at about 4,000 cigarettes consumed annually per capita (more than ten cigarettes per person per day), and has dropped steadily since, with no precipitous drop immediately after 1998 (the year the Master Settlement Agreement passed).[53] In 2016, the per capita number was 1,016.[54] The key turning point was not some new discovery about the harms to smokers but rather one about the harms to those *not* smoking. After all, did the victims of secondhand smoke make a *choice*? Anti-tobacco advocates quickly assumed this line of attack, borrowing language from the Civil Rights Movement about the "rights" of nonsmokers, and bans on smoking in public places proliferated.[55] Despite some last-ditch distraction efforts—including a planned publicity campaign to shift public health advocates' attention away from smoking and toward AIDS—Big Tobacco knew that the good times were over.[56] Knowing all it had taken to bring smoking *into* public spaces, the industry understood well the significance of its banishment *from* public spaces.

A new model of public health was also gaining traction, anchored in the epidemiology of chronic disease (catalyzed, again, by the case of cigarettes). A new terminology of "risk" embedded in different "lifestyles" became common sense, and it was soon being applied to many areas of life, not just smoking.[57] As health consciousness took over American society—or more precisely, as health became a marker of class in America— cigarette smokers quickly became reviled, asocial creatures, unhealthy members of a backward working class. Cigarettes had been successfully revalued as "a loser's drug," and sales plummeted.[58]

That being said, cigarettes are far and away the deadliest drug in existence, not in the *Mad Men* '60s, but today and for the foreseeable future. According to a recent Health and Human Services report, smoking kills 480,000 people in the United States every year.[59] For reference, that's "more than AIDS, alcohol, car accidents, illegal drugs, murders and suicides *combined*."[60] Even more disturbingly, the American epidemic has been exported worldwide: the slow decrease in cigarette consumption in the developed world has been complemented by a sharp increase in the developing world.[61] Today the fastest machines can produce 20,000 cigarettes *in one minute*, and regulations in rich countries certainly aren't turning them off.[62]

This is not simply a case of the "glamor" of American consumption practices being aped by teenagers around the world, but rather one of very pointed efforts to crush foreign, state-run tobacco monopolies—which generally helped keep smoking prevalence down—in the name of "open markets."[63] While reducing cigarette consumption at home, the Reagan and Bush administrations both pushed for a liberalization of the tobacco trade, a move that has been rightly compared to the opium wars of the nineteenth century.[64] Dan Quayle baldly claimed in 1990 that "tobacco exports should be expanded aggressively because Americans are smoking less."[65] Soon after, it became clear that growing cigarette consumption was undermining the marked gains in international public health—especially in China's newly opened market—and the WHO adopted the Framework Convention on Tobacco Control (FCTC) in 2003 to deal with the problem.[66]

The FCTC finally came into effect in 2005, obligating all participating countries to "implement strong evidence-based policies, including five key measures: high tobacco taxes, smoke-free public spaces, warning labels, comprehensive advertising bans, and support for stop smoking services."[67] The FCTC was ultimately silent on the problem of trade liberalization, but that didn't stop British American Tobacco from calling the attempt to "foist" developed-world health standards on the developing world a new "form of moral and cultural imperialism, based on assumptions that 'west is best.'"[68] Out of "respect for cultural diversity," BAT opposed "calls for global regulations and standards" as a "one size fits all" approach.

A recent study on the effectiveness of the FCTC comes to predictable conclusions. While reducing tobacco use in countries that have adopted the key demand-reduction measures (the developed world), the FCTC has not done much to reduce tobacco use in countries that have not adopted such measures (low- and middle-income countries preyed on by the tobacco industry).[69] However, even in developed nations, smoking prevalence rates are drawn along class lines: in 2010, the overall smoking rate in China (28.1 percent), which houses one-third of the world's smokers, was less than that in West Virginia (28.6 percent).[70]

Global cigarette consumption rose steadily until 2010, when it peaked at 5.8 trillion cigarettes consumed. It's fallen in the decade since but was still at 5.2 trillion in 2019. Meanwhile, a younger generation of Americans has switched to e-cigarettes —safer in some ways than their analog forebears, but they are just as addictive and can still cause lung and cardiovascular disease. Juul and Vuse, the two leading e-cigarette brands with 42 percent and 36 percent market share in 2020, are owned by Altria and Reynolds, the two leading cigarette companies with 49 percent and 34 percent of the market share in 2020. *Plus ça change ...*

Sublime

Brandt aptly illustrates the paradox at the heart of the cigarette tragedy:

> It has been conservatively estimated that 100 million people around the world died from tobacco related diseases in the

twentieth century. Through the first half of that century, the health risks of smoking had yet to be scientifically demonstrated. In this century, in which we have known tobacco's health effects from the first day, the death toll is predicted to be one billion.[71]

This projection is largely predicated on the lack of regulatory structure in the developing world, but part of the problem here must be that a good number of people today are taking up smoking in full awareness of its destructive consequences. How do we make sense of the fact that knowledge has proved fatally insufficient?

As we have seen, the story of the cigarette is the story of the blurring of the line between advertising and reality, of the shaping of innermost desires by corporate memoranda, of the intentional obfuscation of the truth in scientific inquiry and in journalism, of the growing responsibility of individuals for social ills, of the breaking down of barriers by crises of overproduction, and, above all, of a pleasure perfectly suited to capitalism. Short and contained like the pop song, a meaning-giving ritual in the absence of meaningful structures, "an ersatz act which absorbs the increasing nervousness of civilized man."[72] As Lord Henry says in *The Picture of Dorian Gray*, "A cigarette is the perfect type of a perfect pleasure. It is exquisite, and it leaves one unsatisfied. What more can one want?"[73]

In *Cigarettes Are Sublime*, Richard Klein argues that we need to appreciate the attractiveness of the cigarette if we are to overcome it. He fears that the straightforward discouragement of anti-tobacco advocates, in ignoring the "sublime" aspect of smoking, does not actually discourage, and in fact "often accomplishes the opposite of what it intends, sometimes inures the habit, and perhaps initiates it. For many, where cigarettes are concerned, discouraging is a form of ensuring their continuing to smoke. For some, it may cause them to start."[74] Klein concludes that

the moment of taking a cigarette allows one to open a parenthesis in the time of ordinary experience, a space and a time of
heightened attention that give rise to a feeling of transcendence,
evoked through the ritual of fire, smoke, cinder connecting hand,
lungs, breath, and mouth.[75]

He calls this experience "*l'air du temps*," the meditative embrace
of situatedness that punctuates the day through ritual exit.

Klein tends to focus on the *meaning* that is acquired through
smoking, though many of his examples offer a darker view.
Jean-Paul Sartre also finds great meaning in the act of smoking,
but describes this meaning in terms of "appropriative, destructive action."

Tobacco is a symbol of "appropriated" being, since it is destroyed
in the rhythm of my breathing, in a mode of "continuous
destruction," since it passes into me and its change in myself is
manifested symbolically by the transformation of the consumed

*The US military's Semi-Automatic Ground Environment (SAGE) com-
puter was designed in the 1950s to protect against Soviet nuclear attack.
A cigarette lighter and ashtray are built into the console. The SAGE
computer is on display at the Computer History Museum in Mountain
View, California. This image was originally posted to Flickr by Joi at
flickr.com/photos/35034362831@N01/494395374. It was reviewed on
May 14, 2007, by FlickreviewR and was confirmed to be licensed under
the terms of the cc-by-2.0.*

solid into smoke. The connection between the landscape seen
while I was smoking and this little crematory sacrifice was
such that as we have just seen, the tobacco symbolized the
landscape. This means then that the act of destructively appropriating the tobacco was the symbolic equivalent of destructively
appropriating the entire world. *Across the tobacco which I was
smoking was the world which was burning, which was going
up in smoke,* which was being reabsorbed into vapor so as to
re-enter into me.[76]

Perhaps beyond calming and meaning-making, it is this
straightforwardly destructive element of cigarette smoking
that is ultimately the source of its appeal. Following Klein's
logic, we should assume that people start smoking today not
in spite of the health risks but *because of them.*[77] How else to
make sense of the glaring insufficiency of knowledge? Every
cigarette puff is a daring "Fuck you" to the neoliberal ethic
of self-care, deadening relief from a deadened society, at the
same time that it is an internalization of the burning earth in
miniature. *L'air du temps*, as Klein seems to know, is also *la
suffocation du temps*, the opening parenthesis followed soon,
with short breath in constricted lungs, by a closing parenthesis.

People today smoke because they are nervous, and they
smoke to lend sense to the day. But they also smoke because
they are hastening an end.

3

Alcohol, or Commodity Fetishism

"I'm on strike, I tell you," he said, "against beer, against whisky, against the saloon, against the men that run the saloon and against the men that spend their earnings in the saloons, when they ought to be supporting their wives and children; and this strike won't be called off as long as I live."

The men stared at him in blank amazement. "The boy's gone daft," said one.

"No, he hasn't," retorted another, "he's sensible enough— more so than we are. It's the saloon that hurts and keeps us poor. I've been wondering all this while why Debs and the rest of the leaders didn't see it."

—A fictional story from the WCTU journal, *Union Signal* (published October 11, 1894, a few months after the Pullman Strike), in which factory workers ask a boy to fetch them a pail of beer and he refuses, citing the above justification

Alcohol was not just a commonly used substance in Western preindustrial societies, it was a fact of life. Beer and wine were always part of meals, even breakfast, and they were consumed in staggering amounts on holidays.[1] You drank at work, you drank at church, and you definitely drank on election days, when it was not just accepted but *expected* that candidates rewarded voters with generous libations.[2] In 1758, George Washington distributed 144 gallons of alcohol to voters in his run for the Virginia House of Burgesses, which earned him a victory with 307 votes.[3] That's about half a gallon per vote.

Though there was some hand-wringing about excessive drunkenness, as well as the cold exploitation of Native

American drinking practices, few criticized alcohol itself before industrialization.[4] Spirits performed a key economic function in preindustrial America: the transformation of perishable and bulky grain into nonperishable and easily traded whiskey.[5] And since no one yet had to worry about handling heavy machinery or drunk driving, there was less cause for concern over a level of per capita consumption that was sometimes more than triple what it is today.[6] Drinking competitions were common, and social obligations around drinking were strict: if you were offered a drink, you either accepted it (and reciprocated), or you suffered the consequences—social marginalization at the very least, with a high likelihood of getting beaten up on the spot. An English visitor to the States in the early nineteenth century observed,

> Americans can fix nothing without a drink ... So much has it become the habit to cement all friendship, and commence acquaintance by drinking, that it is a cause of serious offence to refuse ... It is literally, "Stranger, will you drink or fight?"[7]

These rituals around alcohol are representative of what the anthropologist Marcel Mauss called a "gift economy": a social world united by obligatory rites of giving, receiving, and reciprocating, quite different from the icy calculations of self-interest that are the norm in a capitalist economy.[8] Though we still today feel the compulsions involved in the giving of gifts (including rounds of drinks), a true gift economy can only appear to many contemporaries as regressive and reckless—the inanities and excesses of frat house life but writ large and taken way more seriously.

What these belligerent premodern practices demonstrate is the existence of something that today can only be simulated through constant invocation: *community*. When we look back on the haze of intoxication from which capitalist societies blossomed, any disgust we feel toward its barbaric rituals is in large part a function of our own repressed sociality.

The Royalist Club *and* Mr. Neilson's Battle with the Royalist Club, *attributed to Dr. Alexander Hamilton. In* Gentleman's Progress: The Itinerarium of Dr. Alexander Hamilton, *1744, ed. Carl Bridenbaugh (Chapel Hill: University of North Carolina Press, 1948).*

Industrialization

The temperance movement emerged from the fever of early nineteenth-century evangelical revivals, guided by the aim to eliminate what employers saw as a drag on their workers' productivity, and in response to the extraordinary alcohol consumption of the period (historian W. J. Rorabaugh's account of the time is fittingly titled *The Alcoholic Republic*).[9] The antebellum movement won important local and state victories, including the Maine Law of 1851, which prohibited the manufacture and sale of alcohol in the state. According to a pamphlet of the American Temperance Union released in 1853, the Maine Law had "greatly added to the amount and availableness of human labor. Intemperate, indolent and vicious men have ... become sober, and ready and willing to go into the field and the workshop."[10] Massachusetts crusader Jesse Goodrich nicely prioritized the goods to which drink was a hindrance: "Capital,—Enterprise,—Industry,—Morals,—and Religion."[11]

After the Civil War, during a period of rapid industrialization and capital concentration, the "labor question" was front and center in American life, and the old temperance forces gathered anew to assert their answer. In these changing conditions, the inebriation of the working class, made more visible and concentrated by urbanization, was portrayed as out of place and in fact quite hazardous in an increasingly mechanized world. It was custom for anthracite miners in Pennsylvania, for instance, "to take a day's supply of whiskey down into the mines at the start of each shift."[12] Needless to say, such practices chafed against the capitalist sensibility. In historian Harry Levine's characterization, "The prohibition crusade was justified in terms of the needs of a new, complex, heterogeneous, class-stratified, industrial, efficiency-oriented society."[13] A drunk worker in a complex production process was a danger to himself and society—a position firmly shared by the likes of John D. Rockefeller, Henry Ford, and William Randolph Hearst.[14]

But the drinking practices of the working class were no mere premodern survival. The routinization and exhaustion, not to mention the straightforward immiseration, involved in working in the newly industrialized world led to a new kind of binge drinking.[15] As Rorabaugh explains,

> Factory workers who had previously lived on farms found the discipline of factory work to be new and unsettling. Long, regular hours and dull, unvaried work away from home were in contrast to agricultural labor, with its extensive family contact, variety of tasks, slower pace, and periods of comparative leisure alternating with periods of frenzied activity. It appears that many factory workers met these new conditions by turning to heavy drinking.[16]

Alcohol in preindustrial society flowed with the rhythms of daily life and social obligation. With industrialization, it took on a more instrumental and insidious function: *escape*.

In describing this new situation, Friedrich Engels wrote what is perhaps the most succinct formulation of the "problem" of drug use and abuse in capitalist society, as apt today as it was in his day:

> The worker comes home from his job tired and listless; he finds a residence that is without all comfort, dank, inhospitable and dirty; he urgently needs something to restore him, he must have *something* that compensates for his toil and makes the prospect of the next day tolerable; his tense, harried, hypochondriacal mood, which is the product of unhealthy conditions ... is exacerbated to the point of unendurability by his overall circumstances in life, the precariousness of his existence, his dependence on all manner of contingencies and his inability to introduce any degree of security into his own life ... his need for companionship can be satisfied only in a tavern, since he and his friends have no other place to meet—and all told, how is the worker not to have the strongest temptation towards inebriation, how could he possibly be in any state to resist the allures of drinks? On the contrary, it is a moral and physical necessity that under these circumstances a very great number of workers *must* succumb to drink.[17]

The temperance movement was about many things—evangelical spirit, Progressive reform, status anxiety, anti-immigrant sentiment—but it's perhaps best characterized as a vehicle for the social enforcement of worker discipline in an industrialized age.[18] As historian John J. Rumbarger argues, temperance was about treating labor "as a form of capital to be preserved and improved, according to the needs of enterprise."[19] Much later, on the eve of Prohibition, one manufacturer would state quite plainly, "Until booze is banished we can never have really efficient workmen. We are not much interested in the moral side of the matter as such. It is purely a question of dollars and cents."[20]

But as with most moralized applications of social imperatives, many firebrands of this new movement pursued its aims with undue *élan*, advocating not simply for the regulation of spirits but for *total abstinence*. It was a truly wild idea at first. Cutting down on rum and whiskey, sure, but the notion that one could do without beer and wine was not just unconventional, it was downright lunacy. For one, it wasn't yet commonly understood that the intoxicating essence of beer, wine, and distilled liquor was the same thing. These drinks were considered fundamentally different substances in the early nineteenth century, and it was a self-proclaimed "doctrinal innovation" when English temperance advocate Joseph Livesey spread the word that "whiskey is the soul of beer."[21]

Beer and wine were also seen as health-promoting substances, and compared to the alternatives at the time, they very much were. Drinking water had always been understood as a risky proposition (a certain means of contracting cholera), and for centuries it was common sense to mix wine or spirits in with water before you drank it. This practice was scientifically legitimated by the discovery of the bactericidal properties of wine in 1951.[22] Life insurance companies sometimes refused abstainers in the belief that they were reckless zealots.[23] The appearance of reliably potable water in the mid-nineteenth century was an important precondition of teetotalism. When New York City mayor Philip Hone celebrated the completion in 1842 of an aqueduct bringing fresh Croton River water to the city—"Water! Water! Is the universal note which is sounded through every part of the city, and infuses joy and exultation into the masses"—he wasn't just announcing a massive engineering feat.[24] Temperance ideologues could finally argue legitimately (though they were happy previously to argue illegitimately) that there was no need to drink *any* alcohol as an alternative to water.[25]

Temperance

Thus, when temperance forces first gathered, they encountered both conceptual and pragmatic resistance to their cause. Further developments—like the growth and success of California vintners, the "liquid hospitality" that pervaded the West in general, and the country's love of beer (the production of which increased at more than twice the rate of the population between 1880 and 1910)—made America seem like a particularly inhospitable terrain for this movement to succeed.[26] And yet when veterans returned from the First World War, they found themselves unable to celebrate with anything harder than Bevo—Anheuser Busch's predecessor of O'Douls.[27]

How did that most curious "noble experiment," Prohibition, come to be? In the 1850s, a flood of German immigrants settled in the Midwest, and many of what are still the largest breweries in the country opened in that decade: Miller, Schlitz, Busch. The German brewers were enthusiastic industrialists, introducing new innovations like the steam engine, taking advantage of the new railway network to increase distribution, and vertically integrating their operations through the procurement of saloons.[28]

Unlike the colonial tavern, which lodged visitors and served more as a community hall, the nineteenth-century saloon was more functional and segmented due to a spatial innovation that has been so naturalized to us that it appears quite unremarkable: *the bar*.[29] According to historian Madelon Powers,

> Just as churchgoers in a strange city could enter expecting to find an altar, pews, statues, and stained-glass windows, so saloongoers everywhere could push through the swinging doors expecting to find a long hardwood bar, brass rails, mirrors, and displays of bottles and glasses.[30]

The historian Wolfgang Schivelbusch thinks of the bar as a kind of "*traffic* innovation" that "sped up drinking, just as the railroad sped up travel and the mechanical loom sped up textile production."[31] At a colonial tavern, you sat across from others at a table; at a saloon, you stood across from the alcohol at a bar. While perhaps a bit too formulaic, it doesn't seem wide of the mark to say that, at the bar, you're there to drink first and socialize second (if at all).

Saloons also differed from taverns in being frequented predominantly by men. As with the coffeehouses of the eighteenth century, gendered backlash was inevitable: in 1874, the Woman's Christian Temperance Union (WCTU) formed to represent the "voiceless victims" of male saloon culture.[32] In the temperance reformer's perspective, drunkards had lost their volition and their manhood, having been seduced by the saloonkeeper and invaded by an alien power.[33] The solution was domestic moral suasion: in historian Elaine Frantz Parsons's characterization, "The model of female power as influence posited that women should exercise their power indirectly, by inculcating moral principles into their husbands, sons, and fathers, who would in turn bring those principles to bear in the world of public affairs."[34] Such were the contradictory roots of middle-class women's activism in the nineteenth century.

Unlike the coffeehouses, however, saloons were targeted more particularly as hangouts of *lower-class* men: urban, immigrant Catholics who offended the sensibility of Protestant America (among other things, by hanging pictures of naked women on the walls).[35] Some brands, like Black Cock Vigor Gin, poked the bear. A journal of the Anti-Saloon League, the powerful lobbying organization formed in 1896, put the issue in stark terms: "If we are to preserve this nation and the Anglo-Saxon type we must abolish [saloons]."[36] The saloon embodied in a single institution the poverty, "degeneracy," and social dislocation of industrialized cities in the later nineteenth century, making it a natural target of reform.[37]

Saloons could sometimes be the squalid affairs that reformers painted them as, but many were centers of working-class

Advertisement for Black Cock Vigor Gin (~1905).

social life, providing "public toilets, food, warmth, clean water, meeting space, check-cashing services, newspapers—often otherwise unavailable to workers in the late nineteenth century city."[38] One worker in Denver defended the saloon as supplying "a want—a need. It offers [a] common meeting place. It dispenses good cheer. It ministers to the craving for fellowship."[39] The Chicago Workingmen's Exchange served free lunch and nickel beer. Alderman Michael Kenna used it as a base of operations, where, amid the usual politicking, he helped poor men and women acquire "peddlers' permits" to make ends meet.[40] Unsurprisingly, it was precisely these kinds of clientelist political machines that Progressives saw as corrupt and in need of cleaning up.

On the whole, temperance organizations, though united in the desire to produce "the sober industrious working man," were thoroughly confused in their political orientation.[41] Dominated by middle-class leaders like Frances Willard, the WCTU had both populist and anti-populist, suffragist and nonsuffragist, pro-labor and anti-labor elements.[42] They aped the populists in railing against monopolies of transport, finance, and manufacture that squeezed the farmer and small-town businessman. But they were also supported by many upper-class targets of the populists' rage, who were just as eager to see immigrant workers disciplined.[43] Even in the very root of their mission, the WCTU was not free of contradiction: a survey conducted by the *Ladies' Home Journal*, which "wrote to fifty members of the Women's Christian Temperance Union," "found that three quarters of them were using highly alcoholic patent medicines" (which also contained things like opium and cocaine).[44]

In many ways, this confused period closely resembles the present. The big business tycoons, including the German brewers, had grown fabulously rich. Belief in their corruption was widespread, and typically justified.[45] Moralizing, middle-class progressives were in a headlong crusade for public virtue

Satirizing a slogan of the Woman's Christian Temperance Union, a still from Kansas Saloon Smashers *in* Lapham's Quarterly *(New York, 1895).*

against the "ignorant masses," a blinkered and dogged endeavor for which they were incessantly mocked.[46] Then as now, a confused culture war dominated what passed for politics.

Prohibition

A few early twentieth-century developments pushed the temperance cause over the hump: First, the "antisaloonist" effort to mobilize religious and philanthropic organizations toward curbing working-class unrest had clearly failed.[47] State action was needed. Second, in 1913, the Sixteenth Amendment was finally ratified, allowing for a small income tax on a few wealthy taxpayers. Before this revenue stream became available, the federal government had relied primarily on customs duties on imports and taxes on alcohol.[48] The Sixteenth Amendment finally freed the government of its own dependence. Third, after bitter debates over the use of alcohol as a therapeutic substance, the American Medical Association effectively prohibited its use by physicians in 1917, concluding that *all* forms of drinking, even moderate use, were detrimental to one's health.[49]

Finally, the brewers were predominantly Germans, and on the cusp of war, this fact voided any lobbying power they bore.[50] The prohibitionist campaigner Purley Baker did his best to connect German aggression and beer drinking:

> The primary and secondary and all-compelling cause [of war] is that a race of people have arisen who eat like gluttons and drink like swine—a race whose "God is their belly" and whose inevitable end is destruction. Their sodden habits of life have driven them constantly toward brutality and cruelty until they were prepared to strike for universal conquest, though millions of lives and oceans of blood were to be the price of reaching that unholy ambition. Beer will do for a nation exactly what it will do for an individual.[51]

The Eighteenth Amendment, which prohibited "the manufacture, sale, or transportation of intoxicating liquors," easily passed through Congress and was ratified by the states in 1919. To make things perfectly clear, the Volstead Act, the enforcing act of the Eighteenth Amendment, specified that "intoxicating liquors" meant anything above 0.5 percent alcohol content.

In victory, it was painfully apparent that the dry cause issued from a backward critique of capitalism. Reformers celebrated Prohibition as the beginning of the end of poverty, urban blight, and political corruption. The reverend Billy Sunday rejoiced, "The reign of tears is over! The slums will soon be only a memory. We will turn our prisons into factories and our jails into storehouses and corncribs."[52] Representative Andrew Volstead (the act's namesake) promised that "all men will walk with their heads high, all women will smile, all children will laugh. The doors of hell will forever be closed."[53] Prohibition promised all the goods of capitalism with none of its ills.

With the image of speakeasies, bootlegging, and organized crime in mind, it's common to believe that this dream quickly turned into a nightmare. But for many, it was quite the success. Americans consumed less alcohol in the '20s than at any other time in history, and on the whole, speakeasies weren't nefarious establishments—often they were just restaurants that served alcohol if you asked. Spaghetti and meatballs became an American dish in this decade because Italian restaurants were particularly resistant to the idea that you couldn't serve wine with dinner, and they attracted many customers grateful for their insolence.[54] And unlike the saloon, speakeasies welcomed newly enfranchised women. This wasn't a wholly positive development—one speakeasy in New York City hung a sign out front reading, "Through These Portals the Most Beautiful Girls in the World Pass OUT"—but as intended, the culture of male drinking was broken during Prohibition.[55]

For others, however, Prohibition brought a new kind of

terror. According to historian Lisa McGirr, Prohibition was selectively enforced:

> Uneven enforcement was the hidden reason the white, urbane upper-middle class could laugh at the antics of [New York City Prohibition officers], while Mexicans, poor European immigrants, African-Americans, poor whites in the South, and the unlucky experienced the full brunt of Prohibition enforcement's deadly reality.[56]

Early into the Volstead years, when the federal Prohibition Unit found itself faced with the impossible task of ending the "liquor evil," they called on "grassroots antiliquor warriors" to help with enforcement.[57] Among those who heeded the call were the Ku Klux Klan, revived from the memory of its first Reconstruction-era iteration in 1915. Volstead gave the Klan a mission, and its ranks ballooned beginning in 1920.[58]

By the late '20s, however, the Bureau of Prohibition was less in need of such "citizen enforcers": in order to fight the growing menace of organized crime, the bureau became a sprawling federal apparatus. In 1930, it had a $13 million budget; J. Edgar Hoover's Bureau of Investigation had a $2 million budget that same year.[59] This growth in enforcement spending mirrored the development of the American carceral state: the 1920s and '30s witnessed a first crisis of mass incarceration, when an overcrowding of federal and state prisons led to a rapid increase of prison constructions.[60] Indeed, the War on Alcohol paved the way for the later and more destructive War on Drugs.

Not only did Prohibition organize law enforcement, it also organized crime itself. Anytime you outlaw something that a lot of people want, the suppliers of that good, attracted to wild profits, get real efficient, real quick. The name Al Capone would probably not register in American consciousness today were it not for the Volstead Act. The Saint Valentine's Day Massacre, when Capone's enterprise gunned down seven members of a rival organization in 1929, and which served as a breaking point for the dry cause, was an *effect* of the law, in addition to a violation of it. The crime networks that sprouted during Prohibition traded also in "narcotics," turning the illegal drugs trade into a global business. Though the public eventually would turn against Prohibition, they would continue to see the value in suppressing drug consumption, and much of the institutional knowledge (and corruption) developed in Levi Nutt's Bureau of Prohibition was passed on to Harry Anslinger's Bureau of Narcotics.[61]

Beyond even bootlegging, crime, and the predatory nature of selective enforcement, however, there was something simply *degrading* about Prohibition: where before people could enjoy a good beer in good company, now they snuck bad liquor out of sight.[62] Bootlegged hooch was either harsh "moonshine" (hastily produced liquor from illegal stills) or else derived from industrial alcohol products from which people attempted to remove poisonous adulterants—often unsuccessfully. The worst of it came in 1930, when people started drinking Jamaican ginger extract (colloquially known as "Jake"), which was up to 85 percent alcohol and adulterated with chemicals used in photography. Fifty thousand people were paralyzed for life.[63]

It was all just visibly dehumanizing. One journalist described the Volstead Act as having discouraged "the drinking of good beer in favor of indifferent gin."[64] Another lamented that the art of drinking was now lost on Americans: "Once they drank for the taste, but now they drink only for the effect."[65]

Ultimately though, people read what they want from Prohibition. Drug warriors can point to it as a clear example that banning a substance by law lowers overall use. If continuing users are physically harmed and black market profiteers get organized (two traditionally quite useful phenomena for conservative politicians), these are side effects that we can live with. Decriminalizers and legalizers can point to the obvious human costs, and the fact that America did once, against a constitutional amendment, decide that people shouldn't be paralyzed or shot over a naturally occurring psychoactive substance.[66]

Perhaps the best critique of Prohibition is not that it failed, but that in succeeding, it not only fell miserably short of realizing any of the utopian aims on which it was sold to the American public but also created new social perversions. Prohibition might "work," but always at the cost of extending the rot of contemporary society.

Consumerism

What British economist John Maynard Keynes called the "extraordinary imbecility" of the Great Depression put an end to the more ordinary imbecility of Prohibition. Former "drys" quickly turned against their own cause: What sense was there in funding a corrupt government bureau to enforce a law that led to violence and death, especially when alcohol taxes could be a much-needed source of revenue?[67] In 1930, dry senator Morris Sheppard said there was "as much chance of repealing the Eighteenth Amendment as there is for a humming bird to fly to the planet Mars with the Washington Monument tied to its tail."[68] Three years later, the Eighteenth Amendment was repealed. It's a good reminder that, against the good sense of our political representatives, things can and do change.

The Depression broke the spirit of reformism that fueled temperance, but even before it hit, a new ethos was taking root, which the *Atlantic Monthly* called "consumptionism" in 1924.[69] They incorrectly predicted that this ethos would naturally bolster abstinence (and Prohibition *was* a boon for juice and soft drinks), but they were right that a new consumerism was quickly undermining traditional Protestant values.[70] America no longer needed restraint and sacrifice; it needed a mass consumer base. And having won the vote, women were largely done with the temperance crusade, primed to cast off their old role as guardians of the home for that of *purchasers* of the home.[71]

"Getting The Boat Ready," by Douglas Crockwell. Number 42 in the series "Home Life in America."

Beer belongs...enjoy it

In this home-loving land of ours . . . in this America of kindliness, of friendship, of good-humored tolerance . . . perhaps no beverages are more "at home" on more occasions than good American beer and ale.

For beer and ale are the kinds of beverages Americans like. They belong—to pleasant living, to good fellowship, to sensible moderation. And our right to enjoy them, this too belongs—to our own American heritage of personal freedom.

At mealtime, too!

AMERICA'S BEVERAGE OF MODERATION

This advertisement appears in
Life—May 15, 1950
Collier's—May 6, 1950
Look—May 23, 1950
McCall's—June, 1950
Woman's Home Companion—June, 1950

An ad from the "Beer belongs" campaign of the United States Brewers Foundation that ran from 1945 to 1956. Many of the ads depict a domestic setting with women serving beer. Reprinted with permission.

The new society of consumption exploded in the postwar era: everyone got a TV set and started drinking more at home. New institutions like the cinema and the dance hall appeared, promoting wet values made newly "responsible."[72] What the Frankfurt School philosopher Theodor Adorno called "a new anthropological type" was born: unaffected by the old repressive moral strictures, uncritically receptive of the latest gadgets and cultural slop. Temperance moralizing bounced right off this new type of person.[73] How grotesquely undemocratic and severe the previous age now seemed! And in any event, what a waste it would have been not to employ the newly affordable refrigerator to produce cold beers and ice for cocktails.

At the same time, capitalism couldn't simply accommodate unregulated drinking, and a new paradigm making sense of problem drinking had to be forged. The temperance movement had tried to pin most social problems on liquor.[74] After Prohibition, reformers turned away from alcohol itself—now a socially acceptable beverage—and toward the figure of the *alcoholic*, who was imagined to bear particular personality traits indicating susceptibility to the disease of addiction.[75] The puritanical gaze had shifted from substance to subject. As the old saying goes, "An alcoholic is someone who drinks too much, and you don't like anyway."[76]

Alcoholics Anonymous, formed in 1935, was the perfect expression of this new paradigm. In its view, alcoholics couldn't participate in the broader culture of "responsible drinking" due to their flawed personalities. This "disease conception" of addiction was attractive to a growing medical establishment, but it was also eagerly adopted by the liquor industry, who were, like Big Tobacco, all too happy to pin any problems with their product on the consumers. "Scientific" critics of AA attack its explicitly religious framework—participants work with others through a structured twelve-step process toward spiritual rebirth—but they typically agree with AA's basic conception of the problem: the diseased and irresponsible individual.[77]

To Your Health!

Around the 1970s, California wine so improved that it began to seriously rival French wine, much to the chagrin of European connoisseurs. Wine has a slow, agricultural ethos, much better suited to the decadence of the Old World than the efficiency of the New.[78] Visitors from abroad have long noted the speed and instrumentality with which Americans dine, leaving no time for the languid enjoyment of a shared wine with meals (better to liquor up afterward).[79] Americans do drink wine, of course, but wine is not, and has never been, American.

The drastic increase in American wine consumption since the '90s paradoxically proves this point: in 1991, Morley Safer announced in a now well-known segment on *60 Minutes*, "The French Paradox," that a glass of red wine was practically an elixir of health. It was in response to this public service announcement that the amount of wine consumed every year in the United States more than doubled.[80] The great gift of Dionysus has finally been absorbed by American culture, but as a liquid multivitamin.

The brewers too had to justify themselves within the new culture of fitness. In the early twentieth century, they had portrayed their creation as "liquid bread" in order to emphasize its nutritious rather than intoxicating qualities, a label that would come to haunt them in the '80s.[81] But by then, changes in the industry had well prepared it to meet the moment with a range of colorless, low-calorie beers. In 1983, six breweries—Anheuser Busch, Miller, Heileman, Stroh, Coors, Pabst—controlled 92 percent of the market.[82] As in the cases of coffee and cigarettes, the postwar period had been a time of great corporate consolidation, and the result for consumers was an increasingly bland and flavorless product. All that was needed was a bit more water and the label "lite."

As also with the other licit drugs, middle-class cultural defection ensued. Industrialization had given us crap recreational drugs; deindustrialization in turn offered "craft" alternatives. For a certain class of consumer, Folgers, Camel, and Budweiser were out; Starbucks, Natural American Spirit, and Sierra Nevada were in.

Changing consumer preferences were accompanied by the rise of a "neotemperance" movement, anchored in an organization that formed in 1980, Mothers Against Drunk Driving. MADD was instrumental in raising the drinking age to twenty-one in 1984. The United States today is still home to some of the strictest youth drinking laws in the world, and not uncoincidentally, we also have more youth drinking problems than other industrialized nations.[83] In Andrew Barr's characterization, MADD helped produce "a generation of young people who drink only to get drunk."[84] MADD also held a strict line on drunk driving. According to one chapter president, "Once you've consumed your first drink, you've lost that ability to make a sound judgment."[85] Curiously, they received financial contributions from liquor companies to campaign against drunk driving; a focus on the *abuse* of the substance keeps attention away from the substance itself.[86] One imagines Frances Willard rolling in her grave.

Commodity Fetishism

The history of alcohol in America offers a nice, neat dialectic: from the early alcohol-drenched republic, to the rise and fall of temperance, and then finally to the settling of drink into well-delimited leisure activities and consumer lifestyles. In the first stage, alcohol was abundant: it infused social ties and foundational American ideals—people were free to drink as they liked and "equal before the bottle."[87] Temperance was, among other things, the breaking of traditional life asunder: the teetotaler was out to fashion a progressive culture to match the new society that industrialization forced into existence.[88] Freedom was to be "autonomy exercised within a moral code," and equality an "equal opportunity for all Americans to uphold high moral principles."[89] It all went too far, of course, and post-Prohibition Americans embraced moderate, responsible drinking. The temperance advocates' goal was abandoned for good, but their conceptions of freedom and equality were retained.

Perhaps the greatest change produced in this progression had to do with human sociability. In a much-dissected part of the first chapter of *Capital*, Karl Marx introduces the idea of "commodity fetishism," or the curious transformation of a "definite social relation between men [into] the fantastic form of a relation between things."[90] In a society governed by capital, Marx contends, our social relations are not direct and personal but rather primarily mediated and impersonal, reorganized so as to serve the exchange of commodities. The modern history of alcohol is the story of the sundering of preindustrial communal bonds and their replacement with weaker, more transitory forms of sociability organized by the culture industry. Drinking no longer serves community in the industrialized world; rather, community is now organized around the consumption of commodities, one of which is alcohol.[91]

Commodity fetishism is expressed in our social activities, but also in the weakness with which they bind us together. In a way, it's evident in the simple fact that, in most social settings, we are free to refuse a drink if offered—sometimes simply because we don't drink, but often either because we don't *like* that particular drink or because we don't *feel* like drinking. For such an offense, we would to our forebears be a society of "cold-blooded and uncongenial wretch[es]," deserving of the social isolation that our ridiculous preferences create.[92] Try as we might to rekindle the flame of "community," a "most horrendous distortion of the principle of reciprocity" suffuses our basic social reality.[93] We are the hostile strangers that precapitalist societies feared.

4

Opiates, or Civilizing the Orient

The needle junkie is a magician who can work the conjuring
trick of making a hole and simultaneously fixing it.

—Marek Kohn

There is no better drug than heroin—that is, there is nothing
better at delivering the morphine molecule directly to your
brain, and there is no other molecule that so overwhelms the
mammalian nervous receptors that produce pleasure. If there
is evidence for the existence of a diabolical deity, this is it.[1]

There is also no better drug than heroin through which
to understand the modern history of illicit drugs, given its
preeminent place among the targets of the American drug war.
Chinese opium subcultures shaped most of the connotations
around which moral reformers drummed up American anxieties toward the "drug menace" in the abstract, opiates were
the drugs of concern at the early twentieth-century conferences
that produced global prohibition, and heroin was at the top of
Richard Nixon's list of maligned substances.

Finally, there is no better drug than heroin to treat the pain
and dislocation inherent to capitalist subjectivity. Opiates do
not address the source of alienation—the stresses and insecurity of modern life—but they do very efficiently relieve the
feelings associated with it.[2] To paraphrase Lou Reed (music
copyright is an irritating impediment to the phenomenology
of drugs), heroin offers reprieve from connivance, corruption,
and cruelty.[3] It lets us do the one thing we're all wired not to
do: stop caring about American society.

The Orient

It's easy to forget in the midst of the present opioid scourge—a cold, North American affair, blighting unglamorous towns in Ohio—that the modern history of opium and its derivatives is largely a *Chinese* history. Chinese emigration did not first bring opiates to the West, but most of our lingering cultural associations surrounding opiates still have to do with that era (as one example, the word "hip" goes back to the days of opium dens, when users grew marks on their hips from lying on their sides).[4]

The story begins with a much more innocuous-seeming drug: tea. By the beginning of the nineteenth century, the British had taken to importing massive amounts of it from China, with the workman's cuppa fueling the early Industrial Revolution in England. In return, the Celestial Empire wanted only silver, creating a worrying trade imbalance for the British. At the same time, the production and use of opium was spreading widely in India, so in 1793, the East India Company made itself the sole procurer of opium and prohibited its possession "except for purposes of foreign commerce only."[5] Profiting off a known danger is commonplace in the history of drugs, but this episode is uniquely sinister for curbing Indian consumption (to keep workers efficient) while promoting it abroad. Despite the emperor's proclamation in 1799 banning opium importation, Indian opium poured into China, and soon the outflow of British silver halted.

Thus began almost a century of opium dealing in China, carried out with the tacit approval of the British government.[6] The Chinese authorities hated the British arrogance that the opium trade manifested, but their attempts to stop it made things worse. After 20,000 chests of opium were seized and destroyed by the Chinese in 1839, the British responded by launching the First Opium War in 1840. With vastly superior firepower and tactics, the British won with little effort and forced the Treaty of Nanking on the Chinese, which opened up ports and ceded Hong Kong to the British.[7] A second and bloodier Opium War from 1856 to 1860 would result in the legalization of opium in China. An ambassador reported to the British Parliament that "we forced the Chinese Government to enter into a Treaty to allow their subjects to take opium."[8]

In 1890, the emperor finally legalized Chinese poppy cultivation, a desperate move that curtailed Indian imports, but only at the cost of encouraging an even wider use of opium.[9] The financial benefits from this homegrown production were tremendous for the Kuomintang under Chiang Kai-shek, whose brazen corruption was difficult to match. Payment for government protection of the opium business was euphemistically termed "opium prohibition revenue."[10] By the end of the 1930s, it was estimated that there were some 40 million opium users in China. This was all brought swiftly to an end by the Communists, who burned the poppy fields, executed dealers, publicly destroyed pipes, ran public education campaigns about opium smoking being a capitalist activity, and opened rehabilitation centers for addicts.

It's generally agreed now that reports of the destructiveness of the opium habit in China were greatly exaggerated, in part by missionaries and journalists of the time, and later by the CCP in its campaign to overcome "the century of humiliation." But this *image* of the enslaved Oriental nonetheless bore a historical force of its own.[11] Dependent layabouts dominated ruthlessly by thuggish enterprises, but deserving of their humiliation and exploitation for being weak willed—such was the century-long perception of China, and also the contemporary perception of drug addicts today. Hamilton Wright, eventual architect of the Harrison Act, wrote in 1911: "You see, the whole world had regarded with a shudder China's flat prostration underneath the curse of the drug habit, and our shudders were, perhaps, the most vigorous of all."[12]

The Opium of the People

Before the nineteenth century, opium was primarily known in the West as a medicinal tincture in the form of laudanum, an invention of the seventeenth-century English physician Thomas Sydenham. Strange stories of opium subcultures trickled in from the East, but it otherwise had no special connotations. Doctors weren't even agreed as to whether it was a depressant, a stimulant, or a hallucinogen.[13]

According to historian Richard Davenport-Hines, the modern history of drugs really begins in the 1820s with three events: the publication of Thomas De Quincey's *Confessions of an English Opium-Eater*, the commercialization of morphine, and the intensification of the controversy around the Chinese opium trade.[14] De Quincey's memoirs introduced the Western world to "the marvellous agency of opium, whether for pleasure or for pain."[15] Recounting the high highs and the low lows of his laudanum dependence, De Quincey turned a generation of writers and artists on to the possibility of real escape from their psychic ailments.[16]

> Happiness might now be bought for a penny, and carried in the waistcoat pocket: portable ecstasies might be had corked up in a pint bottle: and peace of mind could be sent down in gallons · by the mail coach.[17]

Before De Quincey, opium was just a substance; after De Quincey, it was an adventure into the "unmapped reaches of the mind" and through a bitter tangle of pleasure and pain. In this, *Confessions* was the model for all subsequent "my drug hell" confessionals in celebrity tabloids.[18]

While De Quincey and the upper classes were testing the bounds of oblivion, cheap and easily obtainable opium had become a medicine cabinet staple in most of Western Europe and America.[19] A wide variety of "patent medicines"—often mixtures of opium and sugar syrups, though sometimes much

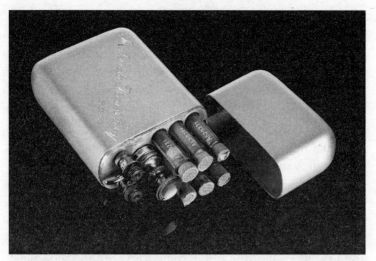

Hypodermic syringe set marketed by Parke, Davis & Company in the 1890s. © Science Museum Group.

more toxic—were quite pervasive in the nineteenth century. Those administered to children were especially popular, like Mother Bailey's Quieting Syrup, Street's Infant Quietness, and Batley's Sedative Solution. The opiate of the masses in the nineteenth century was undoubtedly actual opium.[20]

As opium became the nineteenth century's aspirin, it was also being broken into its component parts by pharmacologists. In 1805, Friedrich Wilhelm Sertürner isolated the alkaloid morphine from raw opium, and it became commercially available fifteen years later.[21] In 1853, Alexander Wood of Edinburgh perfected the hypodermic needle. The next year, one of Wood's family members would be the first person ever to die of an overdose of injected morphine.[22]

And then, just as a clear understanding of the *Morbid Craving for Morphia* (the title of a popular text of 1878) was setting in, a London pharmacist boiled morphine with acetic anhydride to create diacetylmorphine. Five times as potent as morphine, itself the most powerful alkaloid derivative of opium, diacetylmorphine was marketed under a name based on the

German word *heroisch*, or "heroic."[23] Cheaper than morphine, highly concentrated, easy to adulterate and conceal, the closest thing to the Platonic form of an illicit drug was born.[24]

Regulation

The final marker of the inauguration of the modern drug era was the growing concern with both the opium trade abroad and the migration of its influence to the West. The tension that led to the First Opium War did not rouse sympathy but rather disgust for the Chinese, whose smoking shops were described in lurid detail as "the most miserable and wretched places imaginable," frequented by patrons who "are, with very few exceptions, thieves, sharpers and sporting men, and a few bad actors; the women, without exception, are immoral."[25] At a moment when the ideal of male productivity was fetishized, opium smoking was portrayed as making Chinese men indolent and feminine— an association reinforced by the common practice of prescribing opium or morphine for "female complaints."[26]

When the Chinese emigrated west in the late nineteenth century, establishing opium dens as they did, the ground had been well prepared for a full-fledged moral panic—the so-called Yellow Peril, which provided the basic template for all future panics combining drugs and race. Sensationalized stories spread the news of middle-class youth, especially girls, corrupted by the "miserable and grovelling Chinese, who are fed on [opium] almost from the cradle" (rich coming from a people who were dosing their own children with Mother Bailey's Quieting Syrup).[27] In 1888, the writer Edward Dyson published "Mr. and Mrs. Sin Fat," which told the tale of a "curious European on a voyage of discovery," who

> saw in [Mr. Sin Fat's] room, through the clouds of choking evil smelling, opium fumes, debilitated Chinamen, with faces like

Atlanta Georgian, *March 17, 1934. Cartoon by Walter Enright. From Richard J. Bonnie and Charles H. Whitebread II, The Marihuana Conviction: A History of Marihuana Prohibition in the United States (Charlottesville: University Press of Virginia, 1974), 102.*

animals floating to hell in the midst of visions of heaven ... and worst of all, European girls ... of sixteen, decoyed in at the front door by the sheen of silk and the jingle of gold, and then left to percolate through that terrible den.[28]

No one was more repulsed by Oriental vice and its influence than Charles Henry Brent, the Episcopalian bishop of the Philippines during the initial period of its rule by the United States and an important progenitor of the twentieth century's War on Drugs. Brent was a true believer in Christianity and even more fervently in the American civilizing mission abroad. He lamented that "lives of promise have been wrecked ... by the hitherto untried and cruel temptations of the Orient," whose native denizens suffered from "the constitutional fault of ... sensuality."[29] He would eventually serve as the senior American delegate to the International Opium Commission meeting in Shanghai in 1909. Over the protests of congressmen and senators who were reluctant to legislate on moral issues, the Smoking Opium Exclusion Act, which outlawed nonmedicinal opium, was hurriedly passed in Congress just before the convention, to give the US delegation the moral high ground.[30] From this altitude, the proud bishop announced the mission of the new global drug policy: "Our desire is to give the Orient civilization."[31]

A second conference held at The Hague in 1911–12 produced the first international drug control treaty, committing signatories to the swift prohibition of trade in opium and the gradual suppression of it in their countries—a moral obligation that would take many decades of haggling to work into a coherent system.[32] At that conference, US emissary Hamilton Wright committed the United States to passing federal drug legislation, returning to Congress to report "that this new treaty gave them no choice but to enact such a law."[33] In 1914, Congress passed the Harrison Act (authored by Wright), which prohibited the sale of all opium and coca products except by prescription and under tight regulation.

It's no exaggeration to say that the Harrison Act created a fundamentally new paradigm, a novel conceptual and moral universe that would have been unintelligible just two decades before it passed, and in which we reside to this day. In the nineteenth century, morphine use was more respectable than drunkenness, given the oppressive temperance culture.[34] And while those drug users that fell into abuse were moral reprobates, lazy, feminine, sinful, and so on, it was only with these swift legislative actions that they became *dangerous criminals*—at first simply according to the new laws, but inevitably in actual fact as well. Placed on the other side of the law—"by 1930, 35 per cent of all convicts in America were indicted under the Harrison Act"—it was only natural that users turned to actual criminal behavior to produce and consume drugs.[35] The civilization of the Orient had uncovered Orientals all over the country.

The Federal Bureau of Narcotics

The terms "junkie" and "gangster" both originated in New York City in the 1920s, a decade that saw a global eruption of criminal organization thanks to the new incentives of the illegal market in drugs and alcohol.[36] From a relatively minor social nuisance, the United States had fashioned a whole underworld.

World War II made strange bedfellows of the Mafia and the nascent deep state: mobsters Lucky Luciano, Meyer Lansky, Frank Costello, and Vito Genovese all struck deals to help the Allies, and these connections survived the war.[37] One of the CIA's first projects upon its founding in 1947 was to bankroll the Corsican Mafia to disrupt Communist-led unions in France. The Corsicans just so happened to be running laboratories in Marseille that transformed Turkish and Southeast Asian opium into heroin en route to North America. The CIA not only deliberately ignored this infamous "French Connection," but also stifled the efforts of Federal Bureau of Narcotics (FBN) agents to do much about it.

Harry Anslinger, commissioner of the FBN from 1930 to 1962, did a good deal to undermine the success of his own bureau. One of those "men of zeal, well meaning but without understanding" that Louis Brandeis warned of, Anslinger dutifully held the Agency's line in all matters.[38] To divert attention from CIA-supported drug production in Southeast Asia and France, Anslinger liked to point his finger in the direction of the People's Republic of China, at one point claiming knowledge of a secret Chinese twenty-five-year plan "to finance political activities and spread addiction among free peoples through the sale of heroin and opium."[39] According to reports of Anslinger's own agent Ralph Oyler, the Communists were doing no such thing, and in reality engaged in an extensive anti-narcotics campaign, but Anslinger suppressed Oyler's reports.[40]

At home, meanwhile, Anslinger recommended an unforgiving and punitive attitude to all drug users, maligning anyone who

Arlington County Daily Sun, *March 19, 1955. Cartoon by Jesse Taylor Cargill.*

suggested a more compassionate, treatment-focused approach as a naïf. Anslinger pushed an image of "the addict" as a raging and inalterable "dope fiend" for the entirety of his tenure as commissioner, ignoring or attacking academics, physicians, and reformers with alternative models of addiction. Under Anslinger's guidance, FBN agents focused on black neighborhoods because, in the words of one agent, "it was easy. We didn't need a search warrant, it allowed us to meet our quotas, and it was ongoing."[41] Further taking advantage of fears that the late-1940s heroin wave in urban, black, and Latino areas was spreading to the suburbs, Anslinger supported a series of bills in the '50s that increased penalties on heroin dealers and users while giving powers to his FBN akin to those of the FBI.[42]

In addition to being a vicious and conniving drug warrior, Anslinger was also arguably the biggest dealer around. The war had made clear how important the flow of raw materials to US pharmaceutical laboratories was, and access to those materials, along with the promotion of the consumption of American mass-produced drugs abroad, became a key priority of the FBN.[43] As historian Suzanna Reiss demonstrates, the seizure of control over the international drug trade not only allowed the US government to define the boundaries of the licit and the illicit for the entire world, it also laid the foundation for the dominance of the American pharmaceutical industry. With sole authority to approve companies to manufacture narcotic pharmaceuticals, Anslinger was "positioned at the wheel of a gate valve," and naturally this position gained him very powerful defenders in Big Pharma.[44]

It's no surprise that the reign of Harry Anslinger, an unreservedly punitive racist working in the interest of both the CIA and Big Pharma, was a disaster in terms of drug policy. As journalist Douglas Valentine understates the matter, "The existence of CIA-connected FBN agents working with CIA-connected Mafiosi was not, in a word, conducive to effective federal drug law enforcement."[45] It would later be revealed that one in five FBN agents under Anslinger's watch was corrupt, and they were often direct participants in the heroin trade.[46] But these revelations didn't become public until 1975, the year Anslinger died—blind, arteries clogged, and, fittingly, on daily doses of morphine.[47] Historian Jill Jonnes believes that Anslinger's FBN "remains the worst case of corruption ever to hit a federal law enforcement agency."[48]

Nixon's War

The second postwar spike in heroin use, beginning in the late '60s and much bigger than the first wave, was a consequence of the failure of the labor market to absorb sharp increases in the urban population of black and Latino adolescents, many of whom were swept up instead in the underground economies that sprouted from urban divestment.[49] In sociologist Elliott Currie's description, it was "a collective response of a broad segment of the disadvantaged urban young to specific social conditions in postwar America."[50] In the press, however, the causation was reversed: heroin was painted as the *driver* of urban decline and crime, as a "city-killing drug," in historian Eric Schneider's words.[51] Heroin undeniably contributed to the urban crime wave, but it was only one part of the broader tragedy of America's poorest neighborhoods. By 1970, the number of regular users had ballooned back up to 500,000.[52] (Through most of the twentieth century, narcotics numbers were often considerably fudged to suit whatever political cause they were being employed to justify.[53] So it's best to take all figures here with a sizable grain of salt.)

Local police departments had been primed to capitalize on these alarming numbers. The Federal Bureau of Narcotics was finally shuttered and absorbed into the Bureau of Narcotics and Dangerous Drugs (BNDD) in 1968. No longer wishing to deal with the dirty business of local enforcement, BNDD chief John Ingersoll offered local police chiefs a memorandum of understanding in 1970: we'll focus on international trafficking, you deal with local drug dealers.[54] Police were eager to minimize federal intrusion into their work and use drug busts to retain some of the discretion and autonomy encroached upon by a professionalization movement internally and by Civil Rights activism externally. Drug busts shot up with drug use numbers, and they never came down.

While liberals were reduced to calling out "law and order" as dog whistles, and thus seemingly dismissive of concerns about crime, Nixon initiated the acute phase of the War on Drugs with heroin in his crosshairs:

> It is no exaggeration to say that heroin addiction—if not checked by decisive action now—could cripple a whole generation or more of Americans in the critical years ahead. If we do not

destroy the heroin menace, then it will surely and eventually destroy us and our great nation's future.[55]

He had in mind the urban criminal, but even more so returning Vietnam vets, who had turned in droves during their service to readily available heroin. A month before Nixon's well-known speech of June 1971, in which he declared drugs "public enemy number one," *Newsweek* featured a photo of a syringe sticking out of a soldier's helmet. The heroin threat was coming, once again, from the Orient.[56]

The deluge, however, never came. When soldiers returned home, the large majority stopped using altogether. The high remission rates of returning veterans suggested, contrary to the reigning neuroscientific logic that addiction is a brain disease, that drug use is largely situational.[57] In addition, Turkey finally banned opium in 1971, raids on heroin laboratories in Marseille in 1972 shuttered the French Connection, and the adoption of methadone maintenance programs—pushed by Nixon's first drug czar, Jerome Jaffe—had reduced urban crime.[58] In 1974, the year Nixon resigned, it seemed like his war was actually working.

A few years later, heroin was back, and cocaine use was skyrocketing. What happened? When the French Connection finally collapsed, "Mexican mud"—cheap tar heroin—filled in for a while. Turkey also reversed their opium ban in 1974, and opium production was growing rapidly in Southeast Asia, or the "Golden Triangle." A chief distributor of opium in the area was the Kuomintang in exile, which had turned into a brutal opium militia after hopes for a return to China were dashed.[59] They would be supplanted in the '70s by Khun Sa, arguably the first modern "drug lord," who would be in charge of 80 percent of Golden Triangle heroin production by 1987.[60]

In Southeast Asia, the CIA went well beyond financing and feigning ignorance.[61] It was an active participant in the drug trade, building links between different crime networks and even directly transporting "miscellaneous cargo" through its front airline, Air America.[62] When drought in the Golden Triangle moved the center of opium production back to Pakistan and Afghanistan, the CIA was there once again, arming the Mujaheddin Afghan guerrillas who, in now typical fashion, grew poppies and fought the Communists. Scandals at banks like Nugan Hand and the Bank of Commerce and Credit International, both involved in illegal activities with ties to international crime and military figures, point to "an ever larger enterprise, which ... operates under a cover of great respectability and solvency."[63] Perhaps the forceful incentives of the black market would have created a vibrant drug trade whether or not the CIA got involved, but for much of the twentieth century, the global opiates market was very much a planned economy.[64]

Forfeiture

Until crack overtook it in 1986, heroin was the drug of crime. A Reagan critic in 1983 lamented that the White House was wasting its time on high-visibility marijuana and cocaine busts without "making a dent in the heroin trade, which breeds a large proportion of street crime."[65] That same year, a young, new US attorney in Manhattan, Rudolph Giuliani, announced that "heroin is the prime problem that we have and the one that has the most effect on violent crime."[66] People were increasingly alert to the dangers of cocaine, but it was still described then as "the drug of choice of middle-class America: those who hold responsible jobs, those who perform vital services, those we most rely upon for their judgment, skill and experience."[67] The crack scare was still to come.

It was thus in response to the heroin problem that a series of escalating "tough on crime" steps were taken in the '70s and early '80s. They began when a law professor at Notre Dame named G. Robert Blakey came up with a brilliant new legal invention, one that promised victory over the drugs problem at the small cost of making burglary legal. He called it criminal forfeiture. *Civil* forfeiture had long been an important exception to the Fifth Amendment: if the government finds an illegal object, it can confiscate it without "due process." Blakey was searching for a legal tool that would help the state crack down on organized crime, and civil forfeiture just wasn't good enough: illegal assets of the Mafia could be seized, but the cash derived from their sale could not. The government needed some way of taking their money, or it would forever be fighting a losing battle.

In 1970, the Racketeer Influenced and Corrupt Organizations (RICO) Act was enacted, the basics of which were first formulated by Blakey for the Senate Judiciary Committee. Provided a person was proven guilty of a crime, their assets —not just their illegal assets, but *any* assets associated with illegal behavior—could be seized. In 1978, at the behest of the ostensibly liberal drug czar Peter Bourne, Congress eroded the distinction between civil and criminal forfeiture with the Psychotropic Substances Act, which allowed the DEA to seize money and derivative assets *suspected of* being associated with drugs.

For Senator Joe Biden, they hadn't gone far enough. For one, real estate had been excluded from the 1978 law. Assets also couldn't be seized until an indictment was made, an inconvenient hurdle for the police. In addition to establishing mandatory minimum sentences, the 1984 Comprehensive Crime Control Act, the fruit of years of Biden's and Strom Thurmond's efforts to get tough on crime, allowed law enforcement to seize *any* assets on the basis of "probable cause." As journalist Dan Baum summarizes, under the new legislation, law enforcement

> could confiscate, with no more "proof" than was required for a
> search warrant, cash, cars, boats, homes, bank accounts, stock
> portfolios—anything *believed* to have been purchased with drug

money or equal in value to the money *believed* earned from drug sales. No charge, indictment, trial, or conviction was necessary, and the burden of proof was placed on the person whose assets were seized.[68]

The bill also allowed police to keep the proceeds of forfeited assets. Money, cars, homes—anything associated with suspected drug use—were now all potential revenue to bolster local law enforcement budgets.[69]

But police still need enough "proof" to get search warrants, right? Yes, technically, but in the Supreme Court's *Illinois v. Gates* decision in 1983, they ruled that police can get warrants based on anonymous tips. And after *United States v. Leon* in 1984, "evidence seized under tainted warrants is admissible provided the police met a subjective standard of 'good faith.'"[70] With these two precedent-altering cases, nothing prevents police from calling in their own tips or simply lying on their warrant requests.[71] With *Illinois v. Gates, United States v. Leon*, and the 1984 crime bill, the Fourth and Fifth Amendments effectively became optional.[72]

Forfeiture law was reformed in 2000 to make the process of reacquiring one's seized assets clearer, but it also expanded the number of crimes to which forfeiture authority applied. Based on little more than their own "reasonable belief," police today can legally enter your home, take whatever they want (including your home), and not give it back—*ever*. Most Americans take consolation from the idea that while you might not be guaranteed a decent wage, healthcare, any safety net, et cetera, at least the right to the property that you might have is sacred and inviolable. By the early '80s, the generals of the War on Drugs had eviscerated this core tenet of American capitalism.

The Opioid Crisis

With all the media attention on crack, and despite all the punitive measures meant to contain it, heroin use rose steadily throughout the '80s and '90s. It then exploded in the 2000s. This time, the CIA was not the catalyst.[73]

The present opioid crisis is an icy phenomenon. It contains no Anslinger-esque enforcers or blustery crime bosses—just cold market incentives, quiet distribution, and death amid broader decay. Before the 1980s, doctors very rarely prescribed opiates. That decade, the World Health Organization released its first analgesic ladder, outlining a humane approach to alleviating the pain of terminally ill patients, and idealistic young doctors helped establish a new branch of medical specialty: palliative care, or the treatment of the seriously ill. The intentions were good, but the slope was slippery, and soon they were advocating for the alleviation not only of the pain of the terminally ill but also of "chronic pain"—an empty conceptual vessel if there ever was one.

The culture shift was rapid and decisive: doctors who once stood firmly against opiate prescriptions were writing them liberally by the mid-1990s.[74] Much of this had to do with the abominable practices of Purdue Pharma, who employed an army of sales representatives to wine and dine doctors into believing that their newly released product OxyContin, the functional equivalent of heroin, was "'virtually' non-addicting" (a much-propagated descriptor that they knew to be false).[75] Purdue executive David Haddox had coined the term "pseudoaddiction" (an "iatrogenic syndrome that mimics the behavioral symptoms of addiction") to make sense of dependence on OxyContin.[76] Patients weren't addicted, they were just in pain, and the solution was more OxyContin.

In 1993, industry "thought leader" Russell Portenoy told the *New York Times* that OxyContin "can be used for a long time, with few side effects and that addiction and abuse are not a problem."[77] (Portenoy, the "King of Pain," would later serve as a witness against Purdue in exchange for being dismissed as a defendant himself.[78] He has retained his position as a professor of neurology at the Albert Einstein College of Medicine.) Some physicians, under the institutional pressure to control pain, reluctantly abided by the rules of the new paradigm; less morally confined doctors eagerly adopted them, opening up "pill mills" in areas starved for decent healthcare.[79]

At the same time, black tar heroin—much of it traced back to one of Mexico's smallest states, Nayarit—began appearing in places around America that traditionally lacked a trafficking presence. The new dealers from Nayarit were almost the polar opposite of the Colombian cocaine cartels: they avoided the saturated markets of big cities, never carried guns, and only sold in small quantities. They'd make their money and return to Nayarit. It was a clean and quiet business—no kingpins, no violence, just efficient transactions of strong, cheap heroin.

With the disgusting Sackler family to lampoon, Purdue Pharma makes a nice, clean target, and their vilification is certainly well deserved. But the sadder truth is that they were part of what historian Kathleen Frydl has called "the Pharma Cartel," held together by "government agencies incentivized to 'look the other way' when making decisions."[80] Wherever cartel pills were liberally prescribed, abused, and then taken away once the pill mills were shuttered—prominently in the Rust Belt, but all over the country—Nayarit heroin followed. The vast majority of heroin users—about 1 million people in 2016—started on prescription opioids. And now they have a wide variety of means for accessing the morphine molecule, including the synthetic opioid fentanyl, which is about fifty times the strength of heroin.

Synthesized by Belgian chemist Paul Janssen in 1960, fentanyl was for most of its existence an effective intravenous anesthetic. In 2014, while still known only to surgeons and anesthesiologists, it was procurable on the internet from

Chinese chemical companies. In 2019, China banned fentanyl, but by this time it was coming in from Mexico too.[81] In addition to being extremely potent, fentanyl is often mixed poorly in the hands of inexperienced chemists, resulting in what pharmacists call a "failure of content uniformity."[82] Unfortunately, fentanyl's dangers do not end there: increasingly, dealers are cutting it into other drugs like cocaine, methamphetamine, and ketamine in order to create a more reliable customer base. Fentanyl is a surefire way to make a party drug into an all-the-time drug.

In late 2019, Purdue Pharma went bankrupt after settling some 2,000 opioid lawsuits to the tune of $10 billion. That same year, there were about 70,000 drug overdoses in the United States, a new annual high (that number is well over 100,000 as of 2021).[83] The Sackler family, erstwhile owners of Purdue, have not seen criminal charges and remain billionaires. In 2019, after the comedian John Oliver ran a segment on his show *Last Week Tonight* on the Sackler family, Jacqueline Sackler, wife of Purdue co-owner Mortimer Sackler, complained that her children weren't going to get into prestigious schools with her family's name being dragged through the mud. "Lives of children are being destroyed," she concluded.[84]

The Hole

The phenomenology of drugs is a notoriously difficult enterprise. As the sociologist Howard Becker pointed out, "getting stoned" is a skill that one acquires: the raw bodily sensations that drugs produce can be interpreted in terms of subjective feeling in a wide variety of ways.[85] This variety is structured by what Timothy Leary and Richard Alpert first called "set" (the psychological mindset of the person using the drug) and "setting" (the environment in which they take it). Two people taking the same drug at the same dosage delivered through the same route of administration can report wildly different, and even directly opposed, effects.

But in the particular case of opiates, there is something consistently *curt* about the experience: unlike psychedelics, which have spurred countless and painstakingly detailed recollections that are recounted as if meaning itself hung on properly conveying the experience, opiate use affords single word descriptions: "warm," "comfortable," "nice." Perhaps the best way to capture the direct nature of opiates is that *they fill a hole*. No need for a confidence boost, or a high, or a trip. Thomas De Quincey called opium "the master-key" that "can overrule all feelings into a compliance."[86] LSD gets you wondering, "Is this it?" Opiates let you know: "*This* is it."

Many other things can fill this hole—sex, family, God, art, other drugs, a drink and some heartfelt conversation, maybe—but nothing seeps so effortlessly and efficiently into its crevices as the morphine molecule.[87] For some of us, this hole is a minimal intrusion on our lives. We often call it "boredom" or "dissatisfaction," but when it really makes itself felt, we sometimes call it "pain"—an attractive descriptor because it frames all of our many complex problems in the simple terms of needing *relief*, rather than work or communication.

For others, the hole is deep and cavernous, its base the dark and rocky terrain of childhood experience, its opening the abyss of separation from a habitable life. When opiates hit this void, it's a revelation. It's being home around the hearth after years lost out in the cold. It's finding out, as if for the first time, that reality can be *comfortable*.[88]

There's no precise formula determining our lot here. Maybe biology plays some role, but it's mostly some combination of happenstance, early trauma, and adult tragedy. Only one thing is certain about the causality of opiate addiction: the colder and more inhospitable the world becomes, and the more we punish people seeking refuge, the larger those holes will be.[89]

5

Amphetamines, or
Inappropriate Perseverance

> In America, the cars run on high-octane gas, the computers run
> on nanosecond circuits, and the people run on pills.
>
> —Gail Sheehy

Opiates bring you down, they make you comfortable. In a world that demands being uncomfortably energetic, it makes sense that opiates would be irrationally demonized. It also tracks that drugs that produce the opposite "energy feeling" would be irrationally *accepted*, even in the face of undeniably negative effects. Such is the case with amphetamines, which enjoyed a thirty-year period of total normalization (which just so happened to coincide with what social scientists call the Fordist period), and still to this day enjoy widespread use.

Amphetamines, a category in which we can include amphetamine, dextroamphetamine (the right-handed isomer of amphetamine), and methamphetamine, are all very closely related in chemical structure and have even been used interchangeably in medications.[1] At a low dose, they elevate your mood and keep you awake (they were famously first marketed as "pep pills"). They also give you a certain feeling of omnipotence and mental acuity, a focus on *your* tasks and *your* ability to complete them. In journalist Frank Owen's words, amphetamines are "the most utilitarian of all illegal substances."[2]

Over time, larger doses are required for the same feeling, though actual performance degrades: you think you're doing great, but you're making mistakes. You obsess over small, repetitive tasks (what the behaviorists call "inappropriate perseverance") and lose the capacity to follow complex problems to their end.[3] Your trim figure turns gaunt. You become more irritable and volatile, which in turn leads you to take more. Now the smallest offense sets you off. You're twitchy and anxious. You're sure that people are talking about you behind your back, and soon you actually *hear* your paranoid fears—the beginnings of what is called "amphetamine psychosis." It's not far from here to the stereotype: you might not end up covered in sores and chasing imaginary lizards out of your house, but you'll be something equally terrifying and dull.

In sum, amphetamines make you an American.

Blitzkrieg

In 1934, the pharmaceutical firm Smith, Kline & French (SKF) —today GSK—released a new decongestant inhaler called Benzedrine, followed shortly thereafter by Benzedrine Sulfate, a pill containing the same chemical. Its patentee, Gordon Alles, knew he had found something special, and SKF explored a wide variety of possibilities for its use, including mental performance enhancement, weight loss, and mood improvement. It would eventually settle on the last as the primary aim of Benzedrine Sulfate, but these three goals—being thin, smart, and peppy— would remain intertwined.

By 1938, however, stories were coming out about people "addicted" to Benzedrine. Inhalers were easy to crack open, revealing a cotton filler that could be soaked in a beverage or simply swallowed whole to obtain a much stronger (and much more addictive) rush.[4] SKF lawyered up to threaten publications suggesting their drug was addictive. They also worked quietly to introduce into the medical literature a clear line between addiction and mere habituation, a spurious distinction that would confuse drug debates for generations.[5]

While SKF was skillfully managing its (first) Benzedrine

The Benzedrine inhaler. Reprinted with permission.

addiction scare at home, the Nazi machine was romping through Europe, "heavily drugged, fearless, and berserk."[6] The Germans were using massive amounts of methamphetamine under the name Pervitin. According to historian Peter Andreas, the "speed of the Blitzkrieg literally came from speed."[7] By 1942, however, the Germans were beginning to understand the typical consequences of amphetamine abuse. During the siege of Leningrad, an entire SS infantry company surrendered to the Soviets without a fight, having fired all their ammunition the night before in a collective amphetamine psychosis.[8]

As the Germans cut back their amphetamine production, the Allies ramped it up. Beginning around 1942, Benzedrine was widely issued to the US and British militaries and became easily available in emergency kits. Historians estimate that over 250 million "energy tablets" were supplied to American and British troops between 1942 and 1945.[9]

World War II solidified the link between speed and war. Just as many Nazis were absorbed into security apparatuses around the world after the war, so too did blitzkrieg, in defeat, come to be a general principle of modern warfare, with the United States leading the way. Amphetamines were standard issue in the Korean War, were distributed liberally in Vietnam, and

Benzedrine advertisement, Minnesota Medicine *(October 1944): 783. Reprinted with permission.*

remained frequently used even into the period when they fell under tighter domestic control.[10] In 1991, the US Air Force chief of staff proudly banned amphetamines; in 1996, the ban was quietly reversed.[11]

In addition to spending tens of millions of dollars on amphetamines every year, the US military has also more recently taken interest in a new class of nonamphetamine drugs often called "eugeroics" (meaning "good arousal") or "nootropics"—the so-called smart drugs. These include modafinil (marketed as Provigil), adrafinil, and virgil. They are "smart" in promoting the wakefulness and alertness of amphetamines without the jitteriness, risk for abuse, and perhaps most importantly, need for recovery. Amphetamine use is typically followed by a crash; being up for thirty to sixty hours on modafinil seems to only necessitate a normal night's sleep.[12] In modafinil experiments, the military has broken records for sleep deficits, keeping soldiers up for *eighty-five hours straight.*[13]

Though modafinil is a dopamine reuptake inhibitor like cocaine, and though there are no long-term studies verifying its safety, enthusiastic biohackers have been quick to promote it as a drug with virtually no downside.[14] It's been called "Viagra for the brain"—a charming metaphor indicating that human subjectivity can be judged on a spectrum from the humiliatingly flaccid to the chemically erect. (While we're here: the Pentagon today spends about $80 million a year on Viagra for its soldiers and veterans.[15])

Amphetamines and other stimulants are today but one part of the pharmacological cornucopia available to America's military. As journalist Jennifer Senior described in 2011,

> Walk into any of the larger-battalion-aide stations in Iraq or Afghanistan today, and you'll find Prozac, Paxil, and Zoloft to fight depression, as well as Wellbutrin, Celexa, and Effexor. You'll see Valium to relax muscles (but also for sleep and combat stress) as well as Klonopin, Ativan, Restoril, and Xanax. There's Adderall and Ritalin for ADD and Haldol and Risperdal to treat psychosis; there's Seroquel, at subtherapeutic doses, for sleep, along with Ambien and Lunesta. Sleep, of course, is a huge issue in any war. But in this one, there are enough Red Bulls and Rip Its in the chow halls to light up the city of Kabul, and soldiers often line their pockets with them before missions, creating a cycle where they use caffeine to power up and sleep meds to power down.[16]

Amphetamine Democracy

World War II was a godsend to the amphetamine business. According to psychiatrists Lester Grinspoon and Peter Hedblom, "World War II probably gave the greatest impetus to date to legal medically authorized as well as illicit black market abuse of these pills on a worldwide scale."[17] Speed was adult candy in the postwar period—readily available, socially

Benzedrine advertisements, California and Western Medicine 63, no. 2 (August 1945): 21; American Journal of Psychiatry 101, no. 6 (May 1945): xiii. Reprinted with permission.

sanctioned, and much desired.[18] The booming war economy transitioned to a booming warlike economy. Joseph Heller went from satirizing military bureaucracy in *Catch-22* to doing the same for corporate bureaucracy in *Something Happened.* "People in the company like to live well and are unusually susceptible to nervous breakdowns," his narrator Bob Slocum tells us.[19]

Amphetamines were useful in postwar America for the same reason they were useful during the war. According to historian Jonathan Levy, "Mass production and total war developed a strong affinity, as twentieth-century warfare states proved adept at mobilizing the mechanization of capital, bringing factory discipline onto the battlefields (or was it the other way around?)."[20] If Americans were not faster, more alert, and more efficient, our Communist enemies were going to win, and we knew all too well what "losing" involved. The company man and the suburban housewife were at all times a hair's breadth away from the devastation of Europe and Japan. We had a military mindset, and so we took military drugs.

With Benzedrine sales through the roof, SKF aggressively and capably maneuvered to protect its cash cow against imitators, retaining exclusive rights over it until the expiration of Alles's patent in 1949. SKF also successfully fended off proposed regulations, and thanks to their political efforts, amphetamine inhalers would remain over the counter until 1959. Remarkably, *meth*amphetamine inhalers would not be made prescription-only until 1965.[21]

With the expiration of Alles's patent, new amphetamine drugs flooded the market, but once again, SKF was a step ahead. They had long dreamed of a new product that delivered the highs of Benzedrine while also countering the jitteriness to follow, a single pill that brought people up from depression and down from anxiety at the same time. Combining the right-handed (dextro-) isomer of amphetamine, already an SKF bestseller under the name Dexedrine, with the sedative amobarbital, SKF brought its miracle drug to market in 1950. Dexamyl was advertised as it was intended to be—a drug of limitless possibility to be prescribed when other drugs didn't work, or even when they did. Soon amphetamine-barbiturate imitators like Desbutal and Ambar followed, the ultimate compliment to SKF.

Nothing so captures the psychopharmacological dream like the speedball: cocaine or amphetamines to get you up, opiates or tranquilizers to get you down, all in one combined superdrug.[22] In the speedball, we get it *all*.

Doctors in the postwar period knew well the nasty side effects of these drugs, just as the military had known of them during the war. But amphetamines were "America's first mass-marketed lifestyle drug," and as such, just too damn useful. For martial spirit, weight loss, and unjustifiable enthusiasm, nothing beat amphetamines.[23] And not for lack of trying. In the '50s, pharma searched agonizingly for an amphetamine replacement: tricyclics and monoamine oxidase inhibitors for depression, Tepanil and Preludin for obesity ... none lived up to the amphetamine high, nor really avoided the amphetamine low. Until the end of the '60s, amphetamines bore no real social stigma, and they remained the mood lifter of choice for physicians through the early '70s.[24] Amphetamines were not only licit, they were used to remain within the bounds of the licit. As writer Bruce Jackson explained in 1966,

> The thousands of solitary amphetamine abusers take drugs to *avoid* deviance—so they can be fashionably slim, or bright and alert and functional, or so they can muster the *quoi que* with which to face the tedium of housework or some other dull job— and the last thing they want is membership in a group defined solely by one clear form of rule-breaking.[25]

Dexamyl advertisements, Journal of the American Medical Association *170, no. 5 (May 30, 1959): 213; Journal of the American Medical Association 169, no. 13 (March 28, 1959): 251. These ads ran opposite a regular JAMA jokes column called "The Bright Side." Reprinted with permission.*

Regulation

The excesses of the '60s nonetheless spelled the end of the postwar "amphetamine democracy."[26] "Dr. Feelgoods" like Max Jacobson, who kept a long list of celebrities (including JFK) high on his own proprietary combination of uppers and downers; the spread of "splash," or intravenous injection of amphetamine, a practice introduced by servicemen returning from the Korean War; violent speed freaks ruining the peace and love of the acidheads—all brought forth the rage of new "pharmacological Calvinists."[27] In addition, the old story about junkies being hopeless deviants was breaking down. Now suburban housewives could be addicts too. Clearly something had to be done.

In 1959, Tennessee senator Carey Estes Kefauver initiated the assault against Big Pharma. Kefauver was clearheaded and capable: through careful research he demonstrated that drug

Methedrine advertisement, American Journal of Psychiatry *115, no. 2 (August 1958): xii. The tagline reads "Creating the right attitude ... optimism and cooperation are encouraged by 'Methedrine' (Methamphetamine Hydrochloride)." Reprinted with permission.*

companies were not only lying about the supposedly extraordinary expense of R & D but also bribing FDA officials.[28] In 1962, new evidence surfaced proving that thalidomide, millions of samples of which had been distributed to doctors by the US firm Merrell to test its effect on morning sickness, caused birth defects. The anger over the thalidomide scandal made the moment a ripe one for taking pharma down a peg, but the result was much less than Kefauver hoped for. The 1962 amendments to the Food, Drug, and Cosmetic Act gave the FDA a bit more power but included no restrictions on patenting, pricing, or habit-forming drugs. In addition, drugs marketed before 1962, like amphetamine and methamphetamine, were exempt. This basic story repeated itself in 1965 with the Drug Abuse Control Amendments, which essentially left Big Pharma alone.[29]

In its initial form, it looked like the Comprehensive Drug Abuse Prevention and Control Act of 1970 was a third strike for the reformers. This act created the modern drug scheduling system, ranging from the absolutely restricted Schedule I (drugs with no medical use and a high potential for abuse) to Schedule V (medically valuable drugs with a low potential for abuse). This act was remarkably comprehensive, but at first, only liquid injectable methamphetamine was placed under Schedule II, which affected only five of some 6,000 amphetamine products on the market.[30] But the act emboldened the FDA to take on greater regulatory authority, and by 1971, they had moved all amphetamines to Schedule II—recognized to have some medical value but still highly regulated for their potential for abuse.

Naturally, a black market in stimulants, both cocaine and methamphetamine, soon followed. The Hells Angels and other biker outfits dominated West Coast methamphetamine production and distribution beginning in the early '70s and quickly spread into the heartland.[31] (Meth derives its nickname "crank" from the fact that bikers would store the drug in the crankshaft of their motorcycles.[32]) By the '90s, they had been overtaken by Mexican traffickers like the Amezcua brothers, whose superlabs—meth cooking laboratories set up and dismantled after large-scale forty-eight-hour production runs—created 90 percent of the methamphetamine consumed in America.[33] In 1998, the Amezcua brothers were arrested and into the methamphetamine void stepped the now legendary figures of the Sinaloa cartel—Ignacio "Nacho" Coronel, Leopoldo "Polo" Ochoa, and of course, Joaquín "El Chapo" Guzmán, heir to Pablo Escobar's title as the most notorious drug baron until his extradition and imprisonment in 2017.

Meth production also attracted many individual entrepreneurs, who could easily find the required ingredients and recipes, and who couldn't resist the profit margin (typically, to finance their own habits). Small meth labs get a lot of attention: due to the inexperience of their chemists, there are explosions; due to their negligence, there is hazardously discarded toxic waste; and due to their indigence, they are often tragic affairs, easy targets of moral outrage. These DIY cooks produce a tiny percentage of American meth, but their arrests are frequent and well publicized.[34] According to Steve Preisler, better known as Uncle Fester, author of the meth cooking bible *Secrets of Methamphetamine Manufacture*, "It's a prime example of beating up on the little guy while ignoring the heavyweights."[35]

If there is a hard-and-fast rule of the War on Drugs, it's that the low-level offenders must suffer. In Operation Meth Merchant, a particularly cruel application of this principle, forty-nine convenience store clerks in Georgia were charged with selling materials used to make methamphetamine. Forty-four were South Asian immigrants with a transactional command of English.[36]

As with opioids, methamphetamine abuse took off in many areas of the country lacking in decent healthcare. In both cases, it's not difficult to see these phenomena as by-products of unwitting self-medication, a sensible enough option when options are few.[37] The judgment from the outside was not so kind: according to historian Philip Jenkins, "Methamphetamine became a symbol of white degeneracy, of massive downward social mobility."[38]

Still Running

In *On Speed*, the historian Nicolas Rasmussen argues that amphetamine created a dream that we're still trying to realize: the dream of a drug that helps us lose weight, makes us happier and more enthusiastic, and enhances mental and physical performance, without the nervousness, irritability, and dependence to follow. Since all amphetamines were scheduled in 1971, a variety of "nonamphetamine" weight loss drugs have appeared to fill this void, including phenylpropanolamine, a fenfluramine-phentermine combination (fen-phen), and the "all-natural" ephedrine, extracted from ephedra plants that have long been used in Chinese medicine. All are arguably more dangerous and less effective than simple amphetamine.[39] But the spoils are just too attractive: at any given time, about a quarter of men and 40 percent of women in the US are trying to lose weight, and in turn supporting a multibillion-dollar supplement and pill industry.[40]

In the psychiatric field, selective serotonin reuptake inhibitors (SSRIs) like Prozac have replaced amphetamines as the antidepressant of choice. It's unclear if SSRIs do much better than the old tricyclics in terms of relieving clinical depression, but often enough they do increase confidence and lower inhibitions. Ultimately it's this *feeling*, either promised or felt, that is the reason for their popularity, and it is this quality of SSRIs that clearly define them as an heir of amphetamines.[41]

Finally, the increasing normalization of attention deficit hyperactivity disorder (ADHD), diagnoses for which ballooned beginning in the '90s, has boosted demand for drugs that increase mental focus and performance, and remarkably, it's actual amphetamine—and in the case of Adderall, *the exact same molecule* in Benzedrine—that has benefited. (The other major prescription for ADHD, Ritalin, has an "amphetamine spine" and essentially the same effects.) Worried for their children's future in a cutthroat economy, or simply wanting them to sit down and be quiet, parents easily convince doctors of the applicability of the ADHD diagnosis—the boundaries of which have grown broader over the years. They are encouraged to do so by heavy-handed pharmaceutical advertising and supported by lobbyists and ADHD advocacy organizations, themselves sometimes funded by pharmaceutical companies. The game is neatly rigged from all sides, resulting in a steady growth in the prevalence of ADHD in American children (10.2 percent in 2015–16).[42]

More recently, the amphetamine pushers have shifted their marketing to target adults, advertising ADHD as a "lifespan" disorder.[43] An advertisement for Lilly's adult ADHD drug, Strattera, asks: "Distracted? Disorganized? Frustrated? Modern Life or Adult ADD?"[44] What the philosopher Ivan Illich called "the medicalization of social problems" has achieved unapologetic self-consciousness in drug advertising.

At the height of the 1969–70 speed epidemic, Rasmussen estimates that 10 million Americans, or 5 percent of the population, were using amphetamines.[45] Adding up users of diet pills (10 million), SSRIs (17 million), ADHD meds (5 million), methamphetamine (3 million), and ecstasy (2 million), he conservatively estimates that 37 million people, or 12 percent of the population, used amphetamine-like drugs in 2008.[46] Quaint as the old Benzedrine and Dexamyl ads feel, the cultural imperatives they convey are still very much in operation, and in fact today even more demanding, as "smartness," "pep," and "energy" are all required in order to cling to the last vestiges of material security. As long as students and athletes are looking for that extra edge, truck drivers are grinding out "West Coast turnarounds," and pilots and soldiers are acclimating themselves to sleepless environments, amphetamines will be an indispensable part of American society.[47]

But the longer you take amphetamines, the more you start to slip, until you are a parody of what you hoped to be. In the '60s, physician Roger C. Smith noted that

> the speed freak is, in many ways, an outcast in a society of outcasts. He is regarded as a fool by heroin addicts, as insane and violent by those using the psychedelics or marijuana, and as a "bust" by non-drug-using hustlers ... The compulsive speed user is usually incapable of hustles which demand composure, since he is highly agitated, suspicious and fearful that at any moment he may be detected, or the drug effect may leave him so paranoid that he would not take advantage of opportunities.[48]

Most amphetamine users never approach high-dose, compulsive use, but what goes for psychoanalysis also goes for drugs: the truth lies in the exaggerations. Somehow we're becoming stupider taking mountains of "smart" drugs, more depressed with reams of "pep" pills, more incapable of keeping up the necessary appearances in the American hustle.

According to musician and journalist Mick Farren, "Speed is too much a reflection of its time."[49] Capitalism has accelerated social life to a near breaking point, and it's quite fitting that it would also produce a drug to help us keep up. In the postwar era, amphetamine was a staple of American society, propelling productivity and consumption alike. The neoliberal era rediscovered speed in its own right, but without the same collective animating fantasy. We are still in a flat-out sprint, but, to quote social theorist Hartmut Rosa, "We are no longer running towards a bright horizon in the future, we are running away from the dark abyss behind our backs."[50]

6

Psychotropics, or Diagnostic Creeps and Rational Paranoids

We try to remember that medicine is for the patient. We try never to forget that medicine is for the people. It is not for the profits. The profits follow, and if we have remembered that, they have never failed to appear. The better we have remembered it, the larger they have been.

—George Merck, addressing the graduating class
of the Medical College of Virginia in 1950

The psychiatrist Peter Kramer used to see patients, and he still remembers why. When a young woman visits him complaining of being unable to do the laundry, he's nearly lovestruck:

Betty is terribly likable ... She is subtle, generous, self-effacing. In her presence, I feel coarse and overbearing. Betty understands the intricacies of relationships better than I do, has wider tolerance for others' foibles. How lucky I am to be having this conversation.[1]

But it doesn't take long for Kramer to come back to his senses: "When I am charmed, I think depression."[2] And by depression, he means not the characteristics of depressive behavior but rather "glial cells retreating ... neurons withering ... [a] shrunken hippocampus and disordered prefrontal cortex."[3] This is because Kramer, knowing that depression is a brain disease, a problem of neuronal resilience, has trained himself to see beyond the person and into the brain. "No need to look forward to the face," he proudly claims.[4] Just as a "cardiologist sees blocked arteries" when "hearing of chest pain," so too does Kramer see "fragility, brittleness, lack of resilience, a failure to heal" in Betty's brain while being charmed by Betty's self-deprecating persona.[5]

In one sense, Kramer is an extremist (he *is* the guy who insinuated that we ought to consider putting psychiatric medication in the drinking water), but if anything, this depersonalizing and reductive description of Betty is *exemplary* of the contemporary psychiatric view.[6] We are no more than brains in bodies to the psychiatrists. Were it not for a deep material investment in what independent scholar Richard DeGrandpre calls "the cult of pharmacology," it would be pretty clear that this is a terrifying view of human interiority—a form of de-eroticized objectification both bone-chilling and irrational.[7]

While Americans have long drugged themselves to cope with mental stress, it's only in the last forty years or so that this view of psychiatric "care"—manipulating the brain with the aid of pharmaceutical drugs—has come to dominance. This chapter serves as a history of this transformation of mental illness and its pharmacological treatment in America, and is unique in this book for treating very different classes of drugs as one group, within the admittedly unwieldy category "psychotropic." This term is commonly taken to be synonymous with "psychoactive," but Google the two and you'll get very different lists of drugs. This is because psychotropic drugs (the bestselling class of pharmaceutical drugs) are conceptualized first and foremost in terms not of the feeling or experience they produce but of their capacity to alter the function of the brain—which is to say, in the objectifying terms of a professional fantasy.

Neurasthenia, Anxiety, Depression

In the late nineteenth century, *neurology* was the fancy profession, and as such was concerned with sufficiently distancing itself from *psychiatry*, associated at the time with care for the institutionalized. Everyday people with mental troubles wanted no part of the asylum, and so they sought out "nerve doctors," whose cures varied widely. In 1881, George Miller Beard published *American Nervousness*, a text that popularized the term "neurasthenia"—literally "tired nerves," but used to describe a wide range of emotional problems from fatigue and headaches to muscle pain and worry.[8] William James simply called it "Americanitis," and everyone seemed to agree that neurasthenia was a particularly modern condition, something we had to tolerate to enjoy the great bounty of industrial *progress*. In Beard's characterization,

> The capacity of the nervous system for sustained work and
> worry has not increased in proportion to the demands for work
> and worry that are made upon it ... Modern nervousness is the
> cry of the system struggling with its environment.[9]

But Beard was positively proud to live in a country where such struggle ensued: he exclaimed that neurasthenia was "modern and uniquely American; and no age, no country, and no form of civilization, not Greece, nor Rome, nor Spain, nor the Netherlands, in the days of their Glory, possessed such maladies."[10] No one is as sick as us! Beard's contemporary, physician Mary Putnam Jacobi, put the matter starkly:

> Health is like the silent existence of those happy nations that
> have no history. But disease represents the commotion, the
> storm and stress, the drama and the convulsions into which the
> disturbed history of our race has usually been thrown.[11]

Neurasthenia's treatment varied as widely as its symptoms. Most doctors simply recommended rest and a better diet, for which a cottage industry of spas and retreats opened to cater to wealthier neurasthenics.[12] At such retreats Americans were exhorted to cultivate relaxation and repose by learning from the "Oriental people, the inhabitants of the tropics, and the colored peoples generally."[13] But when "colored wisdom" failed,

Advertisement for Carter's Little Nerve Pills (19th c.). Historic New England, *ephemera collection, historicnewengland.org.*

there were also widely available patent medicines, often containing alcohol, opiates, or chloral hydrate (a popular but now forgotten sedative). It's difficult to imagine today, but in the 1880s, you could pretty easily acquire just about any drug you wanted, including medically pure heroin and cocaine, without a prescription. In 1903, the first barbiturate, Veronal, was introduced. Though other drugs available at the local pharmacy would soon be illegal, the barbiturates would remain a pharmaceutical mainstay of American life well into the '70s, keeping up healthy sales even during the heyday of their safer (in the sense of being less easily overdosed) alternative, the benzodiazepines.

Recognizing a catchall term, the psychoanalysts parsed neurasthenia into a number of component parts, but it continued to be a household word into the 1930s. Neurasthenia is best conceptualized as the first instance of a diagnostic dialectic, which includes *anxiety* as its second pole and *depression* as its final one. Neurasthenia was a mess of a category: Beard and others used it to indicate such a wide range of phenomena that really the only way to concisely describe how they understood it at the time would be something like "all of the bad things that capitalist society does to our health." The postwar anxiety that replaced neurasthenia repressed its characteristics of fatigue and enervation, but society remained the cause. The neoliberal period brought back the depressive element of neurasthenia but eliminated the social causes in order to justify pharmacological dependence. Today our *brains* make us sick, only able to process the degradation of society mimetically through the degradations of our prefrontal cortices.

Period	1880s–1930s	1940s–	1980s–
Diagnosis	Neurasthenia	Anxiety	Depression
Cause	Society	Society	The Brain

The Age of Anxiety

As W. H. Auden announced at its outset, the postwar period was an "age of *anxiety*."[14] According to historian Andrea Tone, at the time,

> anxiety was viewed less as a serious psychiatric disorder than as a badge of achievement: an emblem of struggle, but also of success. Anxiety was the predictable yet commendable offshoot of Americans' insatiable hunger to get ahead, their relentless determination to become new and improved.[15]

It was also fueled by the atomic angst of the Cold War, and for its theoreticians, this was all well and good. For figures like the historian Arthur Schlesinger Jr., the existential psychologist Rollo May, and the Cold War strategist George Kennan, anxiety was the price we in the capitalist West paid for our *freedom*.[16] The Soviets weren't anxious, but neither were they free. It's anxiety or Communism, and it sure wasn't going to be Communism.

Advertisement for Hoffmann-La Roche's Librium in 1970. The small print reads: "It is ten years since Librium* became available. Ten anxious years of aggravation and demonstration, Cuba and Vietnam, assassination and devaluation, Biafra and Czechoslovakia. Ten turbulent years in which the world-wide climate of anxiety and aggression has given Librium— with its specific calming action and its remarkable safety margin—a unique and still growing role in helping mankind meet the challenge of a changing world," British Medical Journal 2, no. 5711 (June 20, 1970). Reprinted with permission.

Though theories of anxiety varied widely, it was thus common at this time to think of anxiety, like neurasthenia, in essentially social terms, as the subjective correlate of a particular form of life in the capitalist West. Psychiatrists, who had gained respectability under the aegis of psychoanalysis, understood anxiety as a problem of "daily living" and "the stress of our times," and they saw themselves as helping to shore up a common cultural project.[17] For some, the West's *individualism* was at stake: according to theologian Paul Tillich, "A consequence of the individualization of life is the state of anxiety in every individual."[18] But these same theorists also increasingly viewed anxiety in biological terms, medicalizing what had previously been a predominantly existential and theological conception.[19]

The first anxiolytics (antianxiety drugs) appeared in the '50s: first meprobamate (Miltown), which *Time* memorably dubbed the "Don't-Give-a-Damn Pill," and then the benzodiazepines, including chlordiazepoxide (Librium) and the blockbuster diazepam (Valium)—the most prescribed drug in the world from 1968 to 1981.[20] The Age of Anxiety's tranquilizer boom is often portrayed as a uniquely gendered situation—male doctors prescribing "mother's little helper" to isolated and brutalized housewives—but men too were avid users and were marketed to by drug companies as much as women.[21] All were rightfully anxious and deserving of a pill to take the edge off. Remarkably, it was Arthur Sackler (of the Sackler family criminal enterprise, Purdue Pharma) who designed Librium and Valium's marketing campaigns for their producer, Hoffmann-La Roche.[22] The promotional campaigns directed at doctors' offices he designed for these benzodiazepines prefigured similar tactics the Sacklers would deploy to later sell OxyContin.[23]

Looking back at medical journal advertisements from the '60s and '70s, the degree to which minor tranquilizer promotion predominates is fairly remarkable. Sometimes one and the same drug would be advertised under different names and for different conditions: for instance, on first glance, one might guess that Wallace's Meprospan for heart patients, Wyeth's Equanil for layabouts, and Wallace's Miltown for anxiety—all of which were marketed at the same time—were three different drugs, but the active ingredient in all was meprobamate. The range of forms and uses for the blockbuster benzodiazepines, Librium and Valium, is even more astonishing. Librium and Librax (also chlordiazepoxide) for geriatric anxiety, arthritis, "shadow" cardiovascular and gastrointestinal issues; Valium for insomnia, precordial discomfort, spastic gut, skeletal muscle spasm, and above all "psychic tension." One ad for Valium markets it as the solution to "the third realm of disease," the realm of "'psychosomatic medicine,' such as functional disorders due to excessive psychic tension."[24]

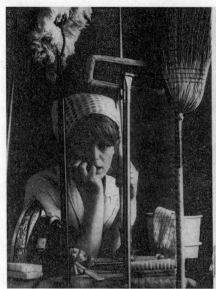

Advertisements for Serax (1967) and Librium (1970), both antianxiety medications. Journal of the American Medical Association *200, no. 8 (May 22, 1967), 206–7;* Journal of the American Medical Association *241, no. 18 (May 4, 1970), 920. Reprinted with permission.*

In other words: for anything that doesn't quite make sense, *Valium*.

By the late '60s, two-thirds of tranquilizer consumers were indeed women, and in fact this belated realization was the beginning of the end of the (first) Valium era.[25] The "over-medicated woman" was seen as victimized by corporate drug pushers, and the understanding of tranquilizer use as femi-nizing reinforced concerns that tranquilizers were muting the "divine discontent of tense men," to quote one physician.[26] Early critics of benzodiazepines worried that Big Pharma was creating a "falsely flaccid race of people."[27] By the '70s, many were beginning to listen. In a 1972 article for *Playboy*, Senator Mike Gravel crystallized this growing realization:

> If tomorrow, by some miracle, every source of illegally grown or manufactured drug were cut off, the U.S. would scarcely feel any withdrawal symptoms, nor would the current drug-abuse epidemic be ended. The sad truth is that our most sophisticated and profitable pushers are the nation's largest pharmaceutical corporations.[28]

Though benzodiazepine sales declined beginning in the late '70s, the Age of Anxiety never really went away, and it came to renewed prominence after 9/11. It's also been escalated in new directions. In the '90s, GlaxoSmithKline (the same company that brought us the first amphetamines in the '30s) launched an awareness campaign around social anxiety disorder (SAD) and received FDA approval to market its drug Paxil as the one and only treatment for SAD.[29] The typical players were involved: an aggressive PR firm (Cohn & Wolfe), an astroturfed advocacy organization (the Social Anxiety Disorder Coalition), and even a celebrity spokesperson (Miami Dolphins running back Ricky Williams).[30] The campaign's tagline? "Imagine Being Allergic to People."

When critics wondered aloud what the difference was between SAD and common shyness, SAD advocates responded that they were destigmatizing a marginalized form of illness (reminiscent of British American Tobacco's claim that world health standards were a form of "cultural imperialism"—if only we just left it to the corporations to carry out social justice).[31] According to historian David Herzberg, the amount of benzodiazepines consumed in 2010 was roughly double that of the drugs' supposed heyday in the '70s.[32]

The Biological Revolution in Psychiatry

A dramatic conceptual transformation separates us from the postwar period. In the '50s, American psychiatrists were mostly in agreement that psychological problems ought to be understood within the complex life history of individual patients. For some, drugging patients was inimical to the therapeutic process; for others, drugs could be a helpful adjunct to talk therapy, but it was the talking that was curative, not the drugs.[33] Only the lowly "directive-organic" psychiatrists (those who worked at state institutions) traded heavily in pills.[34]

Three broad changes, beginning with the psychopharmacological discoveries of the '50s but coalescing into a paradigm shift in the '80s, revolutionized psychiatry. The first was the developments in neuroscience that those discoveries spurred. The idea that neurotic or psychotic symptoms were manifestations of the underlying actions of serotonin, dopamine, or norepinephrine took hold with remarkable speed, ushering in a new era of biological reductionism.[35] The moment of triumph over the old psychoanalytic regime was undoubtedly the release of the third iteration of the psychiatric manual, the *Diagnostic and Statistical Manual of Mental Disorders* (*DSM*), in 1980. The *DSM-III* fully abandoned the old etiological models and introduced a positivist classificatory system of illnesses tied to specific drug treatments.[36] Many critics see this shift as a retreat from the social domain to the biological, but even more immediately, it was a retreat from the *personal* to the biological, as is evident in case histories like Kramer's.[37]

The second related change pertained to drug development. The rapid succession of novel substances peddled by large, profit-hungry corporations prompted amendments to the Food and Drugs Act in 1962, which required drug developers to target specific diseases and prove the efficacy (not simply the safety) of their products through randomized clinical trials (RCTs).[38] As psychiatrist David Healy sadly notes of these well-intentioned amendments,

> One of the great hazards of reforms is that reformers often produce the opposite of what they set out to achieve. The 1962 amendments were passed as part of an effort to guard the people from the unfettered forces of capitalism. It is a moot point whether the reforms have fostered instead the growth of a psychopharmaceutical complex whose power to penetrate markets is now all but comprehensive.[39]

Within psychiatry, the dominance of RCTs fits well with the new biological emphasis: in the view of psychiatric historians Joel Braslow and Stephen Marder, "The RCT shifted the focus from the expertise of the individual clinician and the unique doctor-patient relationship toward an emphasis on results (most often quantitative) and interventions that could be replicated across clinicians, patients, space, and time."[40] In addition, with dogged prodding from Big Pharma, disease categories matched to questionably efficacious drugs have proliferated. The latest iteration of the *DSM* is so broadly pathologizing of normal human behaviors that even its previous authors have come out against it in disgust.[41] The 1962 amendments merely encouraged an even closer bond between dealers and suppliers, ever renewed at the golf and fine-dining getaways that pose as meetings of the American Psychiatric Association.[42]

The third broad change was the rapid closing of large state institutions for the mentally ill. Though justified at the time as an overdue shuttering of inhumane asylums and the birth of a new era of "community" care, the deinstitutionalization of the '60s was first and foremost about state retrenchment.[43] Less-regulated and entrepreneurial smaller care homes emerged to absorb the newly freed, supported in part by funds made available in the War on Poverty, but many of the former hospital inhabitants ended up on the streets or in prison.[44] In 2015, Chicago's Cook County Jail hired a clinical psychologist to be its warden, in recognition of the fact that one-third of the inmates were mentally ill.[45]

Given the overwhelming power accorded to drugs by biological reductionism, it's fitting that many ascribe the genesis of deinstitutionalization to the appearance in the 1950s of the first antipsychotic, chlorpromazine (Thorazine). The closing of state hospitals was a political and economic decision through and through, and yet many choose to remember it as pharmacologically caused.

That said, Thorazine did wake a lot of people up: asylum patients to reality, and their doctors to the untapped power of psychotropics. On Thorazine, institutionalized patients who previously faced physical restraint and extreme treatments like frontal lobotomy became less agitated and more compliant. In an early trial of the drug's efficacy, scientists gave it to rats trained to climb a rope to escape electrical shock. On Thorazine, the rats just stayed put while electrical current coursed through their bodies—impassive, absorbing pain, any urge to escape quieted.[46] If it did not birth deinstitutionalization, it certainly excited the psychiatric imagination. Frank Ayd, the psychiatrist who helped introduce antipsychotics into clinical practice, captured the promise and peril of the moment well: "Biological psychiatry is an important part of the growing technology for controlling human behavior. To some this is cause for cheering, but to others the future is fraught with terrors for man."[47]

The Age of Depression

"Although no major poet has stepped forward to provide an announcement," wrote psychiatrist Leslie Farber in 1979, "sometime during the present decade, the Age of Anxiety became the Age of Depression."[48] Early antidepressants had appeared in the '50s—the tricyclic imipramine and monoamine oxidase inhibitors—but, tellingly, their developers worried about finding a market for them.[49] This definitely had something to do with the wide availability of amphetamines in the postwar period, but it's also the case that while a whole justificatory framework existed for anxiety, nothing similar yet made sense of being clinically *sad*. Indeed, to sell its antidepressant amitriptyline, Merck spent a great deal distributing literature to doctors explaining that long-term depression actually was a real entity.[50] This all seemed rather absurd by 1988 when Eli Lilly released its cash cow Prozac, a drug that is today virtually synonymous with the profession of psychiatry.

What accounts for this profound cultural shift within which depression became *the* prominent psychiatric diagnosis? Part of the power of this new narrative lay in its rejection of the Age of Anxiety. According to Kramer,

> [Prozac] was the opposite of mother's little helper: it got [my patient] Julia out of the house and into the workplace, where she was able to grow in competence and confidence. I see this result often. There is a sense in which antidepressants are feminist drugs, liberating and empowering.[51]

Advertisements for Prozac and Zoloft confirmed this sentiment, illustrating working mothers having and doing it all.[52]

But the ultimate source of the legitimacy of this paradigm lay in the appeal to a new neuroscientific basis. According to historian Edward Shorter, "What made depression epidemic was flogging it to the public as a concept with a firm scientific basis," a basis that the biological revolution supplied.[53] You've

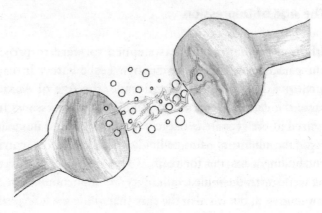

© 2022 *Jaya Rose*

probably seen some version of this picture in a pharmaceutical ad: two mushrooms placed cap to cap with little droplets going back and forth, and maybe some electricity just for fun.

Undergirding anxiety were the Cold War, Western individualism, the Fordist-Keynesian economy, and freedom itself. Depression, meanwhile, has only this sad, goofy image, representing the supposed action of neurotransmitters in response to certain drugs and pushed aggressively in psychopharmaceutical ad campaigns. Even some psychiatrists, like Ross Baldessarini, have indicted the "largely fruitless efforts to support a dopamine excess hypothesis of schizophrenia or mania, a norepinephrine or serotonin deficiency of major depression, a serotonin deficiency hypothesis in obsessive-compulsive disorder, and so on."[54] But this does not stop pharmaceutical companies from endless "neurotransmitter chatter." As Shorter bluntly concludes,

> So how did this public health disaster come about, putting much of the population on pharmacological agents from which they would derive few of the benefits but many of the side effects? It happened because the pharmaceutical companies badly needed these neurotransmitter reuptake theories in their communications with the medical profession and with the public.[55]

But could this be it? Are we all just dupes of Big Pharma? Though we shouldn't, of course, let the Eli Lillys of the world off the hook, there was clearly something in America receptive to the paradigm of depression beginning in the '80s. If there's one thing we know about depression, it's that it's caused by isolation, loneliness, and disconnection—in other words, the atomized affective state brought on by the political economic shifts of the neoliberal period. As described in more detail in the Introduction, during this time unions and membership organizations were gutted, deindustrialization tore apart working-class communities, and a wave of consumerist individualism carried us into the sea of post-politics. We are more alone than ever; no surprise that we are also more depressed than ever.

In the case of all three diagnoses under investigation here, the "cure" definitely played a large role in creating the "disease."[56] There is a remarkable continuity in advertising from the nineteenth-century patent medicines to twenty-first-century pharmaceutical drugs, and the "awareness campaigns" propagated therein have been wildly successful at refashioning conceptions of human health and interiority. But drug producers didn't pull their copy from thin air: neurasthenia, anxiety, and depression, along with the drugs employed for their treatment, were all absorbed by the culture like water on a dry sponge. We all want to know what's wrong with us, and when the word "capitalism" is illegible as an explanation for our generally uncomfortable state of being, easy substitutes must be ready to hand. Drugs provide pharmacological relief, but perhaps more importantly, they provide *explanatory* relief.

Prozac

In addition to being the paradigmatic psychotropic of the neoliberal era, Prozac also encapsulates everything wrong with the pharmaceutical industry today. In a majority of double-blind studies, sugar pills equaled or outperformed Prozac and similar antidepressants.[57] FDA approval is nonetheless possible because only two studies are needed to demonstrate the drug's efficacy. The FDA also doesn't determine how much *more* effective a drug needs to be in comparison to a placebo. According to psychotherapist Lauren Slater, in the forty-seven clinical trials conducted for six major antidepressants,

> when measured on the Hamilton Depression Rating Scale, the tool most clinicians use to measure a person's depression, the average patient improved on the drug only two points better than on the placebo, a difference that Irving Kirsch, a Harvard psychologist and associate director of the Program in Placebo Studies, has called "trivial" and "clinically meaningless" ... Two-thirds of patients on an SSRI would likely have improved on a placebo alone.[58]

In 1991, George H. W. Bush terrifyingly proclaimed the 1990s to be "the decade of the brain." (Coincidentally, Bush had previously served on the board of directors of Eli Lilly, something both Bush and Lilly tried to later downplay.[59]) Perhaps it was this neuroscientific ebullience that minimized the importance of a simple trend, which could have invalidated faith in any other new miracle cure: after the introduction of Prozac, the numbers of depressed patients have steadily increased.[60] Could we imagine deaths from infections growing after the introduction of antibiotics? Or measles outbreaks after the introduction of the measles vaccine?[61]

Of course, many people probably don't think about depression according to a bacteriological model. They take Prozac like aspirin: to treat rather than cure. In some ways, this attitude is a holdover from the postwar period, when psychiatric medications were sold more honestly as a means of coping with the stresses and monotony of daily life. Today, however, the neurobiological paradigm justifying claims about Prozac's efficacy does indeed involve the identification of causes and the promise of cures. But again, even in the more commonsensical view of antidepressants as alleviating symptoms, SSRIs like Prozac just aren't very effective.[62] A moralistic and legal bias against the drugs that get us high and immediately make us feel good has left psychiatrists with dull instruments in their toolbelts. Put simply, they don't have the good stuff (though the psychedelic renaissance might change this).

Unfortunately, there is much more discomfiting news about antidepressants. According to Healy, Eli Lilly knew, even before it sought FDA approval, that in a small but significant number of cases, Prozac causes people to become violent and suicidal, and that the company had gone to a great deal of trouble to hide that fact.[63] On September 14, 1989, in what journalist Mark Ames called "the first modern private workplace massacre in American history," Joseph Wesbecker walked into the office of his former employer, killed eight of his former coworkers, wounded twelve of them, and then shot himself.[64] The previous month he had been put on Prozac. The survivors and families of the victims finally got Eli Lilly in court five years later. While claiming publicly that Prozac was perfectly safe, they privately settled for what one of the lawyers in the case called "a tremendous amount of money."[65]

As if this all isn't enough evidence against the "brain decade" drug, users for whom Prozac *is* effective also get addicted to and develop a tolerance to it, and the majority relapse after they stop taking it.[66] Left in the lurch of pharmacological dependence, psychiatrists will turn to stronger antipsychotics (what used to be called "major tranquilizers") once the typical antidepressants wear off. In 2011, antipsychotics—again, *major tranquilizers* —surpassed statins (cholesterol-lowering medication) as the top-selling category of pharmaceutical drugs in America.[67]

While we're here: the antipsychotic Abilify became the first ever "digital drug" to be approved by the FDA in 2017. The pill contains an ingestible sensor that relays information to a mobile application indicating when it was swallowed.[68]

As many critics have noted, there is scant evidence for the psychiatric conception of depression, according to which the root cause is a chemical brain imbalance.[69] What *is* certain is that once a depressed patient ingests Prozac or similar drugs, they *will* have a chemical imbalance in their brain.[70] In a way, Prozac imbricates its users in the drug's justificatory framework after the fact. Of course, none of this is to say that many people haven't been helped by SSRIs, only that a placebo would work just as well in most cases, that there are better and safer ways of dealing with feelings of depression, and that the paradigm making sense of their efficacy is reductive, dangerous, and obscuring of the social causes of contemporary sadness. If we want to feel better about our lives, we can do better than buy what the psychiatrists are peddling (among other things, by engaging in that old practice of experimental talking that insurance companies have made so difficult to access).

The Age of Rational Paranoia

Though Big Pharma is in many ways the same as it ever was, a typical capitalist industry maximizing profits regardless of "incidental" considerations, its actions today have unique social ramifications and have reshaped subjective understandings, as new diagnostic categories did in the past.

In the postwar period, pharmaceutical companies behaved much like tobacco companies (and often shared PR techniques). They knew their uppers and downers were bad for people (and being abused), but they pretended ignorance and suppressed any information that might damage sales. Their clandestine attempts to replace their best sellers with less harmful substitutes is one of the reasons for the marketing of so many new drugs during this period. Thanks to the sweeping changes in psychiatry and psychopharmacology mentioned previously, pharmaceutical companies increasingly cozied up to both regulatory agencies and medical professionals beginning in the late '60s, and out of this legal racket a new conception of *health* itself emerged.

In the '50s, you went to the doctor when you were sick; today you go for regular maintenance and monitoring of risk factors. The anthropologist Joseph Dumit describes this as the shift from an "inherent health" to an "inherent illness" model. Though the latter may well be more medically valid, it is also a paradigm within which pharmaceutical companies conveniently do quite well. When the target of drug treatment is not sickness but "chronic illness" or mere risk, and when the alleviation of that risk is defined through large RCTs that amplify small treatment effects (see above), Big Pharma unsurprisingly makes a handsome profit.[71] The aim is simply "not to cure people or to identify those who should be cured, but to grow the number of new prescriptions as much as possible."[72]

This was true in the postwar period as well, but the means of doing so today produce what Dumit calls "rational paranoia."[73] Since the target of drug treatment is often not actual sickness but *risk*, illness becomes something you don't necessarily *feel*, but that you *believe* you have to the extent that you have submitted to the proper authorities on the prevention of risk. Unfortunately, those authorities are often not actual doctors but the companies themselves. Indeed, in direct-to-consumer advertising of prescription drugs (something that only exists in the United States and New Zealand), patients are encouraged to challenge their doctors, to press them with information retrieved from advocacy websites that are mostly sponsored by pharma itself. Given the fragmented nature of the American healthcare system, people often *do* have to become self-advocates to receive the care they or their families need; thus the "rational" part of "rational paranoia." This combination of imperatives produces what Dumit calls "the expert patient": the responsible, bordering on obsessive, judge and executor of industry-fashioned expertise, the self-made island of reason in a sea of medical disorganization.

For this cagey monad, immediate reality is not to be trusted; the truth lies elsewhere. The inherent illness paradigm encourages the disregard of one's own feelings and the incorporation of medical facts into one's life. The biological revolution in psychiatry, in fact, provided one new language for this kind of patient, who can often speak effortlessly about dopamine and synapses as if they were describing human interiority as such.[74] The depth hermeneutic of paranoia is thus wedded to a thoroughgoing belief in "the science" and embedded in the structure of everyday life: if you are not taking the pills that address the sickness that you do not yet feel or even have, if you are not scouring the internet for information that you will bring to your doctor about your own condition, if you are not reading about the latest health trends and applying them to your life, then *you are a dupe*—undoubtedly the worst kind of subject to be today.

Pharma is not alone in encouraging us to go beyond deceptive surface appearances to the hidden truth of things (the underlying trends behind market behavior, the real occurrences behind corporate media cover-ups, what men and women *really* want), but it is a key catalyst of a new type of subjective transformation, one accomplished just in time for a new period of political stasis and social regression. Welcome to the Age of Rational Paranoia.

7

Psychedelics, or the Dialectic of Control

To enjoy a drug one must enjoy being a subject.

—Henri Michaux

The psychologist and drug specialist Oakley Ray argued in 1972 that "most of the drugs that have been adopted by western culture are those primarily affecting arousal level"—which is to say, uppers and downers.[1] By contrast, "information processing" drugs—psychedelics—had in his view remained foreign to Western culture because "drugs offering multiple realities and suggesting internal rewards far beyond those in the outside world seem hard to fit into a focused, accomplish-it-because-it's-there orientation. Instead of outward achievements and activation, these drugs would seem to offer inner exploration and passivity."[2]

It's an understandable if overly reductive schematization. While we know what amphetamines and barbiturates are for, at hallucinogenic levels, psychedelics defy instrumentalization and even description.[3] As psychonauts have always held, you either turn on, or you don't know. Brilliant visuals, cosmic love, supreme tranquility, direct contact with the very beginnings and ends of the universe—yes, yes, but not quite. In this sense, psychedelics certainly seem constitutionally opposed to the cold, instrumental logic of capitalism, and as we will see, their enthusiasts have often deployed them as such.

What Ray didn't consider, however, was that the capitalist West has always deeply needed (and deeply exploited) its ostensible other. William Burroughs said of yage (ayahuasca) that "the blood and substance of many races, Negro, Polynesian,

Mountain Mongol, Desert Nomad, Polyglot Near East, Indian —races as yet unconceived and unborn, combinations not yet realized pass through your body."[4] He was speaking to a desire, prevalent especially among the upper and middle classes, to be rejuvenated through exotic intoxication.[5] In the words of writer Andy Letcher, psychedelics enable users "to punctuate the envelope of ordinary consciousness, to transcend the self, and to acquire knowledge that was not known before."[6] They bring us in metaphysical contact with the *Other*, and as such, perform an invaluable function in enchanting the drab confines of capitalist modernity.

The only problem: in this society, there is no outside. "One should not forget," Jean Cocteau reminds us, "that official contacts with the unknown always end as commercial transaction."[7] *Everything* is subject to the grating churn of capital, and anything special about life on planet earth will become fodder for cruelty and control. Our heavens are fated to be earthly, and they also inevitably turn into hells.

Stage One: Controlling the Mind

In 1950, Edward Hunter, a journalist and former "propaganda specialist" for the Office of Strategic Services (the predecessor of the CIA) during World War II, published an article in the *Miami News* entitled "'Brain-Washing' Tactics Force Chinese into Ranks of Communist Party."[8] This term was derived from the Chinese characters *xi nao* (literally meaning "wash brain"), but before long, Americans were also joining the billion-strong ranks of the brainwashed. When US soldiers were released from Communist prisons after fighting ended in Korea in 1953, many of them were critical of the United States; some even praised Communism and wanted to stay behind. Clearly, the Koreans and their allies were performing depraved mind control experiments on captured Americans.[9] In June of that year, a headline

134

in the *New Republic* sounded the alarm: "Communist Brain-washing—Are We Prepared?"[10]

In fact, neither the Chinese nor the Soviets nor the Koreans actually possessed any such tactics, but that didn't stop the CIA from acting on the words of their own propagandist. Such was the fitting justification for CIA research into mind control: the need to master an ability fantasized to be possessed by others.

But while the absolute certainty of this belief was animated above all by the windowless paranoia of Cold War lunacy, CIA officers *did* understand the extraordinary lengths to which their enemies would go in pursuit of global dominance. They knew because they had hired many of them after the war. Through Operation Paperclip, hundreds of Nazi scientists were excused from war crimes and emigrated to the United States to work in the blossoming defense industry.[11] Kurt Blome, director of the Nazis' biological warfare program, was among them. During the war, Blome had worked closely with Japan's own biological warfare department, Unit 731, and its director Shiro Ishii—who also received immunity after the war. Revelations from Blome and Ishii about the extent of human experimentation accomplished on their watch, amounting to some of the most morally abominable acts human beings had ever perpetrated on other human beings, titillated CIA scientists.[12] The bar for depravity had been set, and Americans would not be outdone.

In 1950, the Agency green-lighted Project Bluebird, tasked with finding ways to make an individual "do [the CIA's] bidding against his will and even against such fundamental laws of nature as self-preservation."[13] This project found an early champion in the new CIA deputy director, Allen Dulles. Shortly after assuming full directorship of the CIA in 1953, Dulles lectured to a group of Princeton alumni on "how sinister the battle for men's minds had become in Soviet hands."[14] He was of course describing his own initiatives at the CIA, projected outwards in the terms of the legitimating ideology of the era.

Three days after this speech, he authorized Project MK-ULTRA. The secret project was placed under the aegis of the chemical division of the Technical Services Staff, the head of which, Sidney Gottlieb, was handpicked by Dulles for his "zeal and creative imagination."[15] Gottlieb was given free rein to crack the secrets of the human psyche, and thereby offer America a shortcut to global dominance. Drug experimentation was a crucial part of this work, and after a short time, Gottlieb became convinced that LSD was his miracle drug—perhaps because of his own extensive use of it. Through a variety of "subprojects," whose heads were often unaware of the true source of their funding, Gottlieb "tested" LSD in scenarios that ranged from the merely criminal to the mind-bendingly macabre.

On one end of the spectrum lay Operation Midnight Climax, which established a CIA-funded brothel where clients were unknowingly dosed with LSD for the purpose of studying "how to exploit the art of lovemaking for espionage purposes."[16] A "vastly obese," alcoholic, and sadomasochistic narcotics detective named George Hunter White was put in charge of the project, which predictably he ran as a party house.[17] As he reflected later, "I toiled wholeheartedly in the vineyards because it was fun, fun, fun. Where else could a red-blooded American boy lie, kill, cheat, steal, rape, and pillage with the sanction and blessing of the All-Highest?"[18]

On the other end lay the experiments of Dr. Ewen Cameron, psychology professor at McGill University and director of their psychiatric hospital. Most of Cameron's patients at the Allan Memorial Institute came to him for minor issues, like postpartum depression or anxiety. They left broken by a true monster.

To cleanse unwanted thoughts from a patient's mind, Cameron used a technique he called "psychic driving," in which he administered electroconvulsive shocks that reached thirty to forty times the strength other psychiatrists used. After days of this treatment, the patient was moved to a solitary ward. There he or she was

Sarah Anne Johnson, Black Out, *2008/2020. Bronze and Cardboard, approximately 9 x 5.5 x 2.5 inches. Johnson's grandmother was a victim of Ewen Cameron's.* Black Out *was part of Johnson's exhibition,* House on Fire, *which conveyed the suffering produced by Cameron's brainwashing experiments. Reprinted with permission. © Sarah Anne Johnson, courtesy Yossi Milo Gallery, New York.*

fed LSD and given only minimal amounts of food, water, and oxygen. Cameron fitted patients with helmets equipped with earphones, into which he piped phrases or messages like "My mother hates me," repeated hundreds of thousands of times.[19]

In one report, he discussed a patient who received 101 days of "de-patterning" by psychic driving. Surprisingly—to him —"no favorable results were obtained."[20]

Cameron was no outlier. In another MK-ULTRA-funded experiment, "mentally handicapped children were fed cereal laced with uranium and radioactive calcium."[21] In another, nineteen prisoners were given "LSD nearly every day for fifteen months, without being told what it was."[22] The CIA was running a sophisticated and brutal torture program, modeled on those of the Germans and Japanese during the war.

What are we to do with such information? One of the many reasons "conspiracy theories" tend to be so alienating is that, in addition to often being shocking or repellant, they're difficult to integrate into a coherent worldview. Political scientist Michael Parenti offers perhaps the best means of doing so in situating conspiracy as a component of class analysis:

> No ruling interest could last long if it tried to control an entire society through the manipulations of secret cabals. At the same time, no ruling class could survive if it wasn't attentive to its own interests, consciously trying to anticipate, control, or initiate events at home and abroad, both overtly and secretly. It's hard to imagine a modern state in which there would be no conspiracies, no plans, no machinations, deceptions, or secrecies within the circles of power.[23]

In other words, programs like MK-ULTRA are not *the* way that existing power relations are maintained, but they are nonetheless characteristic expressions of the will of the American ruling class, which does indeed occupy a moral universe so at odds with what most people consider normal that it boggles the mind.

For his perverse dedication, Gottlieb was promoted to chief of Technical Services and eagerly took up other tasks, such as designing poisons to assassinate enemies of the state like Castro and Lumumba.[24] But just as Gottlieb was moving on from his obsession with LSD as a tool of psychic control, many others took an interest in it as a tool of psychic emancipation.

Stage Two: Freeing the Mind

Swiss chemist Albert Hofmann first synthesized LSD in 1938, and his employer Sandoz Laboratories held its secret formula when Gottlieb took interest in the drug. At the behest of the CIA, the American pharmaceutical company Eli Lilly cracked this formula in 1954 and began producing it in "tonnage quantities."[25] Unsurprisingly, portions of this vast reserve escaped the lab, where it quickly became a trendy fixation of the ruling elite and their medical suppliers. Some, like Clare Boothe Luce, wife of Time-Life president Henry Luce, preferred it to stay that way. As she explained after turning on with the likes of Aldous Huxley and Christopher Isherwood, "We wouldn't want everyone doing too much of a good thing."[26]

Huxley felt similarly but couldn't help evangelizing, imagining himself part of a privileged, mind-expanding vanguard.[27] Though psychedelic use is most commonly associated with the '60s, the upper-class "acid hype" of the '50s led the way. Huxley's *The Doors of Perception* (1954), an account of his own mescaline use, piqued interest in peyote. In 1957, self-styled anthropologist and J.P. Morgan vice president for public relations R. Gordon Wasson published an account of his Mexican magic mushroom expedition in *Life* magazine. The article created a psychedelic tourist circuit that ruined the life of María Sabina, the *curandero* with whom Wasson had taken mushrooms.[28] Then in 1959, the *New York Herald Tribune* published an interview with Cary Grant, who described a "born again" experience on LSD: "Already, I feel too happy to stand any more. My saddest moment of today is better than my happiest moment of yesterday."[29] Psychologist Frank Barron observed that "the chemical substance most instrumental in the spread of the psychedelic movement is printer's ink."[30]

Timothy Leary, inventor of the phrase "Turn on, tune in, drop out" and most ready-to-hand representative of the psychedelic counterculture, was a product of this environment. Early on he took media theorist Marshall McLuhan's advice that he was "promoting a product"—"the new and improved accelerated brain"—and that he ought to act as a "basic product endorser," always smiling confidently when photographed.[31] After being removed from his post at Harvard in 1963 for his liberal distribution of psilocybin and LSD, Leary established a psychedelic commune in a sixty-four-room mansion in upstate New York, thanks to the patronage of Billy Hitchcock, heir of the Mellon fortune. There, Leary—now a self-appointed "neurologician"—and his followers plotted their psychic revolution: "Politics, religion, economics, social structure, are based on shared states of consciousness. The cause of social conflict is usually neurological. The cure is biochemical."[32]

This belief in the revolutionary properties of LSD to effect a dramatic change in mass consciousness was shared not only with the CIA but also a disparate band of fellow travelers. The universally beloved cultural ambassador of LSD, Allen Ginsberg; the Eastern philosophy guru Alan Watts; Ken Kesey (an MK-ULTRA test subject) and the Merry Pranksters, whose freewheeling psychedelic circus offered the yang to Leary's intellectualist yin—all labored under the remarkable delusion that they really were changing the world, one trip at a time.[33] As historian Jay Stevens puts it, their aim was nothing less than "to push evolution, to jump the species toward a higher integration."[34] Less well-known figures on the scene were more skeptical. Michael Hollingshead, for instance, who gave Leary LSD for the first time, not only believed that "LSD is not the key to a new metaphysics of being or a politics of ecstasy" but even that it may be "the apotheosis of distractions, the ultimate and most dangerous temptation."[35] But on the whole, the "lysergic Leninists" were neither the danger that conservatives made them out to be nor the misunderstood visionaries of their own self-conception. They were something much more banal, and exactly what they hoped not to be: just kind of dumb.

This all would have been of minimal consequence, however, had the LSD believers followed Leary's advice: "Don't vote. Don't politic. Don't petition. You can't do *anything* about America politically."[36] But of course acid culture made its way into the New Left, amplifying what sociologist Todd Gitlin called the pervasive "as if" mood of the time and helping to turn an already confused campus politics into pseudomillenarian "militancy" within a space of five years.[37] Of course, the Pure Land acidheads and the student militants never quite got along, and it's telling that each was obsessed with the pernicious qualities of the other.[38] The Leary-ites found the New Left "a completely frustrating and pointless exercise of campus politics in a grown-up world."[39] And the New Left saw clearly that the sex, drugs, and rock and roll scene was just a curious niche in the ever-growing culture industry. Each side launched broad missives against the other while degenerating into stereotypy.

There was a decisive downturn for both camps in 1968. San Francisco's Haight-Ashbury district, once the capital of the new psychedelic nation, had been flooded with new drugs, new thrill-seekers, and new hustlers after the previous year's Summer of Love. What Joan Didion called "the desperate attempt of a handful of pathetically unequipped children to create a community in a social vacuum" somehow didn't work out.[40] The wave of the great pharmacological wand had not produced the "epochal event" of Leary and Ginsberg's predictions but rather a frightening and heavily commercialized nightmare. The year 1968 was also when the Yippies (the Youth International Party, an acid-saturated political group founded by Abbie Hoffman, Jerry Rubin, and others) staged a "Festival of Life" to protest the Democratic National Convention in Chicago—"the Convention of Death." Mayor Daley took the Yippies' threats to spike the water supply with LSD seriously and turned Chicago into a military zone. The confrontation to follow crystallized the essence of political struggle for the Yippies and their political kin, while making it clear to everyone else that they represented an absurdist fringe with little interest in mass politics.

The acid-fueled grouplets of zombie '60s radicalism were a caricature of the New Left. One iteration was the "Up Against the Wall, Motherfucker" collective, which disrupted organizing meetings and protests, castigating socialists for their lack of militancy as "armchair book-quoting jive-ass honky leftists."[41] Another was the Weathermen, who sought to shed their white privilege by organizing themselves into secret cells to prepare armed attacks on the state. Even more embarrassing than the insurrectionary fantasies was the gushing upper- and middle-class guilt that suffused the Weather collectives. At a meeting in Cincinnati, an FBI informant confessed while tripping that he was a pig; the group took his expression of guilt to be an authentic coming to terms with his own privilege and accepted him into their ranks.[42]

In retrospect, even "movement" participants had to wonder if the FBI and CIA were behind all this. We know that the RAND Corporation, a CIA-affiliated think tank that designed counterrevolutionary strategies employed in Vietnam, at least contemplated the use of LSD (and other drugs) for the pacification of activists.[43] It was estimated that "nearly one out of six demonstrators at the Chicago convention was an undercover operative."[44] In the end, it's impossible to tell where the New Left ended and the military-intelligence complex's attempts to undermine it began. It all seems of a piece, and destined to crash and burn.

And yet, somehow it didn't. We're still stuck with all the self-destructive tendencies of the late-1960s American left, including

- the idea that the creation of a subcultural "beloved community" would prefigure the future society;
- the fusion of social justice activism with the quest for personal authenticity;
- an obsession with media coverage, leading to symbolic actions and demonstration as a form of ritual theater;
- the rejection of organization in favor of spontaneity;
- a nonstrategic vanguardism deployed as an excuse for the fact that left grouplets represent no real constituency;
- a theatrical confrontationalism, especially with the "pigs," that serves as a test of commitment to "the movement";
- a dismissal of grassroots organizing for being too slow and insufficiently radical;
- and an inattention to the politically feasible, bordering on a lack of a capacity to distinguish reality from fantasy (in

Gitlin's formulation, a "hallucinatory state in which the space between illusion and plausibility has shrunk to the vanishing point").[45]

In the end, the ostensibly "political" response of the New Left to an ugly, crushing, conformist world was not so different from dropping acid: breathless fun, but ultimately just escapism. A century prior, the great hero to the bohemians, Charles Baudelaire, diagnosed the basic issue with the drug-political counterculture as "theomania": "The belief that 'realities' can be reimagined and reconstructed at will through drugs, without such acts of 'creation' entailing any responsibilities."[46]

In 1961, sociologists David Matza and Gresham Sykes wrote,

> The search for adventure, excitement, and thrills, then, is a subterranean value that now often exists side by side with the values of security, routinization, and the rest ... The delinquent may not stand as an alien in the body of society but may represent instead a disturbing reflection or a caricature ... The delinquent has picked up and emphasized one part of the dominant value system, namely, the subterranean values that coexist with other, publicly proclaimed values possessing a more respectable air. These subterranean values ... bind the delinquent to the society whose laws he violates.[47]

The countercultural backlash to the Fordist era, represented in the choice of marijuana and psychedelics over your mom's barbiturates and your dad's amphetamines, did not so much mark the beginning of another period as it did a reaction to the particular *culture* of postwar society that was still very much in line with that society. In this, '60s "counterculture," though celebratory rather than demonizing of psychoactive substances, was not so different from the middle-class temperance reform cause: virtuous in its self-conception, confused in its outrage, and unwittingly committed to leaving the basic structures of capitalism alone.

Stage Three: Freely Controlling the Mind

In that brief window, beginning with the spread of the new hallucinogens in the '50s and ending with the Drug Abuse Control Amendments in 1968, many took an interest in LSD as a tool of neither torture nor rebellion, but their dialectical synthesis: psychotherapy. For some, such as Abram Hoffer and Humphry Osmond (the English psychiatrist who coined the term "psychedelic," meaning "mind manifesting"), madness was the method.[48] Through high-dose LSD conversion experiences, patients could jump out of their compulsive, repetitive routines and into a wholly other life. Others counseled what they called a "psycholytic" approach: traditional psychotherapy in combination with low doses of LSD, which helped lower patients' defenses and thus speed up therapeutic progress.[49] Psychedelic psychotherapy gained many adherents, including Robert F. Kennedy's wife, Ethel. At a Senate hearing in 1966 about LSD experimentation, RFK urged his colleagues to hold off the forces of reaction:

> I think we have given too much emphasis and so much attention to the fact that it can be dangerous and that it can hurt an individual who uses it … that perhaps to some extent we have lost sight of the fact that it can be very, very helpful in our society if used properly.[50]

But of course prohibition came, and with it the end of research into what many psychologists assumed was the future of their profession.[51] Methylenedioxyamphetamine (MDA) and methylenedioxymethamphetamine (MDMA) followed a similar though later and abbreviated trajectory. Thanks to the promotion of these drugs by Alexander Shulgin, and of their use in therapy by Leo Zeff, the development of MDA- and MDMA-assisted psychotherapy techniques began to spread in the late '70s.[52] Shortly after, MDMA became popular as a club drug under the name "Adam" and then "ecstasy"; it was placed on Schedule I in 1985.[53] The therapeutic community again lamented the media hysteria that followed, which shut down further research into these promising new "feeling enhancers."[54]

The inauguration of the Trump era happened to coincide with breakthroughs in what many have called a "psychedelic renaissance": in 2016, major studies were published illustrating the remarkable effectiveness of psilocybin for treating depression and anxiety, and the FDA gave approval to the final trials for the treatment of post-traumatic stress disorder with MDMA.[55] These developments are the fruit of the tireless work of Rick Doblin and the Multidisciplinary Association for Psychedelic Studies (MAPS), which funded many of the twenty-first-century studies in psychedelics—including Swiss psychiatrist Peter Gasser's 2008 research into LSD-assisted psychotherapy, the first of its kind in thirty-six years.[56]

This medical renaissance has been complemented by a cultural one: recreational use of psychedelics is back, but with important differences. The new psychedelic users "microdose"; in other words, they take LSD in small, nonhallucinogenic amounts, as a means of increasing productivity, creativity, and focus. In journalist Hannah Kuchler's characterization, they are typically "highly motivated professionals" who use "LSD as a tool to boost productivity under pressure, to invent the cascade of ideas demanded from knowledge workers, and to improve their focus in a world filled with distractions."[57] They "tune in" without "dropping out." They seek not a cure or an experience but rather to be "better than well."[58] And like MAPS researchers, they often have nothing but contempt for their boomer forebears. Believing "the Summer of Love set back understanding of the drug" by at least a generation, they are "horrified by how the hippies abused LSD."[59] In this they echo psychedelic researchers from the '60s, like the psychiatrist Oscar Janiger, who complained that "Leary and the others ... were ruining what we had worked so hard to build."[60]

It's not just the excess they object to, but also the populist ethos. Terence McKenna, dubbed by none other than Timothy Leary as "the Tim Leary of the Nineties," embodied this new attitude well.[61] He envisioned a "deputized minority—a shamanic professional class, if you will—whose job it is to bring ideas out of the deep, black water and show them off to the rest of us."[62] Whether it's therapists administering MDMA or tech executives responsibly microdosing LSD, the psychedelic renaissance is being carefully curated by this "shamanic guild" rather than being released to the masses—the big mistake of the '60s. This top-down orientation bears a long history: Captain Al Hubbard, a strange psychedelic proselytizer in the '50s with links to the CIA, believed that if only "he could give the psychedelic experience to the major executives of the Fortune 500 companies, he would change the whole of society."[63] Psychedelics are back in elite hands, where they were originally intended to stay.

Patrick Butler of the *Guardian* captures well the new image of a "respectable" drug user:

> It is easy to imagine many of them as smart, respectable, economically productive, holding down jobs in—or preparing to enter—the professions, business, banking, public service, the law, even politics. It's easy to think of these "happy" drug takers as unproblematic: as rational, self-regulating, middle-class "consumers", who are relatively discreet and (on the whole) discriminating in their drug use, and who tend to tidy up after themselves.[64]

Famed mycologist Paul Stamets, touting the "quantum leap in the evolution of the human species" promised by the "paradigm-shifting myco-technology that can literally save billions of lives," concludes that "psilocybin makes kinder, more responsible, more law-abiding people."[65]

If you had to bet on the future of drugs in America, you could do worse than to predict that a number of psychedelics—most likely MDMA, psilocybin, and LSD, in that order—will be legal prescription medications in a few years' time, and that they will rather quickly become *the* means of treating both depression and anxiety, the two most common mental health diagnoses today. In addition to having piqued the interest of investors, they're just plainly better than the alternatives, and there will be enough interest in mitigating the present psychological freefall to overcome any residual propaganda. Liberals who want a "return to normal" amid continuing social decay will become MDMA apostles, telling anyone who will listen about how it saved their marriage or how much it helped turn their suicidal teens into good students again.[66] Boomers will drop acid once more, but now out of paper cups in their retirement homes. Peter Kramer could do a quick "Replace All" and rerelease *Listening to Prozac* as *Listening to Ecstasy*.[67]

Those who want to protect the transformative healing potential of psychedelics are already lamenting their corporatization. They worry that psychedelic experiences will be commodified into a form of "CoolSculpting for the mind," absorbed into the psychiatric machine, and hyped as the great "one weird trick" of the era.[68] Provided exogenous factors don't derail current efforts, all these things will undoubtedly come to pass. A combination of traditional pharmaceutical companies (like Johnson & Johnson) and large market disruptors (like MindMed and Compass Pathways) are ready to capitalize on legalization. Peter Thiel–backed Compass Pathways has been aggressively cornering certain parts of the psychedelics market, including patents on synthetic psilocybin. Some estimate that the psychedelics market will grow to $69 billion by 2025, about two-thirds the size of the global craft beer market today.[69]

What the enthusiasts leave out of their criticisms of such developments, however, is the fact that it is their own unwavering faith in the consciousness-raising and emancipatory value of psychedelics that is one of Big Psych's greatest assets. Compass and MindMed could not ask for better marketing copy than the psychonauts provide. Buoyed by the liberatory characterizations of these true believers, psychedelics can float above the sea of snake oils. It is such believers who hold the "antidote to the current trend of pathologization in service of sales," and thus they who will ultimately help depathologize the sale itself.[70]

In a way, the mainstreaming of "better living through chemistry" will be a perfect fulfillment of the CIA's dream. In their typically bumbling and overeager fashion, CIA luminaries could only imagine "mind control" in terms of wiping clean and starting over. But psychedelic efficacy requires no such extremes: on regulated doses of MDMA or LSD, capitalist subjects can quickly jettison the dysfunctional parts of their personalities and return to their duties sparkling and focused, no longer looking for a lifeboat, but eager and excited to go down with the ship. The quest for control over the psyche was sought by the CIA to undermine Communist society; today it's deployed to tolerate capitalist society. Somewhere, Allen Dulles and Sidney Gottlieb are toasting to their success.

Addendum on Peyote

On New Year's Day in 1889, during a solar eclipse, a Paiute man named Wovoka had a vision: a time would come when God would restore the American Indian tribes to an "aboriginal happiness" in a new world free of white men.[71] To call this new dispensation into being, Wovoka was shown a ritual dance that would bring cleansing rains: the Ghost Dance. This ritual of "mass possession" spread among American tribes and terrified white settlers, for whom the Ghost Dance represented an effervescent barrier to assimilation. In 1890, US Cavalry troops massacred 250 Lakota near Wounded Knee Creek in South Dakota. Accounts vary, but some blame the troops' fear at the commencement of a Ghost Dance.

The event rattled James Mooney, who was working at the time for the Smithsonian's Bureau of Ethnology to preserve fast-dying Indian traditions. Mooney thought the Ghost Dance, predicated as it was on a miracle, to be a dangerous development, and his fears were confirmed at Wounded Knee. He felt the opposite, however, about a different practice that was also creating intertribal networks: peyote ceremonies. The Spanish had encountered peyote rituals upon arrival in the New World, and despite being banned by the Inquisition in 1620, peyote worship survived among tribes like the Huichol and the Tarahumara.[72] Fleeing persecution in the mid-nineteenth century, the Kiowa and Comanche passed through these areas and (it's surmised) brought back peyote to the United States.[73] The Plains peyote ceremony, an invention of the Comanche leader Quanah Parker, was adapted to the American context: unlike the Ghost Dance, it took place inside a tipi instead of out in the open. The Ghost Dance offered salvation; peyote turned transcendence inward. In historian Mike Jay's characterization, "It was a microcosm of the old ways within the shattering trauma of captivity."[74]

In the 1890s and 1900s, peyote religion spread rapidly, much to the chagrin of the federal government, Christian missionaries, and also a significant number of Native nonpeyotists, who saw peyote ceremonies as an unwelcome innovation rather than a rescuing of tradition.[75] To protect this new form of worship, Mooney helped charter the Native American Church in 1918. Among other things, this act involved the reclaiming of a phrase from Anglo-Saxon Protestants, who self-described as "Native Americans" to distinguish themselves from more recent Irish, German, and Italian immigrants.[76] It also helped stave off efforts in 1918 to pass federal legislation banning peyote use, though the antipeyotists remained in organized opposition.

With the election of FDR, the peyote cause appeared safe: Secretary of the Interior Harold Ickes, who was in charge of the Bureau of Indian Affairs, preached tolerance of Indian religious life.[77] But the bureau also supported Indian self-governance, and one of the most vocal critics of peyote religion was the tribal government of the Taos Pueblo. A wealthy New Yorker, Mabel Dodge Luhan, had moved to Taos, where she took on a "proprietary attitude" toward the Taos Pueblo and supported the antipeyotists with letters to her powerful friends.[78] The Taos skirmish produced another bill proposed to ban peyote in 1937, the same year that the Marihuana Tax Act was passed and effectively made cannabis illegal. By this time, the peyote forces were well organized and supported by prominent anthropologists like Weston La Barre and Franz Boas; the antipeyote bill was quietly defeated.

The publication of Aldous Huxley's *The Doors of Perception* in 1954, which explored Huxley's mescaline experience and which La Barre described as propagating a "rather absurd" "sort of instant zen," brought new attention to peyote use.[79]

Mescaline had been isolated from peyote in 1896 and then synthesized in 1918. The crystal was independent of the cactus, and a few generations of Western scientists and writers had already written about peyote and mescaline experiments. But Huxley opened the doors of popular interest—a mixed blessing for the Native American Church, which he praised for defending "the red man's right to spiritual independence."[80]

Mescaline was absorbed into the polydrug scene of '60s counterculture, but it nonetheless retained a kind of sacred aura in its link back to peyote religion. The "primitivism" so attractive to bohemians and beatniks was largely a modern creation: La Barre's 1938 study, *The Peyote Cult*, was used by many tribal groups who adopted peyotism as a kind of ritual handbook.[81] Hippies nonetheless descended on Native communities with atavistic interest, often assuming (incorrectly) that all Indians were peyotists.[82] Some communities eventually went with the flow: the Huichol pilgrimage grounds in Mexico are today booming with "neo-shamanic rituals: organised therapy sessions, drumming circles, temazcal sweat-lodges and spas, spiritual retreats and alternative cancer cures."[83]

In the '50s, the United Nations Narcotics Division described the Native American Church as "an ethnographical curiosity rather than an important movement"; today it is 250,000 members strong.[84] Other groups have sought to emulate their success in seeking similar First Amendment exemptions from the Controlled Substances Act. In 1999, US Customs agents seized thirty gallons of ayahuasca from a US chapter of União do Vegetal, a Brazilian church combining Catholicism with the ritual use of ayahuasca. UDV sued and the case went to the Supreme Court, which ruled in 2006 that UDV's ayahuasca use was indeed an exercise of religious freedom.

A variety of cannabis and psychedelic faith groups have sought similar protections, but thus far unsuccessfully. Psychedelic enthusiasts have been particularly keen on unearthing the spiritual significance of "entheogens"—"Jews, Christians, and

Muslims Are Reclaiming Ancient Psychedelic Practices, and That Could Help with Legalization," reads a headline from *Rolling Stone*—wittingly using the cover of religious exemption to help realize the psychedelic enlightenment.[85] They are, in essence, out to prove James Mooney right: there is no salvation from this world, only well-delimited forms of escape.

Addendum on Dissociative Anesthetics

Dissociative anesthetics like PCP and ketamine are sometimes included in the category of psychedelics, but their effects are quite distinct.[86] Unlike LSD or MDMA, which often result in a starry-eyed fascination with the external world, ketamine offers a retreat from that world to a more carefree state of looseness and disconnection, producing outward symptoms similar to those of alcohol or barbiturates—slurred speech, impaired cognition, memory loss.[87] Higher-dose experiences down the inimitable "K-hole" launch you past the bounds of personal identity and into a strange world of ontological uncertainty and novelty—often compared to a networked cyberspace.

Ketamine's precursor, phencyclidine (PCP), is in numerous ways a model drug, in that it provided the template for other drug perceptions, scares, and uses. A popular party drug for poor and working-class youth in the late '70s and early '80s, PCP was crack before crack, an indefensible monster of a drug that set the basic template for all '80s and '90s drug scares—crack, ice, methcathinone.[88] According to the media portrayal, PCP made you irrationally violent, and despite its sedating qualities, somehow also endowed its users with superhuman strength, echoing similar myths about cocaine and black men in the early twentieth century.[89] Rodney King was referred to by LA police as a "PCP-crazed giant."[90] A favorite tale, conjuring the oedipal specter, held that PCP led you to gouge out your own eyes.[91]

PCP was also known for its zombifying qualities, and the strange movements of a person under its influence were colloquially known as "moonwalking," the origin of the name for Michael Jackson's famous dance move.[92] On account of

This Man Is Really
A Monster With
Superhuman Strength.

It's true. And it's not funny.

He may seem to be a nice, young, talented musician.
And he really is. Until he turns to "Angel Dust."
Then he becomes a madman.

Tonight KABC-TV's dramatic presentation will open
your eyes to the horrors of PCP, the deadly drug.

Now you will understand those stories about people
who jump to their deaths, run in front of automobiles
and attack armed policemen barehanded.

Maybe they don't make sense. But tonight's program does.

"ANGEL DUST:
THE WACK ATTACK"

Starring Vernée Watson and Philip Michael Thomas

10:00 TONIGHT ⑦

Advertisement for Angel Dust: The Wack Attack. *"This Man is Really A Monster with Superhuman Strength," Los Angeles Times, October 25, 1979. The film was later retitled* Death Drug. *"Death Drug (1978/1985) | Phillip Michael Thomas Rosalind Cash," Youtube video, 1:11:45, uploaded January 7, 2020, youtu.be.*

such disorienting and sedating effects, PCP also gained a reputation as a date rape drug, again setting the template for future perceptions of Rohypnol (roofies) and GHB. In all three cases, according to historian Philip Jenkins, these drugs "became a public nightmare not so much because of any objective threat they posed, but because they came to symbolize underlying fears, in this case fears of rape and sexual molestation."[93]

But PCP's most enduring legacy lies in its progeny. In the late '50s, it was marketed by Parke-Davis under the name Sernyl, but it was quickly removed after further tests revealed schizophrenia-like symptoms.[94] The anesthetic promise of PCP nonetheless prompted Parke-Davis to seek out similar chemicals, and from this effort ketamine emerged in 1962. Ketamine first came to market in 1970, was used in Vietnam as a battlefield anesthetic, and then leaked out into the club world in the '80s.[95] It still enjoys widespread recreational use, particularly in East Asia: it's estimated that 73 percent of drug users under the age of twenty-one in Hong Kong have tried it.[96]

Perhaps the most well-known explorer of the ketamine trip was John Lilly, famed neuroscientist, biophysicist, and dolphin whisperer. Lilly began his career as a straight-laced aspiring CIA grantee, promising the possibility of "master-slave controls directly of one brain over another," before falling in with the psychedelic counterculture.[97] After a brief fascination with LSD, which he injected in dolphins at his laboratory for interspecies communication, he next turned to ketamine, through which he believed he made contact with a hierarchy of extraterrestrial beings (the Earth Coincidence Control Office, or ECCO, to be specific). He once came to, after being found floating face down in a pool, believing he was in the year 3001.[98] At one point during his "seduction by K," he was injecting himself with it hourly for twenty hours a day.[99]

With this kind of lore, as well as its reputation in the '80s and '90s as a fashionable party accessory, it's fairly shocking that ketamine was approved by the FDA for use in the treatment of depression in 2019. As with all other antidepressants and anxiolytics, no one really knows how ketamine works, though that doesn't stop pharmacological experts from long neuroscientific digressions that all serve to cover over the only unassailable truth we've discovered so far about drugs: that some of them make some people feel better some of the time. Of course, drugs don't get approved by the FDA simply because they work: Johnson & Johnson first had to patent ketamine's S isomer (esketamine) to market under the name Spravato, even though research has indicated that its R isomer (arketamine) seems to be better at alleviating depression.[100]

The psychedelic shaman D. M. Turner once described the drug as such: "On a Ketamine experience I do not need to 'do' anything. Once administered, the experience simply happens."[101] No need for care, investment, working through— just a quick "subjective time-out," in psychiatrist Phil Wolfson's description.[102] Historically, it's quite odd that a drug enjoying such long-standing recreational popularity would at the same time be the center of a booming legal therapeutic enterprise. This is a clear testament to the great need for what ketamine has to offer—numbness, void, and dissociation, all with little effort and for short, manageable periods of time.

8

Cocaine, or Hyperreality

> Since the world is on a delusional course, we must adopt a
> delusional standpoint towards the world.
>
> —Jean Baudrillard

Heroin has to be called the best drug in existence only so that
cocaine takes offense. In sports, Americans have a conflicted
love for the "I got this" bench player who puts his team on
his back in crunch time when no one wants him to (except
the other team). It's for a similar reason that we love cocaine:
it's the drug of irrational confidence, numbing its users to any
feelings of embarrassment, humility, or basic self-awareness.

Cocaine is often grouped together with the amphetamines
as a "stimulant," and while it's true that the two drugs have
very similar effects, culturally, cocaine fits poorly in this category. Meth smoking aside, the great American appetite for
amphetamines is about accommodating oneself to the strenuous
demands of work. No one would dare say that's what cocaine
is about. One of the earliest American users of cocaine, the
ophthalmologist Herman Knapp, painted his whole body with
the stuff, even injecting it into his penis and, "for the sake of
completeness," his rectum.[1] *That's* what cocaine is about.

Sigmund Freud and Coca-Cola

There are two facts about the early history of cocaine that most
people know: that Sigmund Freud popularized it and that it
used to be in Coca-Cola. Both require some qualification.

In 1884, Freud published *Über Coca*, which he referred to before publication as a "song of praise."[2] In addition to taking it regularly, although seemingly in small amounts, he was also distributing cocaine to just about anyone who would accept it.[3] Freud was, however, only one of a number of researchers investigating its uses, and it was the ophthalmologist Karl Köller (a colleague of Freud's with whom he had conducted research) who sparked an interest in the therapeutic potential of the drug by demonstrating its ability to anesthetize the human eye.[4] It soon seemed a blessing in disguise that Köller was the face of cocaine, as the next year Freud watched his friend Ernst von Fleischl-Marxow struggle through the depths of cocaine addiction. He had earlier introduced him to the drug.

Freud also didn't merely spin his enthusiasm for cocaine out of the rapture of personal experience. He had discovered the drug in the pages of the American journal *Therapeutic Gazette*, which touted cocaine as essentially harmless and encouraged its use as a treatment for morphine addiction (a myth repeated by Japanese cocaine producers to sell cocaine to China in the '20s and '30s).[5] Surprise, surprise—*Therapeutic Gazette* was owned by Parke, Davis & Company, the only American manufacturer and distributor of cocaine (and today a subsidiary of Pfizer). If Freud made a key blunder in the cocaine episode, it was to believe the lies of an American advertising industry that his theories would later bolster.

As for Coca-Cola, it's true that it used to contain a small amount of cocaine, but this was a function of its inclusion of coca leaf extract, not isolated cocaine. A typical line might have fifty to seventy-five milligrams of cocaine. Coca-Cola and similar coca drinks in the late nineteenth century contained only a few milligrams, much like the coca leaves chewed by human beings for thousands of years, or the coca tea that popes enjoy in their visits to South America.[6] Some products at the time were indeed dangerous, like the cures offered for catarrh and asthma, which contained hundreds of milligrams of cocaine

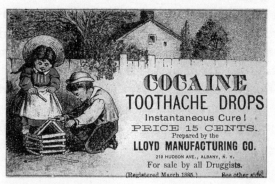

Advertisement for Lloyd's Cocaine Toothache Drops (1885). National Library of Medicine, nlm.nih.gov.

per ounce. In addition, a variety of colas were often spiked with cocaine, and the alcoholic coca wines, like the popular Vin Mariani, packed a combinatory punch.[7] But as today, little distinction was made between relatively harmless coca products and high-potency cocaine.

With their characteristic overzealousness, progressive reformers railed against the nostrum-cure industry. National consumption of cocaine rose 500 percent between 1893 and 1903, and the dangers of "cocainism" became a matter of public debate.[8] In 1906, the Pure Food and Drug Act restricted the use of cocaine in packaged remedies but did nothing to address the actual sale of cocaine. The thriving coca business was eliminated, but you could still walk into a drugstore and get pure cocaine hydrochloride.[9] It wasn't until 1922 that Congress aimed to totally eliminate recreational cocaine use, and here is where Coca-Cola's *real* contribution to the history of cocaine begins.

Knowing regulation was on the way, Coca-Cola partnered with Maywood Chemical Works in 1903 to de-cocainize their coca. Maywood was acquired by Stepan Company in the 1960s, and today they still provide the same service to Coca-Cola, being the one and only legal importer of coca leaves to the United States.[10] With special access to the legal coca export market in South America, Coca-Cola kept the Federal Bureau of Narcotics informed about their dealings there, while the FBN's chief Harry Anslinger protected Coca-Cola's business interests in a variety of ways.[11] This mutually beneficial alliance stifled the Peruvian coca export industry, driving legitimate producers underground.[12] The scandal of Coca-Cola was not in participating in the legal international coca trade, but rather their role in shutting it down.

Demand

When cocaine began trickling into the United States in the '60s, it had been virtually absent from public consciousness since the '30s. This changed decisively with the release of *Easy Rider* in 1969, which opens with Peter Fonda, Dennis Hopper, and Jack Nicholson delivering packages of *"Pura vida!"* to Phil Spector. The subsequent media coverage was an avalanche: *Rolling Stone* called it the "drug of the year" in 1970, *Newsweek* claimed in 1971 that "orgasms go better with coke," and the *New York Times* called it the "champagne of drugs" in 1974. As late as 1981, *Time* called it "the all-American drug."

What accounts for the rapid adoption of cocaine in the '70s after more than a three-decade absence? The demand side of the equation could be chalked up to a lack of familiarity with the early twentieth century's struggle with cocaine, and it's true that the generation-long gap in cocaine use in America meant that people taking it up in the late '60s really had no experiential reference by which to judge its benefits or harms. But if anything, history played too comforting a role in cocaine's resurgence.

Like opium and marijuana, cocaine demonization was heavily racialized in the early twentieth century. The use of cocaine by black workers, particularly stevedores, spurred wildly racist speculation. The *Journal of the American Medical*

Association warned in 1900 that "the negroes in some parts of the South are reported as being addicted to a new form of vice—that of 'cocain sniffing' or the 'coke habit.'"[13] Foreshadowing the militarization of police in the Reagan years, it was rumored that cocaine led black men to be impervious to .32-caliber bullets, leading police to switch to .38-caliber revolvers.[14] Cocaine would soon join opium as one of the first targets of the American drug war with the passage of the Harrison Act. At its congressional hearings, Dr. Christopher Koch of the State Pharmacy Board of Pennsylvania testified that "most of the attacks upon white women of the South are the direct result of a cocaine-crazed Negro brain."[15]

Bringing this history to light for a whole generation, Richard Ashley's *Cocaine: Its History, Uses, and Effects* explained in 1975 that cocaine was not really so dangerous and that prior fears about "cocaine fiends" were simply expressions of the overt racism of white society.[16] It was something like saying, "Snort a line if you're not racist!"

Lingering memories of the "reefer madness" campaigns reinforced such a view. Marijuana was not a target of the Harrison Act and only came under regulation in 1937, when Anslinger's Federal Bureau of Narcotics spread fabulous lies (again, often racialized) about the gruesome killing sprees that could follow from but one puff of marijuana. As historian Richard Davenport-Hines explains, Anslinger paradoxically helped create a receptive environment for the reemergence of cocaine in the '70s: "Americans who remembered the marijuana lies of the 1940s and 1950s treated with fatal disdain warnings about the new fashion for cocaine in the 1970s—with disastrous consequences for American society in the 1980s."[17]

Cocaine was also terribly expensive in the '70s, and while that proved a barrier to some, for the upper and middle classes, it made cocaine a status symbol. When Woody Allen's character Alvy sneezed in the cocaine in *Annie Hall* in 1977, he was surrounded by nice, white professionals talking about their trip out to California. Sting said cocaine was "God's way of saying you have too much money."[18] He might as well have been a paid spokesman for the Colombians.

It's difficult to fathom today, but in the early and mid-1970s, the consensus on cocaine seemed to be that it was *perfectly fine*, really only objectionable if you were a neurotic like Woody Allen.[19] Harvard psychiatrist Lester Grinspoon said it didn't produce serious psychological problems. Yale psychiatrist Robert Byck said cocaine was about as harmful as potato chips.[20] Even Jimmy Carter's own drug czar wrote that "cocaine … is probably the most benign of illicit drugs currently in widespread use."[21] He later made the professionally fatal error of snorting cocaine at a holiday party—generally a bad idea if you're a White House official.

The '70s, needless to say, were the end of the '60s. Hippies gave way to yuppies—in historian Paul Gootenberg's characterization, "Individualistic big-spender hipsters of the next

Advertisement for Easy Liner quality mirrors. Easy Liner Products Inc., "Tonight's Forecast 'snow,'" High Times, 1978, archive.hightimes.com.

'me generation' in the Reagan decade of the 1980s—nurtured, I would suspect, as an elite cultural class on South American cocaine."[22] The confused quest for transcendence was abandoned for quick jolts of ephemeral pleasure. Music producer Paul Rothchild lamented the shift from the culture of marijuana and LSD to that of cocaine, saying: "One consciousness brought about sharing, the other brought about greed."[23] The soft blanket of snow that fell over America didn't inaugurate the neoliberal era, but it symbolized it quite well.

Supply

Cocaine was a Chilean cottage industry until Pinochet's coup in 1973, and much of it passed through Cuban exiles' hands en route to America. Trained by the CIA for the botched Bay of Pigs operation, these Cuban refugees needed money to fight

Advertisement for "The Shotgun Spoon." Shotgun Enterprises, "Shotgun Santa Presents," High Times, 1975, archive.hightimes.com.

against Castro, and as with so many anti-Communist insurgencies in the twentieth century, selling drugs was the answer. By the mid-1970s, however, Colombian traffickers were angling for market dominance, and when they got it, America was swimming in cocaine.

It was a fortuitous moment, coinciding with the drastic reduction in the availability of legal stimulants after the passage of the Controlled Substances Act in 1970.[24] Illegal meth operations quickly popped up to satisfy demand, but speed had a bad rap in drug subcultures ever since Allen Ginsberg's declaration in 1965, "contra speedamos ex cathedra," that "speed is antisocial, paranoid making, it's a drag, bad for your body, bad for your mind."[25] In addition, Nixon's Operation Intercept of 1969 had halted the flow of marijuana across the Mexican border. Then, in the late '70s, it was revealed that Mexican marijuana fields were being sprayed with the herbicide paraquat, which, if inhaled, could do irreversible lung damage. Wary of or without easy access to amphetamines, heroin, and marijuana, Americans were primed to accept what Colombia had to offer.

The Colombian cocaine "cartels" of the '70s and '80s—in reality, tenuous partnerships between distributors located in the cities of Medellín and Cali—are virtually synonymous in the popular imagination with the drug business: big names (Escobar, Ochoa, Ocampo, Gacha), palatial mansions, secret production facilities, government corruption, and most of all, unbelievable violence.[26] But it's clear in retrospect that despite there being a certain market logic to violence in the underground drug economy, the Colombians were an aberration rather than the norm. The heroin trade, for instance, has never been nearly as violent.[27] And unlike most horizontally organized drug trades, where most of the people involved are fine with occupying their link in the chain, the Colombian cartels sought vertical integration like a multinational corporation.[28] In this, perhaps there is a reflection of the drug in the trade. Cocaine gives one a false sense of omnipotence, and the Colombians certainly wanted it all.

Much of the cocaine Colombia dealt was from coca grown in Peru and Bolivia, and as is typical in these kinds of relationships, the distributor often squeezed the producer. In the late '70s, Bolivian coca paste mogul Roberto Suárez hired a crew of fascist mercenaries called the Fiancés of Death to protect his business from Colombian buyers, who would often either underpay or simply steal his product.[29] A prominent associate of the Fiancés of Death was a man named Klaus Altmann—a.k.a. Klaus Barbie, the Nazi gestapo chief known as the Butcher of Lyon.[30] Barbie had been spared punishment for his war crimes thanks to his work for US intelligence services, and then made his way to Bolivia in 1951.

After putting a lid on Colombian chicanery, Barbie and the Fiancés soon set their sights higher: when Hernán Siles Zuazo was elected in 1980 on promises to clean up illicit cocaine operations, the traffickers and their muscle moved quickly to oust Siles and the "Marxist cancer" he represented. The "Cocaine Coup," which installed General Luis García Meza Tejada as president, was one of the bloodiest of Bolivia's many coups d'état. Thousands of trade union leaders and political activists resisting the coup were shot, raped, or jailed. It's a testament to the perverse cunning of history in the twentieth century that a man who reveled in killing thousands of Jews and Resistance members in the 1940s would reappear forty years later and 6,000 miles away to help create the world's first narcocracy.

Crack

Powdered cocaine can't be smoked—it just incinerates when lit; but cooking it with baking soda produces a smokable form of rock cocaine dubbed "crack." While the inflammation of the nasal membranes that powdered cocaine provokes makes snorting a somewhat self-limiting route of administration, crack smoke works through the inviting and comparatively vast surface area of the lungs, producing a much more powerful, if short-lasting, high. By the mid-1980s, the price of powdered cocaine had significantly dropped as supply increased, but it was still rather expensive. Crack rocks, by contrast, could be purchased for a few dollars, and they were—overwhelmingly in economically declining, inner-city ghettos.

In this, the term "epidemic" is misapplied to crack: epidemics are widespread, indiscriminately affecting all kinds of people.[31] The crack scourge, by contrast, was devastatingly concentrated in poor black neighborhoods.[32] For those living through the precarity, drudgery, and sadness of life on the losing end of the neoliberal turn, crack was a cheap and readily available escape. Journalist Jefferson Morley sampled crack for a story and speculated about its appeal:

> You can be a moral tourist in the land of crack and still get a sense of how the drug can make sick sense to demoralized people. If all you have in life is bad choices, crack may not be the most unpleasant of them.[33]

But these neighborhoods weren't simply centers of crack *use*; they were dominated by crack *economies*, which filled part of the void left in the wake of deindustrialization. As anthropologist Philippe Bourgois explains of crack dealers in East Harlem,

> Their macho-proletarian dream of working an eight-hour shift plus overtime throughout their adult lives at a rugged slot in a unionized shop had been replaced by a nightmare of poorly paid, highly feminized, office support work ... They find themselves propelled headlong into an explosive confrontation between their sense of cultural dignity versus the humiliating interpersonal subordination of service work.[34]

In 1990, McDonald's ran an ad about a young black man named Calvin who is portrayed as rejecting the loitering ways of his peers and taking responsibility for his life after getting a job at McDonald's. At the time, McDonald's paid a bit more than three dollars per hour.[35] No surprise that many young people would opt instead for the more lucrative possibilities of street capitalism—the illicit mirror image of the Wall Street hustle. (The Notorious B.I.G.'s "Ten Crack Commandments," codifying the rules of the hardened crack game, happened to be released in the same year as Donald Trump's *The Art of the Comeback*, in which the future president also offers ten tips for success.[36])

Advertisement for a cocaine freebasing kit. Select Industries, "The 'Ultimate High,'" High Times, September 1979, archive.hightimes.com. The name "crack" was new in the 1980s but the substance was not. Candy Sher, the owner of Select Industries, which sold this freebasing system, testified before the House Select Committee on Narcotics Abuse and Control on November 1, 1979: "Our company supports responsible advertising in both trade and consumer magazines and periodicals," Hearing before the Select Committee on Narcotics Abuse and Control, House of Representatives, Ninety-Sixth Congress, First Session (Washington, DC: US Government Printing Office, 1980), 47. Her father, Dr. S. Franklin Sher, also testified that "smoking cocaine has no more propensity for harm than snorting cocaine," ibid., 59.

In addition to being a very real tragedy for areas of pre-existing segregation and poverty, the crack episode was also mediatized through and through, inflated into the prime mover of social chaos such that an astonishing 64 percent of Americans would say in 1989 that dangerous drugs were the number one problem facing the country.[37] As the *New York Times* editorialized in 1988, "America discovered crack and overdosed on oratory."[38] Escalating in 1986 after the deaths of two celebrity athletes, Len Bias and Don Rogers—both of whom likely used powdered cocaine rather than crack—the media coverage of crack was unhinged and grossly irresponsible. Journalists would call drug experts asking about "crack," be told that it sounded like freebased cocaine, and then go on to assume that the experts didn't know anything about it.[39] With no real referent to rein them in, the stories came fast and furious. Crack babies, scarred for life! Never mind that news footage from hospital nurseries often showed babies of *heroin*-addicted mothers.[40] Crack violence, ruining our cities! Never mind that the violence and crime flowed from poverty, not drugs.

This last bit was the primary effect of media hysteria: directing attention away from the larger crisis of impoverished urban areas and toward the pharmacological properties of rock cocaine, which, in their telling, produced "whole body orgasms" in a "state of near psychosis" that led to instant addiction after your first hit.[41] With a drug so devilish, what sense was there in focusing on social and economic root causes? In 1986, Senator Daniel Patrick Moynihan, in a seeming departure from his earlier "culture of poverty" thesis, spelled out quite clearly what was transpiring:

> If we blame crime on crack, our politicians are off the hook. Forgotten are failed schools, the malign welfare programs, the desolate neighborhoods, the wasted years. Only crack is to blame. One is tempted to think that if crack did not exist, someone somewhere would have received a federal grant to develop it.[42]

The 1986 Anti-Drug Abuse Act, delusional as Nancy Reagan's symbolic invocation to "Just Say No," created mandatory five-year sentences for the possession of five grams of crack, a sentence one hundred times more punitive than that for powder cocaine.[43] Eighty-nine percent of crack defendants were black. In historian Elizabeth Hinton's characterization, "Reagan responded to the devastating impact of unemployment and urban divestment as it materialized in crack abuse by attacking social welfare programs and replacing them with punitive ones that targeted racially marginalized Americans."[44] Crack destroyed black neighborhoods, and the response was to destroy them further. Historian David Courtwright says of Reagan's drug war that "it was easily the most dramatic, sustained and controversial governmental response to illicit drug abuse in American history."[45] That's saying something.

When journalist Gary Webb published a shocking story in 1996 about CIA-backed Contras in Nicaragua funding their resistance operation by selling cocaine, thus directly implicating the American government in the creation of the crack scourge, members of the mainstream media launched a despicable assault on the verity of his claims. Exaggerating his argument into the strawman claim that the CIA was directly targeting black people, journalists suggested Webb was stoking the black community's "outright paranoia."[46] In December 1997, the *Los Angeles Times* ran a story with the headline "CIA Clears Itself in Crack Investigation" based on the publication of a report that was mysteriously delayed until 1998.[47] In 2004, Gary Webb was found dead with two gunshots to the head; his death was ruled a suicide.

The severe treatment of Webb's story can be chalked up to the fact that it did not simply reveal American complicity in the drug trade, but directly countered the official lies about it. As Peter Dale Scott and Jonathan Marshall argue, "In the 1980s the Eisenhower-Anslinger propaganda about Red Chinese heroin was replaced by the Reagan-North propaganda about Red

Sandinista cocaine."[48] Both scares mobilized anti-Communist sentiment, and both pinned cocaine production on the wrong side. The hypocrisy reached absurd heights when Panamanian general Manuel Noriega was captured and indicted on cocaine-trafficking charges in Operation Just Cause in 1989. Noriega had long been a CIA asset and had collaborated with the US to undermine the Sandinistas.

How to make sense of the crack episode? Perhaps it's just that media members were (and are) themselves highly coked up, and we're all living in their omnipotent fantasies. A more academic interpretation would employ philosopher Jean Baudrillard's theory of *hyperreality*: for Baudrillard, our models, maps, and representations of reality today *engender* reality itself. It does not make sense to say that the media staged an illusion in this case, because there is no reality against which their stories might be judged illusory; their fabricated stories were and are part of the effective reality.[49]

As a strange bit of evidence for this: if there's a name most associated with the spread of crack cocaine on the West Coast, it's "Freeway" Ricky Ross, "ready rock" kingpin of the early '80s. When he first heard about "crack," he thought it was a new kind of drug. And when accused of peddling crack, he protested sharply: "No it wasn't! It was cocaine! I didn't put no crack in there."[50] The most well-known crack dealer around learned about crack on the news.

The crack explosion was real, and it was devastating; it was also created as a media spectacle, which served as both a veil for economic contraction and a justification for mass incarceration.[51] This is one of those truths that hardened materialists find incredibly uncomfortable, but it's difficult to make sense of the horror-filled surreality of the contemporary world without reference to the maddening simulation we occupy. Cocaine, it just so happens, is a great complement to this mediatized dream world: it lets you stop worrying and just enjoy the ride.

Symbiosis

The cocaine wave crested in the early '80s.[52] Cocaine use roughly tripled between 1977 and 1979, and by 1980, cocaine street dealers outnumbered heroin dealers two to one.[53] In 1982, some 22 million Americans tried cocaine, up from 5 million in 1974.[54] Miami was by this point firmly established as the city of "cocaine cowboys," and Reagan established the South Florida Task Force in 1982 to deal with the huge uptick in homicides and the obvious illegal economic influxes.[55]

In 1973, the Drug Enforcement Administration had been stitched together from a variety of lesser agencies (including Harry Anslinger's now defunct Federal Bureau of Narcotics), and the real cocaine deluge of the '80s helped swell its ranks just as the fictive threat of marijuana had served a similar role for Anslinger's FBN in the '30s and '40s (in this case, first as farce, then as tragedy). In the '80s, the number of DEA special agents nearly doubled; during that same decade, cocaine seizures increased by more than 40 percent per year. One might attribute this to greater DEA effectiveness, but throughout this time cocaine remained widely available and its price consistently dropped, pointing to a massive overall increase in cocaine imports.[56]

According to Davenport-Hines, "The late twentieth-century cocaine boom was chiefly the creation of the presidential drug wars," which established a "symbiotic relationship" between trafficking and enforcing.[57] Cocaine was smuggled into the US by every means available, and smugglers fully expected some of it to be seized. The traffickers got their cargo through, and the DEA in turn got to flaunt the captured cocaine. In a sick way, everyone was satisfied.

Defenders of the War on Drugs can point to a severe dip in US cocaine consumers in the late '80s, but overall cocaine supply didn't dip until the mid-2000s, buoyed past its heyday by heavy users. In addition, a variety of drugs, including heroin, methamphetamine, and ecstasy, quickly came to share in the cultural space where cocaine was once king. George H. W. Bush held up a bag of crack at a news conference in 1989, and his drug czar William Bennett talked openly about beheading drug traffickers.[58] In a fashion that has become standard Democratic fare, Clinton dialed back this punitive rhetoric but continued the drug war apace. One could say this was grasping defeat from the jaws of victory, but only on the assumption that the cocaine scare was really about cocaine.

Extending Charles Tilly's claim that "states made war and war made states," historian Peter Andreas has argued that "states make drug war and drug war makes states."[59] It's true that the crackdown on illegal drugs has justified the enhancement of state security apparatuses (some of which have been involved in the distribution of those very drugs they're ostensibly trying to eliminate), but it would be too simple to say that drug war makes states as such. Drug war makes *punitive* states, states that overmilitarize, states that are unresponsive to anything that is not a "threat." Appropriately, perhaps, drug war makes *paranoid* states.

Narcocracies

As the US ramped up its drug-fighting efforts, our Andean suppliers suffered the consequences of their cocaine economies. The US cut off aid to Bolivia with the Cocaine Coup, and the Fiancés of Death were out of power within a year. Their former ally, Roberto Suárez, supported their ousting, and then kept the national business going in their absence. But the economic fallout was devastating: GDP dropped 10 percent and inflation rose over 100 percent, only to get worse. Under the guidance of the World Bank, 22,000 state-employed miners were laid off in 1985, and as with the collapse of Colombia's textile industry in the late '60s, economic contraction meant more coca growing.[60]

Predictably, as more poor people turned to it for their livelihood, coca became a national "problem." The government sought to eradicate coca in the rural Chapare province (the primary coca-growing region), setting up massive clashes with the coca growers unions. This struggle came to a head in 1999, when the unions blockaded the main arteries between Bolivian cities in response to the passage of a multimillion dollar anti-drugs plan.[61] This display of national power led to one bright spot in the history of cocaine: the coca growers union leader Evo Morales, backed by the militancy of the *cocaleros*, was elected Bolivian president in 2005 with the first absolute majority (53.7 percent) in forty years, beginning fourteen years of social reforms that pulled millions out of poverty. Even a US-backed coup in 2019 couldn't keep Morales's party from resuming power in 2020. Peru, the third great Andean supplier of coca in addition to Colombia and Bolivia, recently elected Pedro Castillo, a trade unionist in the Morales mold.

Colombia rapidly eclipsed Peru and Bolivia as the world's primary coca cultivator in the '90s. After the assassination in 1984 of Rodrigo Lara Bonilla, the popular anti-cocaine crusader, Colombia descended into violence, with the government declaring "war without quarter" on the cartels, and the cartels reciprocating the gesture.[62] When Pablo Escobar was finally gunned down in 1993, the violence and publicity subsided, but the cocaine business did not. The Cali traffickers had learned from the mistakes of their partner-rivals in Medellín: they stayed out of the limelight, ran a quiet business, and most importantly, avoided violence when bribes would do just fine.[63] They owned all the taxis in Cali and had their drivers report on police and foreigners. They bought up about 35 percent of the Colombian Congress. In retrospect, Escobar, fabulously rich though he was, was ultimately a crude operator, not so different from the poor street kids who still idolize him today. The Cali cartel, by contrast, understood the ruling-class principle that everything can and *should* be bought.

Crackdowns on the Caribbean and South Florida smuggling routes pushed cocaine to the Mexican border, where the lion's share enters the United States today.[64] Actually halting the flow of drugs across the border by examining every vehicle for narcotics would amount to a logistical and economic disaster, but "border security" is a good excuse to redeploy some of the high tech tools that private military contractors have rolled out in Iraq and Afghanistan, like new aerial surveillance systems.[65] Increasingly, that justification is about preventing "'spillover' violence": in 2019, Mexico was home to the five cities with the highest homicide rates in the world.[66] The Zetas, the most trigger happy of the traffickers that have proliferated after the arrest of El Chapo, were formed from a Mexican antidrug military unit trained by the US.[67] As ever, the drug war supplies combatants to both sides of its battles.

Around the middle of the 2000s, US cocaine consumption fell dramatically, in what Gootenberg calls "one of the steepest drug use drops ever recorded."[68] Experts have a wide range of competing explanations for what Beau Kilmer names "Uncle Sam's Cocaine Nosedive," covering just about every possible demand and supply-side factor.[69] Whatever the reason, this decline in consumption mirrored a breaking up of Colombia's cocaine dominance, and the whole cocaine market has shifted south, most notably to Brazil. Cocaine was unquestionably the drug symbolizing America's centrality in the neoliberal capitalist world order, rising dramatically in use in the '70s when that of just about every other drug was falling (see appendix A). Today, as US consumption of most psychoactive substances is at a historic high and climbing, cocaine use remains relatively low. Historically, where most drugs zig, cocaine zags.

Real Hallucinations

Doctors say that cocaine is not an aphrodisiac, but users have always felt quite differently. Hans Maier's 1926 treatise on cocaine addiction includes firsthand accounts of men's sexual prowess and women's sexual insatiability while using the drug, but Maier also notes, in men in particular, "an intensification of libido simultaneously with impotence."[70] Maier ultimately concludes that cocaine causes "sexual hallucination," an increase in "mental libido," but curiously adds that this hallucination is not "purely imaginary" in that this faux arousal can and often does lead to sex, though it can just as well lead to impotence.[71] Cocaine, in other words, causes a *real hallucination* of sexual desire—a perfect rendering of the drug's essential paradox.

The entire history of cocaine is one of deception. Freud wasn't the prime mover of the first cocaine binge, but boy is it fun dunking on an intellectual patriarch. Coca-Cola had cocaine in it, but this is only a scandalous fact if we, as our forebears did, ignore the difference between coca and isolated cocaine. The resumption of cocaine use in America in the late '60s and the crack scare of the '80s both might as well have been collaborative efforts of the mainstream press. But in all cases, the lies were effective: our hallucinations bore real consequences. The history of cocaine suggests that there is something essentially fraudulent about our social reality, something demanding to be decoded and laid bare.

How appropriate then that one of the first literary representations of cocaine use appeared in Arthur Conan Doyle's Sherlock Holmes stories. Craving "mental exaltation" to alleviate the "dull routine of existence," Holmes at first embraces cocaine as a harmless habit, but Conan Doyle eventually illustrates the drug's darker side.[72] In "The Final Problem," Holmes descends into full paranoia, with Watson helpless to do much besides absorb the deranged ramblings of his companion. But in his delusion, ever the genius, Holmes pierces through his fantasy-reality to its animating principle, personified in the treacherous figure of Professor Moriarty.

What's strange about Moriarty, whom Holmes only mentions when high, is that he is more system than person: He is described as a "deep organizing power which forever stands in the way of the law, and throws its shield over the wrong-doer." He "does little himself," but "his agents are numerous and splendidly organized." Contemporary hyperreality is similarly structured by an abstract "organizer of half that is evil and of nearly all that is undetected," but sadly for us, it is no cocaine delusion.[73]

9

Marijuana, or Profit Wins in the End

> If pot were legal, it would stop working.
>
> —Old hippie joke

From a strictly pharmacological view, marijuana is just about the most harmless drug one could imagine. It is lethal at a dose at least 1,000 times—and some say as much as 40,000 times —the size of the psychologically effective one (the effective-to-lethal dose ratio for alcohol is one to ten).[1] And yet from the reefer madness hysteria in the 1930s to the absurd "gateway drug" theory and even up to the present, when unethical and unscientific neurobabble still holds that "even casually smoking marijuana can change your brain," marijuana has consistently been portrayed as a menace to society.[2] That pot could have been demonized for so long, despite countless studies and reports over the years showing its relative harmlessness and its effectiveness in treating a variety of medical conditions, goes to show that there is no substance too benign for vilification.[3]

But the history of marijuana—now legal recreationally in nineteen states and counting—also demonstrates that all moral conflicts in a capitalist society can be smoothed over when the conditions for a business opportunity ripen, no matter what taboos, reactionary parents, nervous politicians, or legal obstacles stand in the way. Sensible, scientific opinions couldn't combat the reefer madness campaign or the Reagan onslaught, and in that brief window in the '60s and '70s when sanity was glimpsed, no one thought investing in something disaffected kids grew in their backyard made much sense. The medicalization movement was the crucial turning point not simply

QUICK FIXES

because it broadly destigmatized marijuana, but more importantly because it conveyed to enough people of means the key
lesson required for social revaluation: that there was profit to
be made in the end.

Reefer Madness

In his *Travels*, Marco Polo recounted the story of the ruthless
followers of a mythical Persian leader named the Old Man
of the Mountain. To increase their courage before battles, the
Old Man's murderous gang smoked hashish, and so came to
be known as the *Hashshashin*—the Assassins.[4] The part about
their use of hashish turned out to be fable, but that didn't stop
Federal Bureau of Narcotics chief Harry Anslinger (whom we
met in chapter 4) from recounting this legend in his 1938 contribution to *Reader's Digest*, "Marijuana—Assassin of Youth."[5]
Like opium and cocaine, cannabis had been widely available
as a medicine in the late nineteenth century, but Anslinger side-
stepped any American familiarity with the drug by referring to
it by the name associated with migrant workers: *marijuana*.[6]
Between 1915 and 1930, half a million Mexicans came to the
United States, bringing a penchant for what the papers liked to
call the "loco weed."[7] As with previous drug scares—Chinese
coolies and opium, black stevedores and cocaine—cannabis
became a threat, about which something *had to be done*, in
association with a demonized racial group.[8] That marijuana
was also popular among black jazz musicians in the '30s
virtually assured that it would be a target of Anslinger's rage.[9]

The lies spread about marijuana's violence-inducing effects,
eventually taken to be the official position of Anslinger's
bureau, were so egregious that they would color all subsequent American drug culture. Marijuana was said to make its
users into "bestial demoniacs, filled with a mad lust to kill."[10]
Anslinger particularly liked recounting the story of Victor

178

Licata, a young man from Tampa, Florida, who murdered his whole family with an axe in a supposed "marijuana dream." What Anslinger conveniently avoided was Licata's previous psychiatric record, which included a note about being "frequently subject to hallucinations accompanied by homicidal impulses."[11] No matter—the official government position was that marijuana induced "reefer madness," evident in "savage and sadistic traits likely to reach a climax in axe and ice-pick murders."[12] Anslinger kept a large repository of horror stories linking drugs, violence, race, and sex, which author Larry Sloman refers to as his "gore file."[13] Far as we have come in some ways since Anslinger's time, this connection between drug addiction, violence, and a racialized underclass persists to this day.

Movie Poster for Marihuana: Weed with Roots in Hell *(1936). A good example of what the communications scholar Charles Atkin calls "inadvertent social norming," Charles Atkin, "Promising Strategies for Media Health Campaigns," in* Mass Media and Drug Prevention: Classic and Contemporary Theory and Research, *ed. William D. Crano and Michael Burgoon (Mahwah: Lawrence Erlbaum Associates, 2002), 38–9.*

Early in his career, however, Anslinger had seemed to understand that marijuana was not really such a danger: finding the public outcry over it to be overblown, he had directed his agents to focus on heroin over marijuana. But at hearings for the Marihuana Tax Act of 1937, which effectively made marijuana illegal through aggressive taxation and fines, he testified that the drug led people to "fly into a delirious rage" and "commit violent crimes."[14] In a statement reprehensible even by his own standards, he told Congress that "coloreds with big lips lure white women with jazz and marijuana."[15] Anslinger had come to agree with Judge Alexander MacLeod that

> Marihuana has no therapeutic value whatsoever. It has been responsible for the commission of crimes of violence, of murder, and of rape. Those are major tributaries that flow from the use of marihuana. It has no value of any kind. It is a fungus growth that comes right from the bowels of hell. Each cigarette is a stick of dynamite. Half a dozen of them smoked—no girl walking the streets would be safe with a man under the influence of this devilish drug. Young girls raped, people murdered—that's the story of the highway of marihuana. A marihuana peddler, or a man that peddles any drugs, should be punished, and the only way to punish him is to send him to a penitentiary for a long term.[16]

Why the about-face?[17] It seems Anslinger had been convinced by what historians Richard Bonnie and Charles Whitebread call "the idea of an alien cancer in the social organism ... [and] the inevitable fear that it would spread."[18] But there were more political concerns at work as well: in the mid-1930s, Anslinger's FBN was at risk of being folded into other government agencies, and he needed a new drug menace to boost his budget and his reputation.[19] After the Marihuana Tax Act passed, his bureau got to work. Between 1937 and 1942, the FBN destroyed about 60,000 tons of marijuana.[20] Now that they had a mission, Anslinger worked to ensure that no one would derail it. When New York mayor Fiorello La Guardia commissioned a report

Marihuana

    Colored students at Univ.of Minn.
partying with female students (white)
smoking and getting their sympathy
with stories of racial persecution. Result
pregnancy.

Undercover agent invited to marih.party.
Suggestion that everyone take off their pants
both male and female.　Ⅲ   Agent dropped
blackjack while disrobing and had to arrest
immediately.

*Commissioner of the Federal Bureau of Narcotics from 1930–62, Harry
J. Anslinger, and a close-up from an actual page in his marijuana "gore
files." From the H. J. Anslinger papers, 1835–1975 (01875), Historical
Collections and Labor Archives, Eberly Family Special Collections Library,
Penn State University Libraries, box 14; box 9, file 30.*

on the effects of cannabis, which concluded that "marihuana is essentially a harmless drug," Anslinger suppressed discussion of it and persuaded the *Journal of the American Medical Association* to dismiss it as unscientific.[21]

In 1985, marijuana evangelist Jack Herer published *The Emperor Wears No Clothes*, which laid out a conspiracy between Anslinger, banking tycoon Andrew Mellon, media mogul William Randolph Hearst, and chemical conglomerate CEO Lammot du Pont—an impressive roster! Herer's story went like this: Du Pont and Hearst were up in arms about a new invention, the hemp decorticator, that could make mass hemp usage more feasible and reduce demand for timber—the wood pulp in which both Hearst (the newspaperman) and Du Pont (who had just patented a technology to turn wood pulp into paper) took a material interest.[22] Though it gave countless potheads that "Aha!" moment, Herer's story was later proven to be full of holes by former *High Times* editor Steven Wishnia.[23] But there were two things Herer was right about. First, the Marihuana Tax Act did hurt the legitimate hemp industry, one of the more absurd side effects of the drug war. And second, the outlawing of marijuana was essentially conspiratorial, even if it didn't involve these particular conspirators.

Agents Provocateurs

The 1937 act did not, however, eliminate marijuana use, and in fact, the propaganda around it did a great deal to bring the attention of the nation's youth to irresistibly cool drug subcultures. By the '60s, marijuana was no longer confined to ethnic minorities: white college students were into it, and unsurprisingly, they accorded it undue importance.[24] It became a symbol of rebellion and the casting off of society's cruel logic —a gesture that had gained a positive moral weight in the counterculture. As Yippie Jerry Rubin famously said in 1970,

"Smoking pot makes you a criminal and a revolutionary—as soon as you take your first puff, you are an enemy of society."[25] (He would continue spouting wisdom in his later lucrative career as a Wall Street investor: "Wealth creation," he asserted, "is the real American Revolution."[26]) The days of "reefer madness" hysteria were over, but a new marijuana fear—that it would serve as a "gateway" to harder drugs—settled into common sense. This served both the drug warriors and the young revolutionaries, who were happy for any excuse to playact the dangerous underclass.

The Beats, hippies, and later freaks looked back to bohemians of the past to place themselves in this lineage of deviance. The English poet Samuel Taylor Coleridge and the French Club des Hachichins (a bohemian literary circle in the mid-nineteenth century) were particular inspirations. The United States even had its own homegrown, if more characteristically huckstery, hash-inspired tradition: the novelist and poet Bayard Taylor, whom the *New-York Evening Post* described as having "travelled more and seen less than any man living"; the "hashish eater" and Taylor plagiarist Fitz Hugh Ludlow; and the quack physician Frederick Hollick, whose *Marriage Guide* (1850) encouraged the use of hashish as an aphrodisiac for loveless marriages.[27] But these nineteenth-century enthusiasts were ultimately more ambivalent about drugs. Much like Thomas De Quincey, Ludlow tried throughout his life to give up his drug use. Not so for the children of the '60s, who were unapologetic enthusiasts, out to expose "the great marijuana hoax" (to borrow the title of Allen Ginsberg's 1966 *Atlantic* essay) with a pristine confidence born of middle-class upbringings.

Those same upbringings afforded a form of luxury made technologically possible during their lifetimes: air travel. In search of new exoticisms, the hippie trail extended from Tangier, where kif (a combination of marijuana and tobacco) smoking was common, east to Istanbul, Afghanistan, and eventually Nepal and India, where Western cannabis culture became infused with Eastern mysticism.[28] George Harrison went there in 1966 and brought back the sitar. Harvard psychologist Richard Alpert went in 1967 and brought back a new name, Ram Dass. Still today, the only cultural association for pot devotees more ready to hand than Indian religions is Jamaican Rastafarianism, the dissidence and music of which became no less commercialized.

In all their cultural encounters and appropriations, hippie culture managed effortlessly to turn inside out. As historian Martin Booth summarizes,

> Between them, the war-mongering governments and peace-loving hippies created a well-organized, sustained, international cannabis trade. They caused what had been a cultural phenomenon in Muslim and eastern countries to spread across the planet, altering the economies of those countries and even changing agricultural and production practices. Whilst they liked to see themselves as benign, the hippies were, in effect, *agents provocateurs* for the global capitalism they so abhorred.[29]

Though there was clearly money to be made, it wasn't enough for the pharmaceutical companies to show much interest. Due to the peculiarity of the "active ingredient" in cannabis (THC) among psychoactive drugs—it's not an alkaloid, and so was impervious to the methods of nineteenth-century organic chemistry—it was not isolated until 1964.[30] And when it was, pharmaceutical companies were only interested in it as something on which to model a synthetic copy. As journalist Dan Baum explains, the "problem with THC ... is that it's a natural substance, so it can't be patented, and if it can't be patented, no pharmaceutical company will make it."[31] FDA officials in the '70s were skeptical marijuana would ever become legal simply because "'there's no profit incentive to develop marijuana'; anybody can grow it."[32]

A Fracturing Consensus

Marijuana was normalized in the '70s. Despite Nixon's misguided effort to keep Anslinger's game going, more and more people were using it, and commentators on both sides of the political spectrum were waking up to the silliness of criminalizing pot. *Newsweek* asked in 1970, "Marihuana: Time to Change the Law?"[33] Researchers like Norman Zinberg and Lester Grinspoon both answered with a resounding "Yes!", and the scientific community in general finally snapped out of the fearful daze wrought by Anslinger's machine.[34] The *Washington Post* editorialized in favor of decriminalization.[35] On the right, William F. Buckley's *National Review* urged "American Conservatives [to] revise their position on Marijuana."[36] Even Nixon's own handpicked commission on marijuana and drug abuse concluded that "marihuana use is not such a grave problem that individuals who smoke marihuana, or possess it for that purpose, should be subject to criminal procedures" (a conclusion about which Nixon was understandably furious).[37]

Marijuana smokers got their own advocacy organizations, the most important of which was the National Organization for the Reform of Marijuana Laws (NORML) founded in 1971, and even their own magazine, *High Times*, in 1974. Jimmy Carter was elected in 1976, and he was talking the talk: "Penalties against possession of a drug should not be more damaging to an individual than the use of the drug itself ... Nowhere is this more clear than in the laws against possession of marijuana in private for personal use."[38] By 1978, the high-water mark of the first pro-marijuana movement, decriminalization laws had passed in twelve states. It was a ripe time for legal change, and yet somehow it all fell apart.

When Carter was elected, he brought along Dr. Peter Bourne to be his drug czar. Bourne was first hired by the then Georgia governor in 1970 to manage the state's drug abuse program. Cosmopolitan and liberal, more academic than politician, by many accounts handsome and charming, Bourne made extensive use of the recently legalized methadone maintenance treatment for heroin addicts and was a strong advocate for the decriminalization of marijuana, harm reduction, and other policies that were way ahead of their time. Carter's advisors warned him against taking too soft a stand on drugs, but Carter stuck by the good doctor.

Bourne was a listener to the science: though most Americans at the time still believed pot was an addictive substance, he confidently asserted the drug's essential harmlessness. (He also said *in print* that "cocaine … is probably the most benign of illicit drugs currently in widespread use."[39]) When a group of

Drug Paraphernalia Hearing

Sen. Joseph Biden, D-Del., holds a miniature football that hides a drug pipe as he questions a witness at a special hearing of the Senate Criminal Justice Subcommittee in Baltimore Friday. The panel heard testimony on the sale of drug paraphernalia through legal outlets (UPI).

Senator Joe Biden holds up a miniature football hiding a drug pipe at a special hearing of the Senate Criminal Justice Subcommittee in 1979. The parents' movement was angered by the paraphernalia industry's appeals to children, Hartford Courant, November 17, 1979, 10. Thank you to Sarah Siff for tracking down this image and sharing it with me. See Sarah Brady Siff, "Joe Biden and Drug Control: A More Complete Picture (Part 1 —the 1970s)," Points, October 15, 2020, pointshistory.com.

concerned parents from Atlanta wrote to him to express their anger about their teenagers' pot smoking, he brushed them aside as a bunch of "untrained, hysterical southern parents."[40] Ignored and offended, the anti-marijuana parent lobby got organized, and quickly: soon they had a number of national action groups, their own guide for parents called *Parents, Peers, and Pot*, and the support of National Institute on Drug Abuse head Robert DuPont, who started out pro-marijuana but eventually gave in to the pressure.[41] Needless to say, when Bourne was caught writing a sketchy quaalude prescription and snorting cocaine at a holiday party, the untrained hysterics were only too happy to see him resign in disgrace. And then in 1980, they were of course overjoyed to elect a man who finally *got it*.

With some patience and political savvy, the fracturing of the marijuana prohibition consensus in the '70s could have turned into more rational drug policy. But 1978 proved to be a turning point for the pro-marijuana forces. Just five years later, NORML was in tatters, and all hopes of legalization were dashed, seemingly for good. In 1982, the National Academy of Sciences released a study concluding that short-term marijuana use by schoolchildren caused "amotivational syndrome."[42] The parent movement, which boasted 3,000 active anti-marijuana groups around the country, was celebrated by the White House; their voluntarism was needed to pick up where the Reagan budget cuts left off.[43]

Soon, however, the parents themselves would be left behind as giant corporations took up the cause, and their grassroots education efforts were replaced by the Drug Abuse Resistance Education (DARE) program, which put police officers in elementary and middle schools.[44] The parents had served as the ground troops for state retrenchment and a new punitive paradigm. As parent leader Keith Schuchard would later declare, "*We* were the real counterculture."[45]

Medicine

Not only does the amount of psychoactive material in cannabis go through regular cycles of variation as the plant grows, but marijuana also affects people in very different ways.[46] Some people go inward, or fall asleep; some find they're more creative or focused; some get paranoid, others giddy and sociable. It's for this reason that cannabis fell into disfavor in nineteenth-century medicine.[47] Doctors just didn't know what it was going to do, and they had plenty of other more reliable (and inject-able) drugs at their disposal.[48]

The normalization of marijuana in the '70s coincided with a resurfacing of interest in its medicinal properties. Cancer patients came to hear of it as an antiemetic, counteracting the nausea that goes along with chemotherapy. AIDS patients would later be attracted to cannabis for the same reason. Marijuana also alleviates the eye pressure causing glaucoma, and it helps with a variety of seizure disorders, spastic ailments, and arthri-tis.[49] Drug companies have tried to push synthetic THC (which is patentable) for these purposes, but cannabis contains over 400 chemicals, and to this day, scientists haven't figured out which ones in which combinations address which conditions.

The medical marijuana detractors, however, don't tend to focus on any of these things. Their argument is instead twofold. First, for every case of someone smoking pot for what could be called a legitimate medical reason, there are twenty who buy their "meds" for recreational purposes. When and where people can't simply buy their marijuana legally and without a prescription, this seems undeniably true. But as writer Greg Campbell argues, the medical marijuana "charade" has served a crucial function. Where previous attempts to decriminalize and legalize marijuana the "right" way, through rescheduling petitions and presidential commissions, have miserably failed, the "state-sanctioned hypocrisy" of medical marijuana law has at least shown the average American that cannabis's roots do not, in fact, lie in hell.[50]

The second objection to medical marijuana is a version of the "gateway drug" theory: If our kids learn that marijuana, still to this day scheduled as a drug of high abuse potential and no medical value by the federal government, is not only relatively harmless but an actual *medicine*, what are they going to think of the other drugs grouped for so long in the category of "narcotics"? This is something like the logic the tobacco companies employed well past the point at which they knew they were selling death sticks: "We've been lying for so long, we've got to keep it up!" It's unlikely, however, that any drug deluge will follow a relaxation of attitudes about pot. Polls are pretty clear that people think of marijuana as a categorically different drug than heroin or cocaine.[51] No more than marijuana itself is medical marijuana a gateway to other drugs.

Today, even as recreational use of marijuana is being legalized, its medicalization proceeds apace. The dispensary dosist calls its shops "wellness experiences," where personal "wellness guides" help you achieve one of six "states"—sleep, calm, relief, bliss, passion, arouse—through dose-controlled cannabis therapy.[52] Dennis Peron, coauthor of the 1996 California proposition that allowed the use of medical cannabis, prophetically claimed that "all marijuana use is medical."[53] No one's getting high anymore, we're all just getting better.

The Green Rush

In October 2009, a Justice Department memo suggested that busting medical marijuana patients and businesses would be a low priority, inaugurating the "Great Green Rush."[54] Soon the rich and powerful—philanthropist George Soros, Men's Wearhouse founder George Zimmer, University of Phoenix founder John Sperling—were bankrolling pro-pot ballot initiatives and other efforts, and in 2012, the first states (Washington and Colorado) legalized marijuana for recreational use.[55] As of the summer of 2022, nineteen states have legalized recreational use, and thirty-seven have legalized medical use, but federally, marijuana still remains a Schedule I drug.

Joe Biden or any other American president could change this with a stroke of a pen. Biden, for his part, has made baby steps on the issue, but he hasn't taken decisive action here, likely for fear of the political consequences—specifically the pressure that would naturally follow from marijuana legalization to expunge the records of many of the hundreds of thousands of people in prison for nonviolent drug offenses.[56] Either he would have to live with the contradiction of lots of people behind bars for a legal act, or he'd have governors around the country blaming the Democrats for mass releasing criminals into our communities. With marijuana a low-priority voting issue, not to mention policy itself being increasingly disconnected from electoral politics, Democratic Party strategists have been quite content to signal in the right direction but ultimately kick the can down the road.[57]

In this legal murk, business is still flourishing: in 2021, the legal and illegal cannabis markets together formed a $117.5 billion industry.[58] Residents of Weed, California, who once thought marijuana the "devil's lettuce," have been won over by the inflow of visitors with cash to spend. Licensing their logo might net the city half a million dollars.[59] Where the rational argumentation of liberal reformers has failed for so long, the profit motive has been victorious.

But while renegade growers and egomaniacal distributors used to be the beneficiaries of the marijuana trade, publicly traded corporations are increasingly stepping in to take control. For the moment, this shift has not been decisive: economists Robin Goldstein and Daniel Sumner estimate that 75 percent of the weed sold in California is illegal and about half the price of its legal equivalent.[60] Still, cannabis companies are experiencing near-exponential growth, and the enclosure of what writer June Thunderstorm calls the "marijuana commons" is on the horizon.[61] The alcohol conglomerate Constellation Brands is a major investor, as is Altria (previously Philip Morris). A former Purdue Pharma CEO is now the president and head of the "pharma" division of Emblem, a cannabis company.[62] In 2019, the marijuana industry produced its first billionaire: Boris Jordan, who owns a third of Curaleaf—the "Starbucks of cannabis," according to Jordan.[63]

Many onlookers seem positively shocked "that the emergence of a profitable cannabis market may not necessarily challenge economic and racial inequalities across society," as if there were some inherently ethical nature to green culture that would lead it to *do better*.[64] Part of the problem is in the financing of the cannabis industry: since federally chartered banks fear the possibility of being prosecuted for aiding criminal activity, "ganjapreneurs" must rely on venture capitalists who are generally not interested in seeing cannabis capitalism differ in any way from capitalism itself.[65] But the simple truth of the matter is that legalization efforts around the country are not about righting historic wrongs but rather about benefiting what Edward Forchion Jr., a.k.a. NJWeedman, refers to as the "Caucasian Cannabis Cartel."[66]

At the end of their 1974 history of marijuana prohibition, Bonnie and Whitebread emphasize that "we do *not* endorse the 'alcohol model'; indeed the legal channels of marihuana distribution should *not* resemble those now employed for alcoholic beverages."[67] This conclusion seems odd for a book that carefully lays out the absurdity of Anslinger's America, but their position was not uncommon at the time. Amorphia, an early coalition partner of NORML's, "wanted no part of a commercial, state-controlled, alcohol-model marijuana system."[68] They would "support no initiative that did not permit personal cultivation: free backyard grass."[69] Their fear that large, profit-making enterprises would turn marijuana into a soulless and exploitative industry, akin to that of tobacco or alcohol, was well founded. In many places around the US today, we've got the drug itself, but without all the things that used to make it appealing.

Conclusion

> Man has a certain insatiability for existence itself, a primordial
> insatiability ... Unless it is stamped out, sated through grand
> emotions, work, creativity, power, and so on, it can only be
> smothered by narcotics.
>
> —Stanisław Ignacy Witkiewicz

We are at a turning point in the history of drugs. There is nearly
complete exhaustion with the paradigm of "punitive prohibition" inaugurated at the beginning of the twentieth century,
though, as with neoliberalism, no one is quite sure what comes
after it. Mental health professionals are all overwhelmed and
realizing the traditional pharmacological tools are pretty crude
instruments. And we've reached a technological crescendo that,
in a way, has finally made real the previously illegitimate fears
of anxious parents. Are teenagers going to know the difference
between pot and oregano sprayed with K2? Are they going
to test the cocaine for fentanyl? What new psychedelic thrills
will be plucked with the alphabet soup of synthetics? The high
school pharmacopeia of the '70s looks truly like child's play
compared to what is on offer today.

These changes coincide, unsurprisingly, with a new, if
undefined, phase of American capitalism. The austerity of the
neoliberal era has produced widespread misery and political
instability. The response has been to turn the tap of government
spending on, justified in part by the COVID-19 pandemic, but
with no long-term planning that might begin to mitigate inequality. The forces that one would expect to flex their muscles
in this moment have been demobilized by the disintermediation

of American society, replaced by an ineffective nonprofit world insulating the Washington blob from any popular pressure.[1] Everything must change, but stasis prevails.

In the face of this intransigence, we should expect a wide variety of increasingly baffling fantasies to gain traction in different pockets of American society. In the realm of drugs, one might be a zombified drug warriorism, awoken by the menace of new "super drugs." Another will be an emboldened liberal drug reformism that seeks, with good if blinkered intentions, to undo the damage of the War on Drugs. Both, unfortunately, are simply not up to the tasks they set for themselves. Broader social reform, specifically around jobs and healthcare, is the only way to mitigate the compulsions both to take and to demonize drugs. To refer back to the Introduction, *drug policy is not about drugs*—which means, in turn, that the "problem" of drugs in the abstract cannot be dealt with through drug policy alone.

The Dream of Prohibition

We're now more than a century into the War on Drugs, and, as basically everyone agrees today, it's been a resounding failure, both on its own terms and in its pernicious consequences— hyperincarceration, thuggish police, crime, government distrust, drug-related harms, and so on.[2] Just to be comprehensive, however, as there are still likely some out there who believe in their heart of hearts that there is a better, sane, effective way to fight the drug war, let's quickly review the animating vision here.

There are three ways to attack drug use: by cutting production, by blocking distribution, and by reducing demand. As long as the economic incentives of a lucrative black market are in place, there is no way to sell poor farmers on crop substitution; as historian Martin Booth writes, "Asking them not to grow poppies is like asking a bank manager if he would become a teller once more."[3] The economic gain is just too apparent: "Being poor doesn't make you stupid," as historian Mike Jay puts it.[4] There is thus an "iron law" of the narcotics trade: when supply is cut off in one place, it quickly sprouts in another.[5] This is even truer of the synthetics market, which relies on redirecting precursor chemicals rather than the slower work of soil and seasons.

Targeting the distribution networks, where the real money is made, is just as fruitless. Journalist Mike Gray nicely illustrates why:

> At the great harbors that ring the nation, at Boston, Norfolk, Galveston, Seattle, and a hundred other ports of entry, two million tons of cargo will cross the dock tomorrow. Los Angeles alone will land 130,000 containers this month. Customs inspectors will examine 400. The other 129,600 will pass through without so much as a tip of the hat. And as this tidal wave of heavy machinery, cameras, car parts, and cuckoo clocks moves off the wharf on endless lines of semitrailers and flatcars, it's worth remembering that the entire annual cocaine supply for the United States would fit in just thirteen of those steel boxes. A year's supply of heroin could be shipped in a single container.[6]

And now we've got even more powerful synthetics out there. Forget going through containers, the US mail today does just fine.

Which leaves us with demand. The drug war strategy has been very good at putting people in prison and militarizing the police, but it has not been so good at reducing demand for narcotics. Americans, in general, just *love* drugs. And as even Richard Nixon was made to understand, you can't intimidate addicts out of their addiction. The best way to deal with addicts, and with the issue of crime that addicts commit to maintain their addiction, is through treatment, community support groups, and maintenance prescriptions. (Nixon, it ought to be remembered, was the first president to legalize opiate distribution in the form of methadone clinics.[7])

The dream of drug control is an omnipotent fantasy that, as psychologist Carl Hart has said, only children or naive adults could possibly believe in.[8] You can temporarily stem supply, you can move drug production and distribution around, you can affect drug purity, but you can't stop people from making or taking drugs with either "smart" drug policy or through sheer force. And this is merely to speak of the dream on its own terms, as an effort to curb drug use and abuse. The drug war has also borne all of the perverse symptoms that, ironically, we once recognized quite clearly after the failure of Prohibition. It has led to the exact kind of crime, violence, and death that drug warriors claim to want to eliminate.[9]

Unfortunately, and unlike with Prohibition, these failures have justified further escalation of the drug war, as symptoms are mistaken for causes. This is a vicious cycle of outrage and punishment, but it's also one of defeatism: as sociologist Christina Jacqueline Johns writes, "The violence and pathology of the social order is written off as caused by either drugs or mental illness, and increasingly the populace retreats into its own drugs of choice, or television."[10] It wasn't so long ago that a clear theory of *root causes* was commonplace: an LBJ commission on crime concluded in 1967 that "warring on poverty, inadequate housing, and unemployment is warring on crime … More broadly and importantly, every effort to improve life in America's inner cities is an effort against crime."[11] The great conservative victory in the '80s replaced this theory of root causes with one of *personal depravity*, justifying among other things the expansion of the carceral state (the cheaper alternative to expanding the welfare state).[12]

What exactly inspires the animus of the drug warriors?[13] Hatred of "deviant" subcultures, particularly *youth* subcultures.

A concern that drug use makes one a useless burden on society. Fear of the ravages of addiction and subsequent crime. All of these play a role, but at root, the basic worry is paradoxically that drugs are *too good*, that they satisfy us all too well, and in so doing detract from more noble pursuits: work, love, family, God. "It's so good, don't even try it once," reads the title of a book on heroin from 1972.[14]

Perhaps this is the bubble that really needs popping. There is a recurring fantasy—played out most famously in Aldous Huxley's *Brave New World*, but also in endless speculation about "our posthuman future" and films like *THX 1138* and *Equilibrium*—that we will become a pill- and needle-based society at the cost of freedom, interpersonal relationships, and basic human dignity; that we will be made slavish under the enchanting power of drugs; that we will become, in the words of physician James Wall, "a society where everybody just floats around in his own tub of butter."[15] Perhaps there is some rhetorical value in comparing Prozac to Huxley's soma, but drugs, many might be disappointed to hear, simply aren't *that* good.

Don't get me wrong: drugs—especially the ones we have today—can be very powerful and pleasurable substances. But psychoactive drugs will never take the place of human relationships, though they can numb the pain of disconnection. They will never get people to think in a perfectly determinate and controllable fashion. They will never save the world. And they will never ultimately deliver on the twin promises of meaning and happiness, though they will often deliver quite efficiently on the promise of *fun*. To think they could do any of these things, all of which raise the specter of a new form of evil and slavery that appears as the latent dream-thought to the drug war's manifest lunacy, is to misunderstand the dangers (and the benefits) that drugs *do* pose.

The Blinkers of Liberal Drug Reformism

We've tried punishing and demonizing. It's time to legalize and destigmatize then?

Misguided and destructive as the War on Drugs has been, the key proposals of liberal drug reformism don't inspire much confidence in an alternative. Legalization has, for one, long been the principled position of the libertarian right: from Ludwig von Mises to Milton Friedman, free marketeers have loved pointing to the example of illegal drugs to prove their belief that markets solve everything.[16] Place the drug trade in the stable hands of legal profiteers, they say, and away go the absurd profit margins, the government corruption, the distortion of local economies, the crime, the enforcement budgets, and the drug contamination. The tragedy of the War on Drugs is, in their view, a function of too many visible hands.

Unfortunately for their elegant argument, it's the legal drugs—cigarettes and alcohol, in particular—that are most hazardous to Americans. Letting profit-hungry corporations sell psychoactive drugs virtually assures abuses detrimental to public health. As public policy analysts Robert MacCoun and Peter Reuter conclude in their comprehensive assessment of the costs and benefits of drug legalization: "In projecting the consequences of legalizing drugs like cocaine or heroin, the experience with the alcohol, gambling, and tobacco industries suggests the difficulty of maintaining regulation that is guided by the public interest, particularly public health."[17] Illegal drug dealers can be dangerous sociopaths, but they are nothing compared to CEOs.

Righteous as the liberal critique of the War on Drugs can be, it can quite easily slip into simple libertarianism, or else a misguided faith in the free market to solve all. It's important to keep in mind that there's nothing inherently left wing about liberal attitudes toward drugs, or even downright drug enthusiasm. Paul Staines—a self-declared "anarcho-capitalist" and aide to Thatcher advisor David Hart—was an acid house devotee and even did publicity for one of the largest rave organizers of the '80s and '90s.[18] Peter Thiel is one of the most avid investors in psychedelic start-ups.[19] A more rational society would undoubtedly minimize the impacts of black markets by regulating *all* psychoactive drugs (and, perhaps, controlling their sale through state monopolies or public trust systems), but legalization in *this* society likely means bringing highly potent substances into the purview of profit extraction.[20]

But just as unfortunate as the capitulation to libertarianism is the *idealism* that pervades liberal drug reformism. From sociologist Alfred Lindesmith (who took on Harry Anslinger's erroneous views on opiates) to psychiatrists like Andrew Weil, Norman Zinberg, and Lester Grinspoon (who all tried in their own ways to preempt the backlash to the excess of the '60s) and up to Columbia psychologist Carl Hart in the present, liberal drug reformers have often made it seem like rational drug policy will flow from *awareness* and *destigmatization*: once we know that drugs aren't the menace they're made out to be by the media and enforcement agencies, we won't be prey to their scare campaigns.

There are at least two problems with this position. First, it can appear wildly out of touch with existing social reality. Perhaps it's true, as Dr. Weil stresses, that "any drug can be used successfully, no matter how bad its reputation, and any drug can be abused, no matter how accepted it is."[21] Perhaps it's even true, as Dr. Hart stresses, that most drugs, including heroin, can be used recreationally in a responsible manner.[22] But what comfort is this to someone burdened by heroin or cocaine addiction? Or to their families? Or to their neighborhoods? Poor and working-class people are understandably concerned with drugs and crime, and liberal attempts to destigmatize these things can come off as hopelessly middle class.[23] Worse, the right can easily take advantage of such disregard: as an article in the *Wall Street Journal* mused in 1989, "The unspoken thought behind many of the calls for surrender [to the drug scourge] is that the middle classes can take care of themselves and the ghettos are hopeless."[24]

And besides, *shouldn't* we be concerned that Americans are bingeing on psychoactive drugs? While opioids continue to plague left-behind towns across the Rust Belt, the middle and upper classes are fine tuning their experience with amphetamines and psychedelics. What is so horrible about our social reality that we can only bear it with the aid of chemical enhancements and escapes? Once again, liberals and the left have too often ceded this critique to conservatives: as Dr. Gabriel Nahas, darling of the anti-marijuana parent movement in the '80s, wrote in opposition to drug law reform in 1973, one may "wonder how long a political system can endure when drug taking becomes one of the prerequisites of happiness. If the American dream has lost its attraction, it will not be retrieved through the use of stupefying drugs."[25]

This leads to the more important issue with liberal drug reformism. There are obvious first steps toward a rational drug policy out there—decriminalizing personal possession, eliminating mandatory minimums, prohibiting law enforcement from self-funding through civil forfeiture, descheduling marijuana, and so on.[26] All are policies currently with strong majority support in polls, and they should be pursued so long as they remain genuinely popular and are not a misuse of political capital. Doing some of these things would undoubtedly help reverse, or at least slow, some of the damage done by the War on Drugs, but the problems related to drugs in America, both the excess of their use and the prohibitions against them, are a function of the more fundamental problem of social and economic inequality and alienation.[27] All psychoactive substances could be legal and destigmatized, with medically accurate information about them and perfectly safe routes of administration widely available, but without alleviating poverty, unemployment, stress, and despair, the primary problems we associate with drugs would all still be with us (and arguably would be worse).[28] Real solutions to the "drug problem," in other words, necessarily take up issues that aren't about drugs.

Jobs and Healthcare

Fear and enthusiasm, prohibition and peddling have been the poles between which America has swung wildly when it comes to drugs.[29] One projects a social utopia accomplished through the purging of demonic elements. The other retreats to a personal utopia and leaves the broader social question alone. Both demonstrate a belief in solutions to the problems of capitalist society that do not in any way challenge capitalism itself, and uncoincidentally, both make promises that either can't be kept or can only be temporarily fulfilled. In brief, they both conjure a unique Americanism: *the quick fix*. Anything that covers over, that allows some resumption of "normalcy," that prevents a full reckoning—that's been the stuff for us, for well over a century.

Nobody needs any more of this ill-conceived pushing or restriction. What we need instead is a *free relation* to drugs: not only a clear understanding of their benefits and harms, uncolored by overbearing moralizing, but much more importantly less *compulsion* to use drugs—less stress, less misery, less oppression—so that their use is really a freely made *choice*. In 1910, socialist Hermann Schlüter characterized the problem of intoxication, insofar as it posed a problem at all, in disarmingly simple terms: "Drunkenness has its root in the excessive exploitation of workingmen by capitalism. Every improvement in the condition of the workingmen brings about a diminution in drunkenness."[30] Edward Brecher echoed Schlüter in concluding his comprehensive 1972 overview of *Licit and Illicit Drugs*: "A satisfying way of life is thus the ultimate prescription, and the immediate goal should be improvements in the *quality of life*."[31]

There are two particular improvements that would radically transform American drug consumption, and those are *good jobs* and *universal healthcare*. Research regularly demonstrates the importance of the routine provided by stable employment for avoiding drug abuse. There's a reason we often hear about the heavy drug use of the very rich and the very poor—those *without* jobs.[32] A good job is also an important precondition of the practical and symbolic life reorganization involved in *settling down*, a transition that also typically involves greatly lowered rates of drug abuse.[33] Since capital is unable or uninterested in bringing back the unionized jobs of yesteryear, the United States desperately needs federal jobs programs, or even a federal jobs guarantee, to put people to work rebuilding both its physical and moral infrastructure. "The general principle," according to sociologist Elliott Currie, should be "the direct creation of useful jobs in areas that visibly serve community needs."[34] The excess of opioids, methamphetamine, and other drugs coursing through the country will only be burned off through hard but rewarding *work*.[35]

Improvements in America's disastrous healthcare system would also greatly reduce the country's drug abuse, which is often a form of self-medication, a simple alternative to actual *care*.[36] By far the most important first step in actually providing that care to Americans is killing off the for-profit insurance tapeworm and establishing a universal system like Medicare for All. The latest iterations of Medicare for All legislation include provisions for drug abuse and mental health programs, weakening some of the current incentives toward psychiatric (i.e., drug centered) treatment. And while a single-payer system does not tackle head-on the problem of pharmaceutical company practices, its monopsony buying power does give the federal government the leverage to begin the process.

But we shouldn't think of these kinds of broad social democratic reforms as mere policy fixes. We should instead think about them in the way that American elites think about them:

as policies that would both signal and effect massive *political* shifts in this country. Providing people with jobs and healthcare, in any country and at any time in history, is typically a good thing. But given the historically specific inequities of American society, the precarity and dissatisfaction of employment in a deindustrialized economy, the gross stupidity and obvious cruelty of our healthcare system, and the stifling stasis of culture war politics, a federal jobs guarantee and Medicare for All would be so wildly popular that they would, as many of the New Deal programs did, effect a fundamental change in American political consciousness.

Drug abuse and addiction are exacerbated by social and political malaise: in anthropologist Philippe Bourgois's words, "Self-destructive addiction is merely the medium for desperate people to internalize their frustration, resistance, and powerlessness."[37] A broad swath of the population, and the poor and working classes in particular, have little reason to believe at present that "politics" signifies anything more than tawdry posturing in an arena distant from their everyday lives. They are convinced that political inaction and social decay are reality as such.

Bold policies like a federal jobs guarantee or Medicare for All would change their minds, and not in the abstract. They would open the door to a broader transformation of society and keep that door propped open with near daily reminders of how politics can be in the direct self-interest of the vast majority of people. It is the seeming inalterability of reality that spurs compulsive drug use and irrational drug warriorism. Political possibility means that, at a grand scale, *things can change*.

Human beings will always take drugs, and they'll always rail against their dangers. But the compulsions both to use drugs and to vilify them will ease in a society with more material security, care, and political possibility, for the simple reason that these are three conditions of human freedom.

Appendix A

Psychoactive Drug Use Trends in the United States

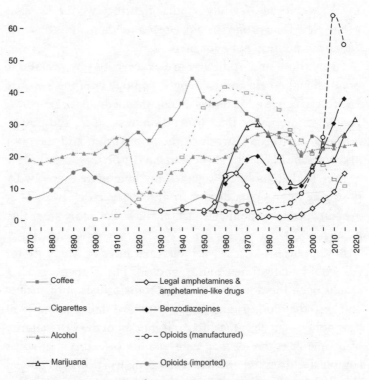

Figure 1 Psychoactive Drug Use 1870–2020

Alcohol = One-tenths of a gallon of absolute alcohol consumed per capita[1]
Amphetamines and amphetamine-like drugs = Ounces per 1,000 population[2]
Antidepressants and antipsychotics = Tens of millions of prescriptions written for antidepressants and antipsychotics[3]
Benzodiazepines = Ounces per 1,000 population[4]
Cigarettes = Hundreds of cigarettes smoked per capita[5]
Cocaine = Tens of metric tons consumed[6]

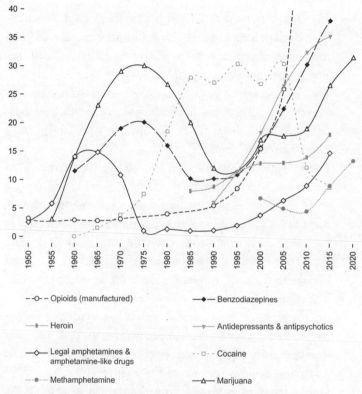

Figure 2 Psychoactive Drug Use 1950–2020

Coffee = Gallons available per capita[7]
Heroin = Metric tons consumed[8]
Marijuana = Millions of regular marijuana users, based on past month use reporting[9]
Methamphetamine = Hundred thousands of regular methamphetamine users, based on past month use reporting[10]
Opioids (imported) = Ounces per 1,000 population[11]
Opioids (manufactured) = Ounces per 1,000 population[12]

These graphs are useful for discerning individual psychoactive drug use *trends*; the comparative *magnitude* of use cannot be deduced here. The scales are really only determined in such a way as to make the trends visually discernible in a single graph. In addition, apples (past month use prevalence, for instance) are often held up for comparison to oranges (estimated metric tons consumed). A few items of note:

- Prohibition more than halved per capita alcohol consumption. Both before and after Prohibition, American alcohol consumption has hovered around two gallons of absolute alcohol per person per year.
- The rise and fall of per capita cigarette consumption was a century-long process, in comparison to the shorter variations of other drugs (thus, the apt title of Allan Brandt's *The Cigarette Century*).
- The marijuana line is based on reliable data from 1979 on, during which the annual National Survey on Drug Use and Health gives us a regular picture of past month use. But since it's generally agreed that marijuana use spiked in the late '70s after a steady rise from obscurity in the late '50s, I have projected the left side of that bell curve to look similar to those of amphetamines and benzodiazepines.
- The sharp rise in marijuana users in recent years is due to the drug's slow legalization, which has made marijuana use less of a youth phenomenon. The V-curve for past month marijuana users aged twelve to twenty-five between 1979 and 2016 is represented in Figure 3.[13]
- One of the most striking features of the whole graph is the intersection of the rise of cocaine with the fall of amphetamine, benzodiazepine, and marijuana use. If one strictly focused on the latter three drugs, one might attribute some success to the regulatory changes of 1965 and 1970, and the initial phase of Nixon's War on Drugs. But it's clear here that Andean cocaine quickly filled the void.

Figure 3 Prevalence Rate of Marijuana Use

- I've included cocaine in terms of metric tons simply because that is how the early data is most readily available, but the sheer quantity consumed shows an interesting trend. The prevalence of past month use of cocaine and crack between 1979 and 2015 looks more familiar (crack was only recorded as a discrete category in 1988):

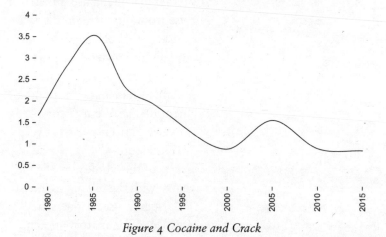

Figure 4 Cocaine and Crack

This graph accords with the common belief that the cocaine binge peaked in the '80s and declined in the '90s. But the overall amount of cocaine coming into the country did not slow with the decrease in the number of users, indicating an increasing concentration of use among high-frequency cocaine users. This seems important to represent given the cocaine addict's role as a central target justifying the continuation of the War on Drugs, as well as the clear failure of that war to stem the supply of available cocaine.

- Prozac was introduced in 1988, at the moment when benzodiazepine, amphetamine, and marijuana use are all bottoming out.

Appendix B

Timeline of Drug Discovery

Year Distilled/ Isolated*/Synthesized	Drug	Derived From
13th c.	Brandy/Whiskey	Wine/Grain
17th c.	Rum	Molasses
1805	Morphine	Opium
1819	Caffeine	Coffee
1828	Nicotine	Tobacco
1859	Cocaine	Coca
1874	Heroin	Opium
1881	Barbital†	Synthetic
1887	Amphetamine	Synthetic
1893	Methamphetamine	Synthetic
1896	Mescaline	Peyote
1912	MDMA	Synthetic
1926	Phencyclidine (PCP)	Synthetic
1938	LSD	Synthetic
1944	Methylphenidate (Ritalin)	Synthetic
1946‡	DMT	*Mimosa tenuiflora*
1950	Meprobamate (Miltown)	Synthetic
1951	Chlorpromazine (Thorazine)	Synthetic
1957	Psilocybin	Psilocybe mushroom
1959	Diazepam (Valium)	Synthetic
1960	Fentanyl	Synthetic
1962	Ketamine	Synthetic
1964	THC	Cannabis
1971	Fluoxetine (Prozac)	Synthetic

* It's important to note that in the case of the isolation of the "active ingredients" in naturally occurring substances, this process has been essentially reductive: we tend to think of cocaine as the "essence" of coca, but coca itself contains at least fourteen different alkaloids, most of which have largely gone unstudied. In the '70s, when it was well known that marijuana relieved glaucoma and nausea, pharmaceutical giant Eli Lilly tried to push its synthetic THC (nabilone) through the FDA as a patentable alternative to medical marijuana. However, there are over 400 distinct chemicals in marijuana, and to this day, researchers are not entirely sure which ones reduce eyeball pressure.[1]

† Diethyl-barbituric acid, the first barbiturate to be brought to market.

‡ DMT was actually synthesized in 1931 before it was isolated. DMT is perhaps best known as the primary psychoactive drug in ayahuasca, brewed from *Banisteriopsis caapi*, *Psychotria viridis* (chacruna), and sometimes other herbs.

Appendix C

Key Dates in Psychoactive Drug History

1874 The Woman's Christian Temperance Union is formed.

1875 San Francisco bans opium smoking and opium dens; it is the first ever narcotic ban in the United States.

1881 George Miller Beard publishes *American Nervousness*, a text that popularizes the term "neurasthenia."

1895 The Anti-Saloon League is formed.

1898 Heroin is introduced by Bayer.

1903 The first barbiturate, Veronal, is introduced by Bayer.

1906 The Pure Food and Drug Act, requiring patent medicines to list ingredients if they contain more than a certain amount of opium, morphine, heroin, cocaine, alcohol, chloral hydrate, or cannabis, is enacted.

1909 The Smoking Opium Exclusion Act, banning the importation, possession, or use of "smoking opium," is enacted; it is the first national law to ban a nonmedical substance. The Shanghai Opium Commission, the first international narcotics control conference, meets; it is presided over by the US chief delegate Charles Brent.

1911 *United States v. American Tobacco Company* breaks the ATC into four companies.

1912 Twelve nations agree to controls on the manufacture and export of opium and cocaine at The Hague International Opium Convention.

1914 The Harrison Act, regulating and taxing the production, importation, and distribution of opiates and coca products, is enacted.

1916 *United States v. Jin Fuey Moy* excuses physician Jin Fuey Moy from any wrongdoing in prescribing opiates to an addict. This decision is essentially overturned in Jin Fuey Moy's second time before the Supreme Court in 1920.

1918 The Native American Church is chartered in Oklahoma.

1920 The Eighteenth Amendment, prohibiting the manufacture and sale of alcohol, and the Volstead Act, carrying out its intent, go into effect.

1922 The Jones-Miller Act, or the Narcotic Drugs Import and Export Act, aimed at eliminating any recreational consumption of opiates and cocaine and tightly regulating the quality of drugs used for medical purposes, is enacted.

1925 The Geneva International Opium Convention cracks down further on opium production and imposes international controls over a wider range of drugs.

1929 Prices plummet at the New York Coffee Exchange; two weeks after, the stock market crashes.

1930 The Federal Bureau of Narcotics is formed; Harry Anslinger is appointed its first commissioner.

1931 Third Panama Canal Zone study of marijuana finds no evidence linking marijuana and delinquency.

1933 The Benzedrine inhaler is introduced by Smith, Kline & French.

The Eighteenth Amendment is repealed.

1935 Alcoholics Anonymous is founded.

1936 The Geneva Treaty urges all countries to create a "specialised police service" committed to "severely punishing, particularly by imprisonment or other penalties of deprivation of liberty" both trafficking and possession.

1937 The Marihuana Tax Act, taxing and regulating the sale of marijuana, is enacted.

1938 The federal Food, Drug, and Cosmetic Act, giving the Food and Drug Administration the authority to regulate food, drugs, medical devices, and cosmetics, is enacted.

1946 The UN Commission on Narcotic Drugs is created; it is

still today the central drug policy–making body of the
UN.

1950 Dexamyl is introduced by Smith, Kline & French.

1951 The Durham-Humphrey Amendment to the 1938 Food,
Drug, and Cosmetic Act, making a wide range of drugs
prescription-only, is adopted.

The Boggs Act, amending the 1922 Jones-Miller Act to
set mandatory sentences for drug convictions, is enacted.

1953 Allen Dulles authorizes Project MK-ULTRA.

1954 Thorazine is introduced by Smith, Kline & French.

1955 Miltown is introduced by Wallace.

Ritalin is introduced by Ciba (now Novartis).

1956 The Narcotic Control Act, providing heavier penalties
for drug offenders, is enacted.

1961 The Single Convention on Narcotic Drugs, an international treaty prohibiting the production of some drugs
and licensing others for medical treatment and research,
is adopted.

1962 Anslinger steps down as head of the FBN.

The International Coffee Agreement, protecting international coffee producers, is adopted.

The Kefauver-Harris Amendment, requiring drug developers to target specific diseases and prove the efficacy
(not simply the safety) of their products through randomized clinical trials (RCTs), is adopted.

1963 Valium is introduced by Hoffmann-La Roche.

The Community Mental Health Act, providing the first
federal assistance for local treatment of addiction, is
enacted.

1964 The surgeon general's report, *Smoking and Health*, concludes that cigarette smoking is a cause of lung cancer.

1965 The Drug Abuse Control Amendments, prohibiting the
illicit manufacture of stimulants and depressants, are
adopted.

The Federal Cigarette Labeling and Advertising Act,

requiring warning labels on all cigarette packaging, is enacted.

1966 California and Nevada both ban the manufacture, sale, or possession of LSD; many states soon follow suit.

The Narcotic Addict Rehabilitation Act, allowing for civil commitment for treatment rather than criminal prosecution, is enacted.

1968 The Bureau of Drug Abuse Control (BDAC) and the Federal Bureau of Narcotics (FBN) are merged into the Bureau of Narcotics and Dangerous Drugs (BNDD).

The Alcoholic and Narcotic Addict Rehabilitation Amendments, providing federal funding for treatment, rehabilitation, prevention, and education, are adopted.

1969 *Leary v. United States* declares the Marihuana Tax Act unconstitutional.

Operation Intercept cracks down on marijuana trafficking at the Mexican border.

1970 The Public Health Cigarette Smoking Act, banning cigarette advertising from radio and television, is enacted.

The Racketeer Influenced and Corrupt Organizations (RICO) Act, cracking down on organized crime, is enacted.

The Comprehensive Drug Abuse Prevention and Control Act, replacing all previous federal drug legislation and creating the modern schedule of controlled substances, with associated penalties, is enacted.

The National Organization for the Reform of Marijuana Laws (NORML) is founded.

1971 The Convention on Psychotropic Substances expands the scope of drugs covered by the 1961 Single Convention on Narcotic Drugs.

1972 The National Commission on Marihuana and Drug Abuse announces it is "of the unanimous opinion that marihuana use is not such a grave problem that individuals who smoke marihuana, and possess it for that purpose, should be subject to criminal procedures."

The Drug Abuse Office and Treatment Act, setting up federally funded programs for prevention and treatment, is enacted.

The French Connection is broken up.

1973 The Drug Enforcement Administration (DEA) is created, supplanting the BNDD.

1978 The Psychotropic Substances Act, stipulating mechanisms by which substances can be added to the schedule of controlled substances, is enacted.

1980 The third iteration of the *Diagnostic and Statistical Manual of Mental Disorders* is published, completing the biological revolution in psychiatry.

1981 The Posse Comitatus Act is amended, allowing military involvement in civilian law enforcement.

1982 The South Florida Task Force is formed to crack down on crime and cocaine smuggling.

1983 *Illinois v. Gates* allows police to get warrants based on anonymous tips.

1984 *United States v. Leon* allows evidence seized on the basis of a mistakenly issued search warrant to be introduced at trial.

The National Minimum Drinking Age Act raises the drinking age to twenty-one years old.

The Comprehensive Crime Control Act, increasing penalties on marijuana, expanding civil forfeiture, and creating mandatory minimums, is enacted.

1985 The DEA declares an emergency ban on MDMA.

1986 The Anti-Drug Abuse Act, increasing the use of mandatory minimums and creating the one-hundred-to-one crack-to-cocaine sentencing disparity, is enacted.

1987 *United States v. Salerno* rules that the Eighth Amendment does not guarantee the right to pretrial bail.

1988 Prozac is introduced by Eli Lilly.

"The National Defense Authorization Act of Fiscal Year 1989," charging the Defense Department with leading

the effort to detect drug traffic into the US and boosting
the military's drug enforcement activities and budget, is
enacted.

The Anti-Drug Abuse Act, creating the policy goal of a
drug-free America and establishing the Office of National
Drug Control Policy (ONDCP), is enacted.

The United Nations Convention Against Illicit Traffic
in Narcotic Drugs and Psychotropic Substances creates
additional mechanisms for enforcing the 1961 Single
Convention on Narcotic Drugs and the 1971 Convention
on Psychotropic Substances.

1989 The International Coffee Agreement collapses.

Operation Just Cause deposes Panamanian general
Manuel Noriega.

The CIA creates the Counter Narcotics Center.

1990 The Crime Control Act, regulating drug precursors,
allowing seizure of drug trafficker assets, and controlling
drug paraphernalia, among many other things, is enacted.

1991 *California v. Acevedo* permits police to conduct a warrant-
less search of containers in a car with probable cause.

Harmelin v. Michigan rules that severe mandatory penalties may be cruel, but not unusual, and thus not in violation
of the Eighth Amendment (the ruling pertained to a life
sentence for a first-time cocaine possession offense).

1992 The Prescription Drug User Fee Act, allowing the FDA
to collect fees from drug manufacturers, is enacted.

1993 Pablo Escobar is shot and killed.

1996 Adderall is introduced by Richwood (now Shire).

Clinton decertifies Colombia, making it ineligible for US aid.

OxyContin is introduced by Purdue.

California passes Proposition 215, allowing the use of
medical cannabis.

1997 The Drug-Free Communities Act, creating federal grants
for community organizations to reduce substance abuse,
is enacted.

The FDA suggests ways in which pharmaceutical advertisements could meet regulatory broadcast requirements, opening the door for direct-to-consumer advertising.

1998 The Amezcua brothers are arrested.

The Master Settlement Agreement, settling dozens of state lawsuits against tobacco companies, is reached.

2000 California passes Proposition 36, allowing probation and treatment for first-time nonviolent drug offenders in lieu of incarceration.

2003 The Illicit Drug Anti-Proliferation Act, prohibiting individuals from owning, managing, controlling, etc., any place used to sell, make, or use drugs, is enacted.

The Framework Convention on Tobacco Control, a WHO treaty intended to make clear the dangers of tobacco and limit its use, is adopted.

2006 *Gonzales v. O Centro Espírita Beneficente União do Vegetal* establishes that UDV's ayahuasca use is indeed an exercise of religious freedom.

The Combat Methamphetamine Epidemic Act (passed with the newly reauthorized PATRIOT Act), which increases criminal penalties for making, possessing, and distributing methamphetamine, is enacted.

2009 The Family Smoking Prevention and Tobacco Control Act, giving the FDA authority to regulate tobacco products, is enacted.

The Justice Department releases a memo suggesting that busting medical marijuana patients and businesses is a low priority.

2010 The Fair Sentencing Clarification Act, reducing the sentencing disparity between crack and cocaine from one hundred to one to eighteen to one, is enacted.

2012 Washington and Colorado legalize marijuana for recreational use; they are the first states to do so.

2017 El Chapo is extradited to the United States.

Acknowledgments

For help with research and editing, thank you to Ritika Anand, Chris Crawford, Kyle Delashmutt, Joshua Dubler, Thomas Field, Jorge Hernandez, Taylor Hines, Andrew Hudson, Sam Kriss, Melissa Naschek, Kiera Riley, and Elizabeth Whiteman. Thanks also to all the SPIs and the participants in the Historical Capitalisms and Social Theory workshop at the University of Chicago for reading and responding to drafts of previous chapters; to my students at Arizona State University for the enlightening conversations; to Barrett, the Honors College, the Center for Work and Democracy, and the Drescher Fund for institutional support; to editors at *The Outline* and *Current Affairs* for revisions to the coffee and cigarettes chapters, respectively; to Asher Dupuy-Spencer and everyone else at Verso and *Jacobin* for helping the book along; and finally to Alison, Jaya, Ziggy, and Noam for keeping my priorities straight.

Notes

Introduction

1 "Opioids: Perception of Pain," Minnesota Department of Health, health.state.mn.us; Brian J. Piper et al., "Trends in Use of Prescription Stimulants in the United States and Territories, 2006 to 2016," *PLoS One* 13, no. 11 (2018).

2 Alyssa Fowers and William Wan, "A Third of Americans Now Show Signs of Clinical Anxiety or Depression, Census Bureau Finds amid Coronavirus Pandemic," washingtonpost.com, May 26, 2020; Sara G. Miller, "1 in 6 Americans Takes a Psychiatric Drug," scientificamerican.com, December 13, 2016; *Depression and Other Common Mental Disorders: Global Health Estimates*, World Health Organization, 2017, apps.who.int.

3 Matej Mikulic, "Total Nominal Spending on Medicines in the U.S. from 2002 to 2019," *Statista*, August 18, 2020, statista.com; "Spending on Illicit Drugs in US nears $150 Billion Annually," *Science Daily*, August 20, 2019, sciencedaily.com.

4 "Long-Term Trends in Deaths of Despair," United States Congress Joint Economic Committee, September 5, 2019, jec.senate.gov.

5 *The Transatlantic Cocaine Market*, United Nations Office on Drugs and Crime, April 2011, unodc.org; that would be about $150 billion in 2022 dollars.

6 "Cures and Curses: A History of Pharmaceutical Advertising in America," University of Saint Augustine for Health Sciences, library .usa.edu.

7 Quoted in P. E. Caquet, *Opium's Orphans: The 200-Year History of the War on Drugs* (London: Reaktion Books, 2022), 131.

8 Mike Jay, *Emperors of Dreams: Drugs in the Nineteenth Century* (Sawtry: Dedalus, 2000), 221.

9 Echoes of our scare tactics can still be recognized all around the world. When President Rodrigo Duterte of the Philippines recently claimed that meth shrinks your brain, a "fact" used to justify his proud admission of "extrajudicial killings" of drug offenders, he cited the authority of an American forensic study; Howard Johnson and Christopher Giles, "Philippines Drug War: Do We Know How

Many Have Died?," bbc.com, November 12, 2019; Leila B. Salaverria, "Duterte Insists Shabu Can Cause Brain Damage," *Inquirer.net*, May 10, 2017, newsinfo.inquirer.net.

10 Richard Davenport-Hines, *The Pursuit of Oblivion: A Global History of Narcotics* (New York: W. W. Norton, 2004), 167; historian David Musto calls the American obsession with prohibiting narcotics the "American disease," David F. Musto, *The American Disease: Origins of Narcotic Control* (Oxford: Oxford University Press, 1999).

11 The chapters should not be confused for informational guides or collections of "straight facts" about different drugs. For those, see Cynthia Kuhn, Scott Swartzwelder, and Wilkie Wilson, *Buzzed: The Straight Facts About the Most Used and Abused Drugs from Alcohol to Ecstasy* (New York: W. W. Norton, 2014); Andrew Weil and Winifred Rosen, *From Chocolate to Morphine: Everything You Need to Know About Mind-Altering Drugs* (Boston: Mariner, 2004); Darryl S. Inaba and William E. Cohen, *Uppers, Downers, All Arounders: Physical and Mental Effects of Psychoactive Drugs*, 7th ed. (Medford, OR: CNS Productions, 2011).

12 Virginia Berridge, *Demons: Our Changing Attitudes to Alcohol, Tobacco, and Drugs* (Oxford: Oxford University Press, 2013), 15.

13 David T. Courtwright, *Forces of Habit: Drugs and the Making of the Modern World* (Cambridge, MA: Harvard University Press, 2001), 167; Mark Lawrence Schrad, "How Europe's Temperance Movement Saved Beer," *Foreign Policy*, September 26, 2021, foreignpolicy.com.

14 Courtwright, *Forces of Habit*, 178.

15 David Harvey, *The Condition of Postmodernity: An Enquiry into the Origins of Cultural Change* (Cambridge, MA: Blackwell, 1989), 135.

16 Suzanna Reiss, *We Sell Drugs: The Alchemy of US Empire* (Oakland: University of California Press, 2014).

17 David Herzberg, "Between the Free Market and the Drug War," in *The War on Drugs: A History*, ed. David Farber (New York: New York University Press, 2022), 274.

18 Quoted in Emily Dufton, *Grass Roots: The Rise and Fall and Rise of Marijuana in America* (New York: Basic Books, 2017), 49.

19 Cedric G. Johnson, "The Panthers Can't Save Us Now," *Catalyst* 1, no. 1 (Spring 2017): 82, 81.

20 John Clegg and Adaner Usmani, "The Economic Origins of Mass Incarceration," *Catalyst* 3, no. 3 (Fall 2019): 36.

21 Berridge, *Demons*, 214.

22 See Michael Shiner, *Drug Use and Social Change: The Distortion of History* (Basingstoke: Palgrave Macmillan, 2009), chap. 2, for a

discussion of the sociological debate on the normalization of drugs in postindustrial society.

23 Harvey, *The Condition of Postmodernity*, 133.

24 Karl Marx, *Capital: A Critique of Political Economy, Volume I*, trans. Ben Fowkes (Harmondsworth: Penguin Books, 1982), 503.

25 Benjamin Y. Fong and Melissa Naschek, "NGOism: The Politics of the Third Sector," *Catalyst* 5, no. 1 (Spring 2021); Robert D. Putnam, *Bowling Alone: The Collapse and Revival of American Community* (New York: Simon and Schuster, 2001).

26 It is thus too simple to say that drug consumption levels are straightforwardly a kind of social misery index, as they are determined by a wide range of factors, including what other drugs are on the market, technological advances, regulatory measures, their social uses, etc. American alcohol consumption was at its historical high *before* industrialization. Marijuana and psychotropics use bottomed out during the neoliberal period. But it's also hard not to see changing patterns of drug consumption (see appendix A) as rooted in broader shifts in regimes of capital accumulation.

27 Aldous Huxley, "A Treatise on Drugs," in *Moksha: Aldous Huxley's Classic Writings on Psychedelics and the Visionary Experience*, ed. Michael Horowitz and Cynthia Palmer (Rochester, VT: Park Street Press, 1999), 4.

28 Pierre-Arnaud Chouvy, *Opium: Uncovering the Politics of the Poppy* (Cambridge, MA: Harvard University Press, 2010), 1.

29 This is something of a simplification: coca, for instance, is often used in the context of ritual.

30 Edward Slingerland lays out the case for why "getting drunk, high, or otherwise cognitively altered must have, over evolutionary time, helped individuals to survive and flourish, and cultures to endure and expand" in *Drunk: How We Sipped, Danced, and Stumbled Our Way to Civilization* (New York: Little, Brown Spark, 2021), 11.

31 Mike Jay, "Why Do People Take Drugs," *International Journal of Drug Policy* 10, no. 1 (February 1999): 5–7; see *International Journal of Drug Policy* 19, no. 5 (October 2008) for an issue devoted to pleasure and drugs.

32 Theodore Roszak, *The Making of a Counter Culture: Reflections of the Technocratic Society and Its Youthful Opposition* (Garden City, NY: Anchor Books, 1969), 171.

33 Quoted in Jerrold Winter, *Our Love Affair with Drugs: The History, the Science, the Politics* (Oxford: Oxford University Press, 2020), 66.

34 Quoted in H. Wayne Morgan, *Drugs in America: A Social History, 1800–1980* (Syracuse: Syracuse University Press, 1981), 47.

35 Peter Andreas, *Killer High: A History of War in Six Drugs* (Oxford: Oxford University Press, 2020), 207.

36 Cf. Courtwright, *Forces of Habit*, chap. 7.

37 Alejandro Badel and Brian Greaney, "Exploring the Link between Drug Use and Job Status in the U.S.," Federal Reserve Bank of St. Louis, July 1, 2013, stlouisfed.org; Wilson M. Compton et al., "Unemployment and Substance Outcomes in the United States 2002–2010," *Drug and Alcohol Dependence* 142 (September 1, 2014).

38 Quoted in Johann Hari, *Chasing the Scream: The First and Last Days of the War on Drugs* (New York: Bloomsbury, 2015), 166.

39 C. Wright Mills, "The Competitive Personality," *Damage Magazine*, November 5, 2018, damagemag.com.

40 Inaba and Cohen, *Uppers, Downers, All Arounders*, 10.2.

41 See samhsa.gov.

42 Benjamin Y. Fong, Jeremy Cohan, and Moishe Postone, "Behind Our Backs, Part Two," *Damage Magazine*, January 21, 2019, damagemag.com.

43 See Benjamin Y. Fong and Scott Jenkins, "Society, Regression, Psychoanalysis, or 'Capitalism *Is* Responsible for Your Problems with Your Girlfriend': On the Use of Psychoanalysis in the Work of the Frankfurt School," *SAGE Handbook of Frankfurt School Critical Theory*, ed. Beverley Best, Werner Bonefeld, and Chris O'Kane (London: Sage Publications, 2018): 952–69.

44 Cf. Richard Wilkinson and Kate Pickett, *The Spirit Level: Why Greater Equality Makes Societies Stronger* (New York: Bloomsbury, 2010), chap. 5.

45 Philippe Bourgois, *In Search of Respect: Selling Crack in El Barrio* (Cambridge: Cambridge University Press, 2003), 326.

46 Sam Quinones, *Dreamland: The True Tale of America's Opiate Epidemic* (New York: Bloomsbury, 2015), 55.

47 Dominic Streatfeild, *Cocaine* (London: Virgin Books, 2005), 261.

48 Wendy Sawyer and Peter Wagner, "Mass Incarceration: The Whole Pie 2020," prisonpolicy.org, March 24, 2020; Enrique Desmond Arias and Thomas Grisaffi, "Introduction: The Moral Economy of the Cocaine Trade," in *Cocaine: From Coca Fields to the Streets*, ed. Enrique Desmond Arias and Thomas Grisaffi (Durham: Duke University Press, 2021), 10.

49 Bourgois, *In Search of Respect*, 24.

50 See Mark Thornton, *The Economics of Prohibition* (Auburn, AL: Mises Institute, 2014).

51 Mills, "The Competitive Personality."

52 Cf. Thomas Szasz, *Ceremonial Chemistry: The Ritual Persecution of Drugs, Addicts, and Pushers* (Garden City, NY: Anchor Press,

1974), 14; David T. Courtwright, *Dark Paradise: Opiate Addiction in America before 1940* (Cambridge, MA: Harvard University Press, 1982), 3; Troy Duster, *The Legislation of Morality: Law, Drugs, and Moral Judgment* (New York: Free Press, 1970), 247.

53 David Herzberg, *White Market Drugs: Big Pharma and the Hidden History of Addiction in America* (Chicago: University of Chicago Press, 2020), 17, 23.

54 This goes back to the beginning of the modern period: "Seventeenth-century texts relating to the drug trade are rich with epithets and slanders directed at the supposed deceitfulness of the members of what we might call this 'drug underground': empirics, cunning women, African healers, crypto-Jews. It is in this push and pull over the respectability, trustworthiness, and 'purity' of the drug seller that some of the first signs of a division between illicit and licit drugs begins to appear," Benjamin Breen, *The Age of Intoxication: Origins of the Global Drug Trade* (Philadelphia: University of Pennsylvania Press, 2019), 44.

55 Jack Shafer, "Crack Then. Meth Now.," slate.com, August 23, 2005.

56 Martin Torgoff, *Can't Find My Way Home: America in the Great Stoned Age, 1945–2000* (New York: Simon and Schuster, 2004), 320; Jill Jonnes, *Hep-Cats, Narcs, and Pipe Dreams: A History of America's Romance with Illegal Drugs* (New York: Scribner, 1996), 314.

57 Courtwright, *Forces of Habit*, 191; German Lopez, "The War on Drugs, Explained," vox.com, May 8, 2016.

58 Quoted in Davenport-Hines, *The Pursuit of Oblivion*, 366–7.

59 Alex Lockie, "Top Nixon Adviser Reveals the Racist Reason He Started the 'War on Drugs' Decades Ago," businessinsider.com, July 31, 2019.

60 Cf. Christina Jacqueline Johns, *Power, Ideology, and the War on Drugs: Nothing Succeeds Like Failure* (New York: Praeger, 1992), 57–8.

61 Cf. Kathleen J. Frydl, *The Drug Wars in America, 1940–1973* (Cambridge: Cambridge University Press, 2013), 2; cf. John Helmer, *Drugs and Minority Oppression* (New York: Seabury Press, 1975), 152.

62 Helmer, *Drugs and Minority Oppression*, 61.

63 Theodor W. Adorno, "Culture Industry Reconsidered," in *The Culture Industry: Selected Essays on Mass Culture*, ed. J. M. Bernstein (London: Routledge, 1991), 103.

1. Coffee, or the Serene Delight

1 Wolfgang Schivelbusch, *Tastes of Paradise: A Social History of Spices, Stimulants, and Intoxicants*, trans. David Jacobson (New York: Pantheon Books, 1992), 22.
2 Ibid., 23.
3 Jonathan Morris, *Coffee: A Global History* (London: Reaktion Books, 2019), 46.
4 Schivelbusch, *Tastes of Paradise*, 35.
5 Ibid., 48.
6 Ibid., 39.
7 David T. Courtwright, *Forces of Habit: Drugs and the Making of the Modern World* (Cambridge, MA: Harvard University Press, 2001), 19.
8 Quoted in Mark Pendergrast, *Uncommon Grounds: The History of Coffee and How It Transformed Our World* (New York: Basic Books, 2010), 143.
9 Ibid., 19–20.
10 Ibid., 23.
11 Nina Luttinger and Gregory Dicum, *The Coffee Book: Anatomy of an Industry from Crop to the Last Drop* (New York: New Press, 2006), 16.
12 William H. Ukers, *All about Coffee* (New York: The Tea and Coffee Trade Journal Company, 1922), 18; cf. Jeanette M. Fregulia, *A Rich and Tantalizing Brew: A History of How Coffee Connected the World* (Fayetteville: University of Arkansas Press, 2019), 120.
13 Brian Cowan, *The Social Life of Coffee: The Emergence of the British Coffeehouse* (New Haven, CT: Yale University Press, 2005), 79; Courtwright, *Forces of Habit*, 2; coffeehouses in America, the first of which appeared in 1669 in New York City, were largely modeled on their European counterparts. The "men living in the colonies who retained ties to England, France, and other parts of Europe were instrumental in the popularity of the coffeehouse on the other side of the ocean," Fregulia, *A Rich and Tantalizing Brew*, 147–8.
14 Cowan, *The Social Life of Coffee*, 228, 87.
15 Ibid., 225, 232–3.
16 Guy Faulconbridge and Kate Holton, "Update: Lloyd's of London Apologizes for Its 'Shameful' Role in Atlantic Slave Trade," *Insurance Journal*, June 18, 2020, insurancejournal.com.
17 Luttinger and Dicum, *The Coffee Book*, 28; Philippe Girard, *Paradise Lost: Haiti's Tumultuous Journey from Pearl of the Caribbean to Third World Hotspot* (New York: Palgrave Macmillan, 2005),

22; Eric Williams, *From Columbus to Castro: The History of the Caribbean, 1492–1969* (New York: Vintage Books, 1984), 245.

18 Girard, *Paradise Lost*, 22.

19 Quoted in Williams, *From Columbus to Castro*, 191.

20 Morris, *Coffee*, 88–9.

21 Heinrich Eduard Jacob, *Coffee: The Epic of a Commodity*, trans. Eden Paul and Cedar Paul (Short Hills, NJ: Burford Books, 1998), 103; Luttinger and Dicum, *The Coffee Book*, 29.

22 Quoted in Robert Edgar Conrad, *The Destruction of Brazilian Slavery, 1850–1888* (Berkeley: University of California Press, 1972), 48.

23 Morris, *Coffee*, 104.

24 Jacob, *Coffee*, 225.

25 Robert C. Tucker, ed., *The Marx-Engels Reader* (New York: W. W. Norton, 1978), 417.

26 Pendergrast, *Uncommon Grounds*, 161.

27 Ibid., 163.

28 Quoted in ibid., 166.

29 Ibid., 171.

30 Luttinger and Dicum, *The Coffee Book*, 137.

31 Morris, *Coffee*, 113.

32 Luttinger and Dicum, *The Coffee Book*, 83.

33 Quoted in ibid., 85.

34 Quoted in ibid., 86.

35 Pendergrast, *Uncommon Grounds*, 146, 211.

36 Quoted in Luttinger and Dicum, *The Coffee Book*, 92.

37 Pendergrast, *Uncommon Grounds*, 220.

38 Quoted in Robert W. Thurston, "The Long Debate over Coffee and Health," in *Coffee: A Comprehensive Guide to the Bean, the Beverage, and the Industry*, ed. Robert W. Thurston, Jonathan Morris, and Shawn Steiman (Lanham: Rowman and Littlefield, 2013), 344.

39 Quoted in Cowan, *The Social Life of Coffee*, 42.

40 Quoted in Luttinger and Dicum, *The Coffee Book*, 19.

41 Schivelbusch, *Tastes of Paradise*, 37; Morris, *Coffee*, 73.

42 Alecia Swasy, *Soap Opera: The Inside Story of Procter & Gamble* (New York: Touchstone Books, 1993), 118.

43 Jean C. Buzby and Stephen Haley, "Coffee Consumption over the Last Century," USDA Economic Research Service, June 1, 2007, ers.usda.gov.

44 Quoted in Pendergrast, *Uncommon Grounds*, 199.

45 Luttinger and Dicum, *The Coffee Book*, 156.

46 Ibid., 170.

47 Benoit Daviron and Stefano Ponte, *The Coffee Paradox: Global Markets, Commodity Trade, and the Elusive Promise of*

Development (London: Zed Books, 2005), 37.

48 Luttinger and Dicum, *The Coffee Book*, 168.

49 Morris, *Coffee*, 28.

50 Pendergrast, *Uncommon Grounds*, 328.

51 Nick Brown, "A Brief History of Coffee Price Volatility in the Modern Era (1963–2013)," *Daily Coffee News*, October 6, 2014, dailycoffeenews.com.

52 Morris, *Coffee*, 149.

53 Luttinger and Dicum, *The Coffee Book*, 107.

54 Ibid., 108.

55 Ibid., 131.

56 Ray Oldenburg, *The Great Good Place: Cafes, Coffee Shops, Bookstores, Bars, Hair Salons, and Other Hangouts at the Heart of a Community* (New York: Marlowe, 1999).

57 Quoted in Luttinger and Dicum, *The Coffee Book*, 11.

58 Harriet Agerholm, "Coffee Could Be Extinct by 2080 Due to Climate Change Destroying Areas Suitable for Growing Beans," independent.co.uk, September 5, 2016.

59 Luttinger and Dicum, *The Coffee Book*, 38.

2. Cigarettes, or Knowledge Is Not Power

1 Jason Hughes, *Learning to Smoke: Tobacco Use in the West* (Chicago: University of Chicago Press, 2003), 109.

2 Industry documents joke that smoking is "the major cause of statistics," quoted in Robert N. Proctor, *Golden Holocaust: Origins of the Cigarette Catastrophe and the Case for Abolition* (Berkeley: University of California Press, 2011), 2.

3 Allan M. Brandt, *The Cigarette Century: The Rise, Fall, and Deadly Persistence of the Product That Defined America* (New York: Basic Books, 2007), 12.

4 Proctor, *Golden Holocaust*, 561.

5 Sidney Mintz, *Sweetness and Power: The Place of Sugar in Modern History* (New York: Penguin Books, 1985), 185.

6 Wolfgang Schivelbusch, *Tastes of Paradise: A Social History of Spices, Stimulants, and Intoxicants*, trans. David Jacobson (New York: Pantheon Books, 1992), 111.

7 A third might be considered the cardboard matchbook, invented in 1892.

8 Gary S. Cross and Robert N. Proctor, *Packaged Pleasures: How Technology and Marketing Revolutionized Desire* (Chicago: University of Chicago Press, 2014), 62, 79; for most of human history,

tobacco was drawn only into the mouth and nose, not the lungs, Proctor, *Golden Holocaust*, 32.

9 Cross and Proctor, *Packaged Pleasures*, 80.

10 Ibid., 71.

11 Ibid., 72.

12 Brandt, *The Cigarette Century*, 53.

13 Cassandra Tate, *Cigarette Wars: The Triumph of "The Little White Slaver"* (Oxford: Oxford University Press, 1999), 66.

14 Quoted in Proctor, *Golden Holocaust*, 44.

15 Tate, *Cigarette Wars*, 84–5.

16 Quoted in ibid., 153.

17 Brandt, *The Cigarette Century*, 98.

18 Quoted in Tate, *Cigarette Wars*, 99.

19 Adam Curtis, "Happiness Machines," *The Century of the Self* (London: BBC, 2002).

20 Quoted in Brandt, *The Cigarette Century*, 67.

21 Sarah Milov, *The Cigarette: A Political History* (Cambridge, MA: Harvard University Press, 2019), 72.

22 Ibid., 387.

23 Ibid., 37, 96; Virginia Berridge cautions against attributing too much power to advertising and the media, ostensibly to uplift the "voice of the consumer" and the complex ways in which consumer habits, culture, and industry efforts collide. Along with Brandt, I have fewer reservations about describing the cigarette boom as a kind of mass indoctrination, Virginia Berridge, *Demons: Our Changing Attitudes to Alcohol, Tobacco, and Drugs* (Oxford: Oxford University Press, 2013), 151–3.

24 David T. Courtwright, *Forces of Habit: Drugs and the Making of the Modern World* (Cambridge, MA: Harvard University Press, 2001), 18.

25 Quoted in Brandt, *The Cigarette Century*, 79.

26 Richard Kluger, *Ashes to Ashes: America's Hundred-Year Cigarette War, the Public Health, and the Unabashed Triumph of Philip Morris* (New York: Alfred A. Knopf, 1996), 105.

27 Ibid., 294; Brandt, *The Cigarette Century*, 73.

28 Ibid., 156.

29 Proctor, *Golden Holocaust*, 343.

30 Quoted in ibid., 340.

31 Ibid., 355.

32 "As Imperial Tobacco once confided to the Tobacco Institute, 'Research must go on and on,'" quoted in ibid., 263.

33 "A Frank Statement to Cigarette Smokers," Campaign for Tobacco-Free Kids, tobaccofreekids.org.

34 Brandt, *The Cigarette Century*, 204.

35 Jonathan M. Samet, "Epidemiology and the Tobacco Epidemic: How Research on Tobacco and Health Shaped Epidemiology," *American Journal of Epidemiology* 183, no. 5 (March 2016): 394–402.

36 Quoted in Proctor, *Golden Holocaust*, 289.

37 Brandt, *The Cigarette Century*, 241.

38 Ibid., 256.

39 Ibid., 347.

40 Jerrold Winter, *Our Love Affair with Drugs: The History, the Science, the Politics* (Oxford: Oxford University Press, 2020), 7.

41 Brandt, *The Cigarette Century*, 320.

42 Quoted in Proctor, *Golden Holocaust*, 332.

43 Quoted in Kluger, *Ashes to Ashes*, 510.

44 Brandt, *The Cigarette Century*, 330.

45 Ibid., 369.

46 Mark Landler, "The Media Business; ABC News Settles Suits on Tobacco," nytimes.com, August 22, 1995.

47 Brandt, *The Cigarette Century*, 380.

48 Ibid., 383.

49 Carrick Mollenkamp et al., "The People vs. Big Tobacco: How the States Took On the Cigarette Giants," Bloomberg Press, 1998, archive.nytimes.com.

50 Brandt, *The Cigarette Century*, 427.

51 Ibid., 434–5.

52 Thomas Farragher, "Most States Use Tobacco Payout to Balance Budgets," *SFGATE*, August 12, 2001, sfgate.com.

53 Erich Goode, *Drugs in American Society*, 9th ed. (New York: McGraw Hill, 2015), 241; about 40 percent of the population smoked at the time, which means that number is about 10,000 cigarettes consumed annually per smoker (more than 27 cigarettes per smoker per day); Lydia Saad, "U.S. Smoking Rate Still Coming Down," news.gallup.com, July 24, 2008.

54 Wikipedia, "Tobacco Consumption by Country," en.wikipedia.org.

55 Milov, *The Cigarette*, chap. 5.

56 Brandt, *The Cigarette Century*, 470.

57 Berridge, *Demons*, 169.

58 Courtwright, *Forces of Habit*, 206.

59 US Department of Health and Human Services, *The Health Consequences of Smoking—50 Years of Progress: A Report of the Surgeon General* (Atlanta: Centers for Disease Control and Prevention, 2014), ncbi.nlm.nih.gov.

60 "The Toll of Tobacco in the United States," Campaign for Tobacco-Free Kids, tobaccofreekids.org; my italics.

61 Brandt, *The Cigarette Century*, 450.

62 "Making Cigarettes," Philip Morris International, pmi.com.

63 Brandt, *The Cigarette Century*, 460.

64 Glenn Frankel, "Thailand Resists U.S. Brand Assault," washington post.com, November 18, 1996.

65 Quoted in Kluger, *Ashes to Ashes*, 714.

66 Brandt, *The Cigarette Century*, 474.

67 "The Global Tobacco Control Treaty Has Reduced Smoking Rates in Its First Decade, but More Work Is Needed," *Lancet*, March 22, 2017, sciencedaily.com.

68 Quoted in Brandt, *The Cigarette Century*, 484.

69 Shannon Gravely et al., "Implementation of Key Demand-Reduction Measures of the WHO Framework Convention on Tobacco Control and Change in Smoking Prevalence in 126 Countries: An Association Study," *Lancet* 2, no. 4 (April 1, 2017).

70 Nan Enstad, *Cigarettes, Inc.: An Intimate History of Corporate Imperialism* (Chicago: University of Chicago Press, 2018), 266.

71 Brandt, *The Cigarette Century*, 487.

72 Schivelbusch, *Tastes of Paradise*, 129.

73 Oscar Wilde, *The Picture of Dorian Gray* (New York: Penguin Books, 2003), 77.

74 Richard Klein, *Cigarettes Are Sublime* (Durham: Duke University Press, 1993), 1.

75 Ibid., 16.

76 Jean-Paul Sartre, *Being and Nothingness: A Phenomenological Essay on Ontology*, trans. Hazel E. Barnes (New York: Washington Square Press, 1992), 761; my italics.

77 "Maybe the Marlboro cowboy knew [the perils of smoking], too, but indulged nonetheless, fatalistically, as if in possession of the core secret of the great happy hunting ground he roamed: Life is a terminal disease," Kluger, *Ashes to Ashes*, 297.

3. Alcohol, or Commodity Fetishism

1 Wolfgang Schivelbusch, *Tastes of Paradise: A Social History of Spices, Stimulants, and Intoxicants*, trans. David Jacobson (New York: Pantheon Books, 1992), 22.

2 Mark Edward Lender and James Kirby Martin, *Drinking in America: A History*, rev. and expanded ed. (New York: Free Press, 1987), 10.

3 Susan Cheever, *Drinking in America: Our Secret History* (New York: Hachette Book Group, 2015), 40.

4 In Barr's telling, "The Indians assumed that alcoholic drinks served

the same purpose as hallucinogenic plants and tobacco, and treated them in the same way. They imagined that they were possessed of magical powers, which would be made available to the drinker only if he consumed them in sufficient quantity to fall entirely under their influence. The Indians therefore drank spirits, not by the shot, but by the bottle," Andrew Barr, *Drink: A Social History of America* (New York: Carroll and Graf, 1999), 6.

5 W. J. Rorabaugh, *The Alcoholic Republic: An American Tradition* (Oxford: Oxford University Press, 1979), 74.

6 Lender and Martin, *Drinking in America*, 53.

7 Quoted in Barr, *Drink*, 375.

8 Marcel Mauss, *The Gift: The Form and Reason for Exchange in Archaic Societies*, trans. W. D. Halls (New York: W. W. Norton, 2000).

9 John J. Rumbarger, *Profits, Power, and Prohibition: Alcohol Reform and the Industrializing of America, 1800–1930* (Albany: State University of New York Press, 1989), chap. 1.

10 Quoted in ibid., 38–9.

11 Quoted in Maureen Ogle, *Ambitious Brew: The Story of American Beer* (Orlando: Harcourt, 2006), 25.

12 Quoted in Amy Mittelman, *Brewing Battles: A History of American Beer* (New York: Algora Publishing, 2008), 51.

13 Harry Gene Levine, "The Alcohol Problem in America: From Temperance to Alcoholism," *British Journal of Addiction* 79 (1984): 113.

14 Ryan Grim, *This Is Your Country on Drugs: The Secret History of Getting High in America* (Hoboken: John Wiley and Sons, 2009), 24; Rockefeller Jr. would later reluctantly join the repeal forces and offer one of those veiled critiques of capitalism that only the history of drugs has to offer: "Only as the profit motive is eliminated is there any hope of controlling the liquor traffic in the interest of a decent society," quoted in John C. Burnham, *Bad Habits: Drinking, Smoking, Taking Drugs, Gambling, Sexual Misbehavior, and Swearing in American History* (New York: New York University Press, 1993), 64.

15 Schivelbusch, *Tastes of Paradise*, 149.

16 Rorabaugh, *The Alcoholic Republic*, 131.

17 Quoted in Schivelbusch, *Tastes of Paradise*, 149, 152; cf. Merrill Singer, "Toward a Political-Economy of Alcoholism: The Missing Link in the Anthropology of Drinking," *Social Science and Medicine* 23, no. 2 (1986): 113–30.

18 Rumbarger has been criticized for overemphasizing the role of the capitalist class in driving the temperance movement; William J. Rorabaugh, "Review of *Profits, Power, and Prohibition: Alcohol Reform and the Industrializing of America, 1800–1930* by John J.

Rumbarger," *Journal of Southern History* 57, no. 2 (1991): 321–2; my claim here is not, however, that Prohibition was ultimately the machination of the business elite, but rather, in Harry G. Levine's reformulation of one of Rumbarger's theses, that "temperance ideas functioned as a very effective procapitalist ideology," and that the broad structural transformation of American society lay at the roots of temperance's moral power, Harry G. Levine, "Preface," in Rumbarger, *Profits, Power, and Prohibition*, xiii.

19 Rumbarger, *Profits, Power, and Prohibition*, 186.

20 Quoted in Lisa McGirr, *The War on Alcohol: Prohibition and the Rise of the American State* (New York: W. W. Norton, 2016), 29.

21 Iain Gately, *Drink: A Cultural History of Alcohol* (New York: Gotham Books, 2008), 248; the principle was first demonstrated by the chemist William Thomas Brande in 1811.

22 Ibid., 425.

23 Barr, *Drink*, 214.

24 Quoted in ibid., 207.

25 Rod Phillips, *Alcohol: A History* (Chapel Hill: University of North Carolina Press, 2014), 322.

26 Gately, *Drink*, 344, 346.

27 Ibid., 369.

28 Ibid., 317.

29 According to Sharon Salinger, taverns became more stratified in the eighteenth century, eventually giving way to upper-class hotels on the one hand, and lower-class saloons on the other. "During most of the colonial period in the port city, the rich drank alongside the poor and Congregationalists imbibed with Anglicans. In the second half of the eighteenth century, a distinctive stratification and specialization of tavern culture gradually emerged. Men drank and conversed only with those from the same socioeconomic stratum," Sharon V. Salinger, *Taverns and Drinking in Early America* (Baltimore: Johns Hopkins University Press, 2002), 5.

30 Madelon Powers, *Faces along the Bar: Lore and Order in the Workingman's Saloon, 1870–1920* (Chicago: University of Chicago Press, 1999), 70.

31 Schivelbusch, *Tastes of Paradise*, 202.

32 Gately, *Drink*, 319; like the coffeehouse, the saloon was also seen as a hangout of political radicals: one observer noted of the "working man's club": "The names of Karl Marx and leaders of social and political thought are often heard here," quoted in Rumbarger, *Profits, Power, and Prohibition*, 117.

33 Elaine Frantz Parsons, *Manhood Lost: Fallen Drunkards and Redeeming Women in the Nineteenth-Century United States* (Baltimore: Johns Hopkins University Press, 2009).

34 Ibid., 56.
35 Joseph R. Gusfield, *Symbolic Crusade: Status Politics and the American Temperance Movement* (Urbana: University of Illinois Press, 1963), 110.
36 Quoted in ibid., 100.
37 McGirr, *The War on Alcohol*, xvii, 12.
38 Roy Rosenzweig, *Eight Hours for What We Will: Workers and Leisure in an Industrial City, 1870–1920* (Cambridge: Cambridge University Press, 1983), 53.
39 Quoted in Mittelman, *Brewing Battles*, 51.
40 McGirr, *The War on Alcohol*, 46.
41 Quoted in Rumbarger, *Profits, Power, and Prohibition*, 124.
42 Edward Behr, *Prohibition: Thirteen Years That Changed America* (New York: Arcade Publishing, 1996), 46.
43 Gusfield, *Symbolic Crusade*, 108.
44 Barr, *Drink*, 135.
45 Political scientist Mark Lawrence Schrad believes railing against the liquor traffic was the equivalent of attacking Big Pharma today, Mark Lawrence Schrad, *Smashing the Liquor Machine: A Global History of Prohibition* (Oxford: Oxford University Press, 2021), 16.
46 Genevieve M. Ames, "American Beliefs about Alcoholism: Historical Perspectives on the Medical-Moral Controversy," in *The American Experience with Alcohol: Contrasting Cultural Perspectives*, ed. Linda A. Bennett and Genevieve M. Ames (New York: Plenum Press, 1985), 31.
47 Rumbarger, *Profits, Power, and Prohibition*, 175.
48 W. J. Rorabaugh, *Prohibition: A Very Short Introduction* (Oxford: Oxford University Press, 2020), 49.
49 Barr, *Drink*, 212.
50 Lender and Martin, *Drinking in America*, 129; Behr, *Prohibition*, 60.
51 Quoted in Barr, *Drink*, 332.
52 Gately, *Drink*, 373.
53 Quoted in Antonio Escohotado, *A Brief History of Drugs: From the Stone Age to the Stoned Age*, trans. Kenneth A. Symington (Rochester: Park Street Press, 1999), 82.
54 Barr, *Drink*, 113.
55 Mark Forsyth, *A Short History of Drunkenness: How, Why, Where, and When Humankind Has Gotten Merry from the Stone Age to the Present* (New York: Three Rivers Press, 2017), 220–1.
56 McGirr, *The War on Alcohol*, 71.
57 Ibid., 122.
58 Ibid., 133.

59 Ibid., 69.
60 Ibid., 202–4.
61 Ibid., 216.
62 Barr, *Drink*, 239.
63 Gately, *Drink*, 375, 395.
64 Quoted in Barr, *Drink*, 239.
65 Quoted in ibid., 239.
66 Lender and Martin, *Drinking in America*, 161.
67 Gusfield, *Symbolic Crusade*, 128; "Tax revenues had fallen to $1.5 billion in 1932—the lowest collection since 1917; following Repeal they began to rise. In the first six months that legal 3.2 beer was available, Americans drank 7,037,969,264 eight-ounce glasses. This gave the government $84,917,539 in revenue," Mittelman, *Brewing Battles*, 100.
68 Quoted in Lender and Martin, *Drinking in America*, 156.
69 Gately, *Drink*, 380.
70 Lender and Martin, *Drinking in America*, 152.
71 Ibid., 166.
72 Ames, "American Beliefs about Alcoholism," 33.
73 Robert Hullot-Kentor, "A New Type of Human Being and Who We Really Are," *Brooklyn Rail*, November 10, 2008, brooklynrail.org.
74 Harry G. Levine, "The Discovery of Addiction: Changing Conceptions of Habitual Drunkenness in America," *Journal of Studies on Alcohol* 39, no. 1 (1978): 165.
75 Ibid., 162.
76 Quoted in Oakley S. Ray, *Drugs, Society, and Human Behavior* (Saint Louis: C. V. Mosby, 1972), 78.
77 Cf. Mittelman, *Brewing Battles*, 177.
78 Barr, *Drink*, 71.
79 Ibid., 95.
80 "US Wine Consumption," Wine Institute, wineinstitute.org.
81 Burnham, *Bad Habits*, 56.
82 "Chronology of the American Brewing Industry," beerhistory.com.
83 Barr, *Drink*, 269.
84 Ibid., 266.
85 Gately, *Drink*, 492.
86 Burnham, *Bad Habits*, 81.
87 Rorabaugh, *The Alcoholic Republic*, 151; cf. Barr, *Drink*, 370.
88 Rorabaugh, *The Alcoholic Republic*, 151.
89 Ibid., 200–1.
90 Karl Marx, *Capital: A Critique of Political Economy, Volume I*, trans. Ben Fowkes (New York: Penguin Books, 1976), 165.
91 Marianna Adler, "From Symbolic Exchange to Commodity Consumption: Anthropological Notes on Drinking as a Symbolic

Practice," in *Drinking: Behavior and Belief in Modern History*, ed. Susanna Barrows and Robin Room (Berkeley: University of California Press, 1991), 379.

92 Rorabaugh, *The Alcoholic Republic*, 151.

93 Michael T. Taussig, *The Devil and Commodity Fetishism in South America* (Chapel Hill: University of North Carolina Press, 2010), 37.

4. Opiates, or Civilizing the Orient

1 Opium was referred to as "God's Own Medicine" in the nineteenth century, Arnold S. Trebach, *The Heroin Solution* (New Haven: Yale University Press, 1982), 38.

2 Following Sam Quinones's convention in *Dreamland*, I've chosen to use the word "opiate" to describe all opium derivatives (including morphine and heroin) as well as synthetic drugs that resemble morphine in their effects (often called opioids).

3 The Velvet Underground, "Heroin," *The Velvet Underground & Nico*, Verve Records, 1967.

4 Jill Jonnes, "Hip to Be High: Heroin and Popular Culture in the Twentieth Century," in *One Hundred Years of Heroin*, ed. David F. Musto (Westport, CT: Auburn House, 2002), 229.

5 Quoted in Richard Davenport-Hines, *The Pursuit of Oblivion: A Global History of Narcotics* (New York: W. W. Norton, 2004), 47.

6 Martin Booth, *Opium: A History* (New York: St. Martin's Griffin, 1996), 115.

7 Peter Andreas, *Killer High: A History of War in Six Drugs* (Oxford: Oxford University Press, 2020), 145.

8 Quoted in Booth, *Opium*, 145.

9 Andreas, *Killer High*, 147.

10 Quoted in Booth, *Opium*, 166.

11 Mike Jay, *Emperors of Dreams: Drugs in the Nineteenth Century* (Sawtry: Dedalus, 2000), 71; Virginia Berridge, *Demons: Our Changing Attitudes to Alcohol, Tobacco, and Drugs* (Oxford: Oxford University Press, 2013), 122; Richard K. Newman, "Opium Smoking in Late Imperial China: A Reconsideration," *Modern Asian Studies* 29, no. 4 (October 1995): 765–94.

12 Quoted in H. Wayne Morgan, *Drugs in America: A Social History, 1800–1980* (Syracuse: Syracuse University Press, 1981), 50.

13 Davenport-Hines, *The Pursuit of Oblivion*, 54.

14 Ibid., 61.

15 Quoted in Booth, *Opium*, 36.

16 Wolfgang Schivelbusch, *Tastes of Paradise: A Social History of Spices, Stimulants, and Intoxicants*, trans. David Jacobson (New York: Pantheon Books, 1992), 210.

17 Thomas De Quincey, *Confessions of an English Opium-Eater and Other Writings* (Oxford: Oxford University Press, 2013), 39.

18 Jay, *Emperors of Dreams*, 62, 65.

19 Schivelbusch, *Tastes of Paradise*, 206; De Quincey himself observed that workers at Manchester cotton manufacturers "were rapidly getting into the practice of opium-eating; so much so, that on a Saturday afternoon the counters of the druggists were strewed with pills of one, two, or three grains, in preparation for the known demand of the evening," quoted in Benjamin Breen, *The Age of Intoxication: Origins of the Global Drug Trade* (Philadelphia: University of Pennsylvania Press, 2019), 174.

20 Mother Bailey's Quieting Syrup was sold for $0.25 in 1868 (roughly $5 today).

21 Sertürner was in fact the first person to isolate an alkaloid (the term given by K. F. W. Meissner for nitrogenous organic compounds derived from crude drug sources), and his method was later applied to isolate other drugs like codeine, quinine, scopolamine, atropine, and caffeine, Ronald D. Mann, *Modern Drug Use: An Enquiry on Historical Principles* (Lancaster: MTP Press, 1984), 471.

22 Wood and others were the victims of a false linguistic inference: drug addiction was understood in terms of "appetite" in the nineteenth century, and they assumed that the avoidance of ingestion that injection offered would create no addiction.

23 Thomas Dormandy, *Opium: Reality's Dark Dream* (New Haven: Yale University Press, 2012), 196.

24 Julian Durlacher, *Heroin: Its History and Lore* (London: Carlton Books, 2000), 17.

25 Quoted in Davenport-Hines, *The Pursuit of Oblivion*, 83; David T. Courtwright, *Dark Paradise: Opiate Addiction in America before 1940* (Cambridge, MA: Harvard University Press, 1982), 73.

26 Quoted in Davenport-Hines, *The Pursuit of Oblivion*, 112; cf. Diana L. Ahmad, *The Opium Debate and Chinese Exclusion Laws in the Nineteenth-Century American West* (Reno: University of Nevada Press, 2007).

27 Quoted in Davenport-Hines, *The Pursuit of Oblivion*, 125.

28 Quoted in Booth, *Opium*, 178.

29 Quoted in Davenport-Hines, *The Pursuit of Oblivion*, 204.

30 Dormandy, *Opium*, 205.

31 Quoted in Davenport-Hines, *The Pursuit of Oblivion*, 209.

32 William B. McAllister, *Drug Diplomacy in the Twentieth Century: An International History* (London: Routledge, 2000), 100.

33 Mike Gray, *Drug Crazy: How We Got into This Mess and How We Can Get Out* (New York: Routledge, 2000), 50.

34 Andrew Barr, *Drink: A Social History of America* (New York: Carroll and Graf, 1999), 12.

35 Booth, *Opium*, 202.

36 Dormandy, *Opium*, 240; "During the early 1920s a number of New York City addicts supported themselves by picking through industrial dumps for scraps of copper, lead, zinc, and iron, which they collected in a wagon and then sold to a dealer. Junkie, in its original sense, literally meant *junkman*," Courtwright, *Dark Paradise*, 113.

37 Tim Newark, *The Mafia at War: Allied Collusion with the Mob* (London: Greenhill Books, 2007).

38 McAllister, *Drug Diplomacy*, 147; Anslinger worked for the Office of Strategic Services, the predecessor of the CIA.

39 Quoted in Eric C. Schneider, *Smack: Heroin and the American City* (Philadelphia: University of Pennsylvania Press, 2008), 68; cf. Jill Jonnes, *Hep-Cats, Narcs, and Pipe Dreams: A History of America's Romance with Illegal Drugs* (New York: Scribner, 1996), 176.

40 Douglas Valentine, *The Strength of the Wolf: The Secret History of America's War on Drugs* (Douglas Valentine, 2018), 67.

41 Ibid., 62.

42 Schneider, *Smack*, 57, 74.

43 Suzanna Reiss, *We Sell Drugs: The Alchemy of US Empire* (Oakland: University of California Press, 2014), 97.

44 Gray, *Drug Crazy*, 75.

45 Valentine, *The Strength of the Wolf*, 261.

46 Jonnes, *Hep-Cats, Narcs, and Pipe Dreams*, 197

47 Johann Hari, *Chasing the Scream: The First and Last Days of the War on Drugs* (New York: Bloomsbury, 2015), 298.

48 Jonnes, *Hep-Cats, Narcs, and Pipe Dreams*, 197.

49 Schneider, *Smack*, 99, 102.

50 Elliott Currie, *Reckoning: Drugs, the Cities, and the American Future* (New York: Hill and Wang, 1993), 67.

51 Schneider, *Smack*, ix.

52 Booth, *Opium*, 204.

53 Gray, *Drug Crazy*, 95.

54 Kathleen J. Frydl, *The Drug Wars in America, 1940–1973* (Cambridge: Cambridge University Press, 2013), 315–16.

55 Schneider, *Smack*, 124; quoted in Andreas, *Killer High*, 168.

56 Ibid., 167; see also Jeremy Kuzmarov, *The Myth of the Addicted Army: Vietnam and the Modern War on Drugs* (Amherst: University of Massachusetts Press, 2009).

57 Andreas, *Killer High*, 169; Davenport-Hines, *The Pursuit of Oblivion*, 429; Christopher Caldwell, "American Carnage: The New

NOTES FROM PAGES 89 TO 93

Landscape of Opioid Addiction," *First Things*, April 2017, first things.com.

58 Jonnes, *Hep-Cats, Narcs, and Pipe Dreams*, 281.

59 Booth, *Opium*, 264.

60 P. E. Caquet, *Opium's Orphans: The 200-Year History of the War on Drugs* (London: Reaktion Books, 2022), 241.

61 See Alfred W. McCoy, *The Politics of Heroin: CIA Complicity in the Global Drug Trade* (Chicago: Lawrence Hill Books, 2003).

62 See Alexander Cockburn and Jeffrey St. Clair, *Whiteout: The CIA, Drugs and the Press* (London: Verso, 1999), chap. 10.

63 Antonio Escohotado, *A Brief History of Drugs: From the Stone Age to the Stoned Age*, trans. Kenneth A. Symington (Rochester: Park Street Press, 1999), 155; it's been alleged that the Shakarchi Trading Company, for instance, cleaned $25 million for the CIA en route to the Mujaheddin, Booth, *Opium*, 338.

64 Cf. Pierre-Arnaud Chouvy, *Opium: Uncovering the Politics of the Poppy* (Cambridge, MA: Harvard University Press, 2010), 95.

65 Stuart Taylor Jr., "Is the Battle against Crime Mostly a War of Words?," nytimes.com, January 9, 1983.

66 Arnold H. Lubasch, "U.S. Attorney to Stress Fight Against Heroin," nytimes.com, July 3, 1983.

67 Leslie Maitland Werner, "Crime Panel Told of Cocaine Abuse," nytimes.com, November 28, 1984.

68 Dan Baum, *Smoke and Mirrors: The War on Drugs and the Politics of Failure* (Boston: Little, Brown, 1996), 203–4.

69 Branko Marcetic, "Joe Biden Was a Leader in Building Up the Carceral State," *Jacobin*, February 26, 2020; Biden's stance here has been extremely consistent. Later, criticizing George H. W. Bush for being soft, Biden asserted that we needed a *real* war on drugs: "We need another D-Day. Instead you're giving us another Vietnam: a limited war, fought on the cheap, financed on the sly, with no clear objectives, and ultimately destined for stalemate and human tragedy," quoted in David Farber, *Crack: Rock Cocaine, Street Capitalism, and the Decade of Greed* (Cambridge: Cambridge University Press, 2019), 147.

70 Baum, *Smoke and Mirrors*, 202; cf. Michelle Alexander, *The New Jim Crow: Mass Incarceration in the Age of Colorblindness* (New York: New Press, 2010), 62.

71 Baum, *Smoke and Mirrors*, 203.

72 Cf. Steven Wisotsky, "Crackdown: The Emerging Drug Exception to the Bill of Rights," *Hastings Law Journal* 38, no. 5 (1987): 889–926.

73 Ryan Grim, *This Is Your Country on Drugs: The Secret History of Getting High in America* (Hoboken: John Wiley and Sons, 2009), 76; Cockburn and St. Clair, *Whiteout*, 261; Jennifer Robison,

"Decades of Drug Use: The '80s and '90s," news.gallup.com, July 9, 2002; Arline Kaplan, "Resurgence of Illicit Drug Use in '90s Poses Challenge for Physicians," *Psychiatric Times* 15, no. 4 (April 1, 1998).

74 Sam Quinones, *Dreamland: The True Tale of America's Opiate Epidemic* (New York: Bloomsbury Press, 2015), 96.

75 Ibid., 127.

76 Patrick Radden Keefe, *Empire of Pain: The Secret History of the Sackler Dynasty* (New York: Doubleday, 2021), 341; David E. Weissman and J. David Haddox, "Opioid Pseudoaddiction—an Iatrogenic Syndrome," *Pain* 36, no. 3 (March 1989): 363–6.

77 Elisabeth Rosenthal, "Patients in Pain Find Relief, Not Addiction, in Narcotics," nytimes.com, March 28, 1993.

78 Radden Keefe, *Empire of Pain*, 377.

79 Quinones, *Dreamland*, 156.

80 Kathleen J. Frydl, "The Pharma Cartel," in *The War on Drugs: A History*, ed. David Farber (New York: New York University Press, 2022), 332; the Sacklers claimed that OxyContin's market share was never more than 4 percent, and it's certainly true that there were a wide range of opioids also being abused: Nucynta, Duragesic, Opana, Roxicodone, Fentora, Actiq. But Purdue's market share of *all* opioid painkillers was closer to 30 percent, and in any event, they were the market leaders after which other opioid-producing pharmaceutical companies followed, Radden Keefe, *Empire of Pain*, 364–5.

81 Emily Feng, "'We Are Shipping to the U.S.': Inside China's Online Synthetic Drug Networks," npr.org, November 17, 2020.

82 Sam Quinones, *The Least of Us: True Tales of America and Hope in the Time of Fentanyl and Meth* (London: Bloomsbury, 2021), 78.

83 Jesse C. Baumgartner and David C. Radley, "The Drug Overdose Toll in 2020 and Near-Term Actions for Addressing It," The Commonwealth Fund, August 16, 2021, commonwealthfund.org.

84 Radden Keefe, *Empire of Pain*, 390–1.

85 Howard S. Becker, "Becoming a Marijuana User," *American Journal of Sociology* 59 (1953): 235–42.

86 De Quincey, *Confessions*, 48.

87 "Certainly I want heroin; but almost anything else would do just as well. It's boredom and A[nno] D[omini]! A girl or a game of chess would fill the gap," Aleister Crowley, quoted in John Symonds, *The Great Beast: The Life of Aleister Crowley* (London: Rider, 1951), 295.

88 Eric Detzer, *Monkey on my Back: The Autobiography of a Modern Opium Eater* (London: Abacus, 1988), 48.

89 Hari, *Chasing the Scream*, 166.

5. Amphetamines, or Inappropriate Perseverance

1 We might also include here methylphenidate (Ritalin), bupropion (Wellbutrin), and other "pep pills" that are similar to amphetamine in their structures and effects.

2 Frank Owen, *No Speed Limit: The Highs and Lows of Meth* (New York: St. Martin's Press, 2007), 7.

3 Nicolas Rasmussen, *On Speed: The Many Lives of Amphetamine* (New York: New York University Press, 2008), 185.

4 Lester Grinspoon and Peter Hedblom, "A Historical Overview of Amphetamines," in *Amphetamines*, ed. Nancy Harris (Detroit: Greenhaven Press, 2005), 24.

5 Rasmussen, *On Speed*, 48.

6 Quoted in Peter Andreas, *Killer High: A History of War in Six Drugs* (Oxford: Oxford University Press, 2020), 188.

7 Peter Andreas, "How Methamphetamine Became a Key Part of Nazi Military Strategy," time.com, January 7, 2020.

8 Rasmussen, *On Speed*, 55.

9 Richard Davenport-Hines, *The Pursuit of Oblivion: A Global History of Narcotics* (New York: W. W. Norton, 2004), 308; David T. Courtwright, *Forces of Habit: Drugs and the Making of the Modern World* (Cambridge, MA: Harvard University Press, 2001), 78.

10 "From 1966 to 1969, American soldiers swallowed more amphetamines than all the American and British soldiers combined for the whole of the Second World War," Jim Hogshire, *Pills-A-Go-Go: A Fiendish Investigation into Pill Marketing, Art, History, and Consumption* (Venice, CA: Feral House, 1999), 106.

11 Andreas, *Killer High*, 199–202.

12 Lukasz Kamienski, *Shooting Up: A Short History of Drugs and War* (Oxford: Oxford University Press, 2016), 278.

13 Ibid., 279.

14 Daniel Oberhaus, "Why Can't We All Take Modafinil?," vice.com, November 30, 2016.

15 "Why Does the US Military Buy So Much Viagra?," bbc.com, July 27, 2017.

16 Jennifer Senior, "The Prozac, Paxil, Zoloft, Wellbutrin, Celexa, Effexor, Valium, Klonopin, Ativan, Restoril, Xanax, Adderall, Ritalin, Haldol, Risperdal, Seroquel, Ambien, Lunesta, Elavil, Trazodone War," *New York Magazine*, February 4, 2011.

17 Lester Grinspoon and Peter Hedblom, *The Speed Culture: Amphetamine Use and Abuse in America* (Cambridge, MA: Harvard University Press, 1975), 18.

18 Miriam Joseph, *Speed: Its History and Lore* (London: Carlton Books, 2000), 22.

19 Joseph Heller, *Something Happened* (New York: Simon and Schuster, 1997), 21.
20 Jonathan Levy, *Ages of American Capitalism: A History of the United States* (New York: Random House, 2021), 341.
21 Rasmussen, *On Speed*, 104.
22 Energy drinks spiked with alcohol are essentially speedballs, though they're not typically thought of as such.
23 Owen, *No Speed Limit*, 85.
24 Rasmussen, *On Speed*, 162.
25 Quoted in Davenport-Hines, *The Pursuit of Oblivion*, 342.
26 Courtwright, *Forces of Habit*, 79.
27 Edward M. Brecher and the editors of *Consumer Reports*, "Speed Freaks of the Late 1960s," in *Amphetamines*, ed. Nancy Harris (Detroit: Greenhaven Press, 2005), 58.
28 Rasmussen, *On Speed*, 206.
29 Ibid., 212.
30 David Herzberg, "Between the Free Market and the Drug War," in *The War on Drugs: A History*, ed. David Farber (New York: New York University Press, 2022), 281; Rasmussen, *On Speed*, 215.
31 Mick Farren, *Speed-Speed-Speedfreak: A Fast History of Amphetamine* (Port Townsend, WA: Feral House, 2010), 100.
32 Owen, *No Speed Limit*, 17.
33 Ibid., chap. 7; Farren, *Speed-Speed-Speedfreak*, 146, 148.
34 Farren, *Speed-Speed-Speedfreak*, 145.
35 Quoted in Owen, *No Speed Limit*, 74.
36 Farren, *Speed-Speed-Speedfreak*, 144.
37 Rasmussen, *On Speed*, 225.
38 Philip Jenkins, *Synthetic Panics: The Symbolic Politics of Designer Drugs* (New York: New York University Press, 1999), 142.
39 Rasmussen, *On Speed*, 243.
40 Darryl S. Inaba and William E. Cohen, *Uppers, Downers, All Arounders: Physical and Mental Effects of Psychoactive Drugs*, 7th ed. (Medford, OR: CNS Productions, 2011), 3.31.
41 Rasmussen, *On Speed*, 248.
42 "General Prevalence of ADHD," Children and Adults with Attention-Deficit/Hyperactivity Disorder, chadd.org.
43 Ray Moynihan and Alan Cassels, *Selling Sickness: How the World's Biggest Pharmaceutical Companies Are Turning Us All into Patients* (New York: Nation Books, 2005), 69.
44 Ibid., 73.
45 Rasmussen, *On Speed*, 237.
46 Ibid., 250.
47 Andreas, *Killer High*, 202.
48 Edward M. Brecher and the editors of *Consumer Reports, Licit*

and Illicit Drugs: The Consumers Union Report on Narcotics, Stimulants, Depressants, Inhalants, Hallucinogens, and Marijuana —Including Caffeine, Nicotine, and Alcohol (Boston: Little, Brown, 1972), 287–8.

49 Farren, *Speed-Speed-Speedfreak*, 196.

50 Claudio Gallo and Hartmut Rosa, "Social Acceleration and the Need for Speed," *Los Angeles Review of Books*, June 28, 2015, lareviewofbooks.org.

6. Psychotropics, or Diagnostic Creeps and Rational Paranoids

1 Peter D. Kramer, *Against Depression* (New York: Penguin Books, 2006), 65.

2 Ibid., 65.

3 Ibid., 62.

4 Ibid., 61.

5 Ibid., 62, 61.

6 Jacob M. Appel, "Beyond Fluoride: Pharmaceuticals, Drinking Water and the Public Health," *Huffington Post*, March 18, 2010, huffpost.com.

7 Richard DeGrandpre, *The Cult of Pharmacology: How America Became the World's Most Troubled Drug Culture* (Durham: Duke University Press, 2006).

8 Andrea Tone, *The Age of Anxiety: A History of America's Turbulent Affair with Tranquilizers* (New York: Basic Books, 2009), 8.

9 George Miller Beard, *American Nervousness, Its Causes and Consequences* (New York: G. P. Putnam's Sons, 1881), 138.

10 Quoted in Richard DeGrandpre, *Ritalin Nation: Rapid-fire Culture and the Transformation of Human Consciousness* (New York: W. W. Norton, 1999), 111.

11 Quoted in Barbara Sicherman, "The Paradox of Prudence: Mental Health in the Gilded Age," *Journal of American History* 62, no. 4 (March 1976): 893.

12 Tone, *The Age of Anxiety*, 11.

13 Quoted in T. J. Jackson Lears, *No Place of Grace: Antimodernism and the Transformation of American Culture, 1880–1920* (New York: Pantheon Books, 1981), 52.

14 W. H. Auden, *The Age of Anxiety: A Baroque Eclogue* (New York: Faber and Faber, 1947), 3.

15 Tone, *The Age of Anxiety*, xvii.

16 Simon Taylor, "The Modern Condition: The Invention of Anxiety,

1840–1970" (PhD diss., Columbia University, 2014), 19–20.

17 Quoted in Mickey C. Smith, *Small Comfort: A History of the Minor Tranquilizers* (New York: Praeger, 1985), 54, 17.

18 Paul Tillich, "The Significance of Kurt Goldstein for Philosophy of Religion," *Journal of Individual Psychology* 15, no. 1 (May 1959): 22.

19 Cf. Taylor, "The Modern Condition."

20 Smith, *Small Comfort*, 69; Joel T. Braslow and Stephen R. Marder, "History of Psychopharmacology," *Annual Review of Clinical Psychology* 15 (2019): 33.

21 Tone, *The Age of Anxiety*, 106.

22 Barry Meier, *Pain Killer: A "Wonder" Drug's Trail of Addiction and Death* (New York: St. Martin's Press, 2003), 201.

23 Gerald Posner, *Pharma: Greed, Lies, and the Poisoning of America* (New York: Avid Reader Press, 2020), 202.

24 *Journal of the American Medical Association* 211, no. 4 (January 26, 1970), 595–6.

25 Tone, *The Age of Anxiety*, 179.

26 Ibid., 197; quoted in David Herzberg, *Happy Pills in America: From Miltown to Prozac* (Baltimore: Johns Hopkins University Press, 2009), 64.

27 Quoted in Tone, *The Age of Anxiety*, 86.

28 Mike Gravel, "Corporate Pushers: The Only Thing Amusing about the Ethical Drug Industry Is Its Name," in *Uppers and Downers*, ed. David E. Smith and Donald R. Wesson (Englewood Cliffs: Prentice Hall, Inc., 1973), 124.

29 Tone, *The Age of Anxiety*, 217.

30 Ray Moynihan and Alan Cassels, *Selling Sickness: How the World's Biggest Pharmaceutical Companies Are Turning Us All into Patients* (New York: Nation Books, 2005), chap. 7.

31 Tone, *The Age of Anxiety*, 222.

32 David Herzberg, *White Market Drugs: Big Pharma and the Hidden History of Addiction in America* (Chicago: University of Chicago Press, 2020), 292.

33 Herzberg, *Happy Pills in America*, 37.

34 Andrew Scull, *Madness in Civilization: A Cultural History of Insanity from the Bible to Freud, from the Madhouse to Modern Medicine* (Princeton: Princeton University Press, 2015), 341.

35 Braslow and Marder, "History of Psychopharmacology," 37.

36 Scull, *Madness in Civilization*, 389.

37 David Healy, *The Creation of Psychopharmacology* (Cambridge, MA: Harvard University Press, 2002), 173.

38 Ibid., 367.

39 Ibid., 368.

40 Braslow and Marder, "History of Psychopharmacology," 39.

41 Michael Mechanic, "Psychiatry's New Diagnostic Manual: 'Don't Buy It. Don't Use It. Don't Teach It.'" *Mother Jones*, May 14, 2013.

42 Moynihan and Cassels, *Selling Sickness*, 26.

43 Scull, *Madness in Civilization*, 375.

44 Ibid., 376–7; Braslow and Marder, "History of Psychopharmacology," 41.

45 Timothy Williams, "A Psychologist as Warden? Jail and Mental Illness Intersect in Chicago," nytimes.com, July 30, 2015.

46 Healy, *The Creation of Psychopharmacology*, 80.

47 Quoted in Smith, *Small Comfort*, 20.

48 Quoted in Herzberg, *Happy Pills*, 152.

49 Lauren Slater, *Blue Dreams: The Science and the Story of the Drugs That Changed Our Minds* (New York: Little, Brown, 2018), 139.

50 Braslow and Marder, "History of Psychopharmacology," 32.

51 Peter D. Kramer, *Listening to Prozac: The Landmark Book about Antidepressants and the Remaking of the Self*, rev. ed. (New York: Penguin Books, 1997), 40.

52 Prozac Advertisement, *American Journal of Psychiatry* 155, no. 5 (April 1998); Zoloft Advertisement, *American Journal of Psychiatry* 155, no. 11 (November 1998).

53 Edward Shorter, *How Everyone Became Depressed: The Rise and Fall of the Nervous Breakdown* (Oxford: Oxford University Press, 2013), 152.

54 Quoted in ibid., 157.

55 Ibid., 157.

56 Clayton J. Mosher and Scott Akins, *Drugs and Drug Policy: The Control of Consciousness Alteration* (Thousand Oaks, CA: Sage Publications, 2006), 344.

57 Slater, *Blue Dreams*, 226.

58 Ibid., 172–3, 217; cf. Scull, *Madness in Civilization*, 404.

59 Scull, *Madness in Civilization*, 392; Jim Hogshire, *Pills-A-Go-Go: A Fiendish Investigation into Pill Marketing, Art, History and Consumption* (Venice, CA: Feral House, 1999), 56–7.

60 Qingqing Liu et al., "Changes in the Global Burden of Depression from 1990 to 2017: Findings from the Global Burden of Disease Study," *Journal of Psychiatric Research* 126 (2020): 134–40.

61 Slater, *Blue Dreams*, 163.

62 That the blockbuster drug of the '90s is not what it announced itself to be is hardly surprising. Since the postwar era, there's actually been very little in the way of real drug breakthroughs. Like the rest of American industry, in the neoliberal period, Big Pharma was financialized, investing less and less in productive research and development, and more and more in "scooping up government-funded science, gaming the system to extend licenses and delay

generic competition, and aggressively seeking short-term stock boosts through maximum pricing, mergers, acquisitions and take-overs," Alexander Zaitchik, "How Big Pharma Was Captured by the One Percent," *New Republic*, June 28, 2018.

63 DeGrandpre, *The Cult of Pharmacology*, 38–9; for grisly accounts of antidepressant-induced psychotic episodes, see DeGrandpre, *The Cult of Pharmacology*, 49–50.

64 Slater, *Blue Dreams*, 188–9.

65 Quoted in ibid., 190.

66 Ibid., 195; Healy, *The Creation of Psychopharmacology*, 170.

67 Slater, *Blue Dreams*, 51; cf. Scull, *Madness in Civilization*, 402.

68 "FDA Approves Pill with Sensor That Digitally Tracks If Patients Have Ingested Their Medication," US Food and Drug Administration, fda.gov.

69 DeGrandpre, *The Cult of Pharmacology*, 56.

70 Slater, *Blue Dreams*, 194.

71 Joseph Dumit, *Drugs for Life: How Pharmaceutical Companies Define Our Health* (Durham: Duke University Press, 2012), 113.

72 Ibid., 15.

73 Ibid., 40.

74 Joseph E. Davis, *Chemically Imbalanced: Everyday Suffering, Medication, and Our Troubled Quest for Self-Mastery* (Chicago: University of Chicago Press, 2020).

7. Psychedelics, or the Dialectic of Control

1 Oakley S. Ray, *Drugs, Society, and Human Behavior* (Saint Louis: C. V. Mosby, 1972), 271.

2 Ibid., 274.

3 I'm including in this category LSD, psilocybe mushrooms (and their isolate, psilocybin), ayahuasca (and its isolate, DMT), peyote (mescaline), and MDMA. There are many other drugs, particularly the ever-proliferating number of synthetics, that could be included in this category (see the Vaults of Erowid at erowid.org for a remarkably comprehensive catalog). One might question my inclusion of MDMA here—to certain drug connoisseurs, it's unquestionably an "empathogen" rather than a psychedelic, and in any event, its chemical structure is that of an amphetamine—but I've included it here because it is a key component of the contemporary "psychedelic renaissance."

4 William S. Burroughs, *Naked Lunch* (New York: Grove Press, 1992), 96.

5 A thesis on "extoxication" is out there waiting for a literary scholar to write it.

6 Andy Letcher, *Shroom: A Cultural History of the Magic Mushroom* (London: Faber and Faber, 2006), 270.

7 Jean Cocteau, *Opium: The Diary of an Addict*, trans. Ernest Boyd (London: Longmans, Green, 1932), 35.

8 Stephen Kinzer, *Poisoner in Chief: Sidney Gottlieb and the CIA Search for Mind Control* (New York: Henry Holt, 2019), 53.

9 Ibid., 82.

10 "Communist Brainwashing—Are We Prepared?," *New Republic*, June 8, 1953, 5–6.

11 Alexander Cockburn and Jeffrey St. Clair, *Whiteout: The CIA, Drugs and the Press* (London: Verso, 1999), chap. 6.

12 "For the brave of heart and strong of stomach," see Kinzer, *Poisoner in Chief*, 25–6, for accounts of the experiments run in Unit 731.

13 Quoted in Cockburn and St. Clair, *Whiteout*, 195.

14 Quoted in Martin A. Lee and Bruce Shlain, *Acid Dreams: The Complete Social History of LSD: The CIA, the Sixties, and Beyond* (New York: Grove Press, 1985), 27.

15 Kinzer, *Poisoner in Chief*, 51.

16 Lee and Shlain, *Acid Dreams*, 33.

17 Kinzer, *Poisoner in Chief*, 74.

18 Quoted in Jill Jonnes, *Hep-Cats, Narcs, and Pipe Dreams: A History of America's Romance with Illegal Drugs* (New York: Scribner, 1996), 225.

19 Kinzer, *Poisoner in Chief*, 138–9.

20 Quoted in ibid., 139.

21 Ibid., 131.

22 Ibid., 98.

23 Michael Parenti, "Conspiracy and Class Power," recorded on cassette from a radio broadcast in 1993 in Berkeley, California, YouTube video, April 20, 2020.

24 Cockburn and St. Clair, *Whiteout*, chap. 4.

25 Quoted in Kinzer, *Poisoner in Chief*, 130.

26 Quoted in Lee and Shlain, *Acid Dreams*, 71.

27 Which is funny, of course, given that most people associate Huxley with the drug dystopia portrayed in *Brave New World*. Huxley's final novel, *Island*, describes a chemical utopia made possible by a mushroom called *moksha*, and is much more in line with his own beliefs. But as writer Marcus Boon notes, there is something creepy in the progression: "What separates the drugged utopia of *Island* from the drugged dystopia of *Brave New World* is more a change of sentiment than anything else. The old goal of social control, which Huxley denounced in the 1930s, was reconfigured as the

new goal of 'health,'" Marcus Boon, *The Road of Excess: A History of Writers on Drugs* (Cambridge, MA: Harvard University Press, 2002), 253.

28 See Andy Letcher, *Shroom: A Cultural History of the Magic Mushroom* (London: Faber and Faber, 2006), chap. 5–6; Stephen Siff, *Acid Hype: American News Media and the Psychedelic Experience* (Urbana: University of Illinois Press, 2015), 73.

29 Quoted in Siff, *Acid Hype*, 100.

30 Frank Barron, "Motivational Patterns in LSD Usage," in *LSD, Man, and Society*, ed. Richard C. DeBold and Russell C. Leaf (Middletown, CT: Wesleyan University Press, 1967), 4.

31 Quoted in Siff, *Acid Hype*, 149.

32 Quoted in Lee and Shlain, *Acid Dreams*, 79.

33 See Tom Wolfe, *The Electric Kool-Aid Acid Test* (New York: Farrar, Straus and Giroux, 1968).

34 Jay Stevens, *Storming Heaven: LSD and the American Dream* (New York: Grove Press, 1998), xiii.

35 Quoted in Lee and Shlain, *Acid Dreams*, 109.

36 Quoted in ibid., 166; Watts echoed Leary: "Whenever the insights one derives from mystical vision become politically active, they always create their own opposite ... a parody," quoted in Todd Gitlin, *The Sixties: Years of Hope, Days of Rage* (New York: Bantam Books, 1987), 211.

37 Gitlin, *The Sixties*, 253.

38 Ibid., chap. 8.

39 Quoted in Lee and Shlain, *Acid Dreams*, 253.

40 Joan Didion, *Slouching Towards Bethlehem: Essays* (New York: Farrar, Straus and Giroux, 1968), 122.

41 Quoted in Lee and Shlain, *Acid Dreams*, 227.

42 Ibid., 232.

43 Ibid., 197; cf. Theodore Roszak, *The Making of a Counter Culture: Reflections of the Technocratic Society and Its Youthful Opposition* (Garden City, NY: Anchor Books, 1969), 176.

44 Lee and Shlain, *Acid Dreams*, 224.

45 Gitlin, *The Sixties*, 243.

46 Boon, *The Road of Excess*, 264

47 David Matza and Gresham M. Sykes, "Juvenile Delinquency and Subterranean Values," *American Sociological Review* 26, no. 5 (October 1961): 716–17.

48 Erika Dyck, *Psychedelic Psychiatry: LSD from Clinic to Campus* (Baltimore: Johns Hopkins University Press, 2008), 56; in 1956, Aldous Huxley proposed the term "phanerothyme" for drugs that induce mystical consciousness to Osmond in a couplet: "To make this trivial world sublime / Take half a Gramme of phanerothyme."

Osmond replied: "To fathom hell or soar angelic / Just take a pinch of psychedelic."

49 Harold A. Abramson, "Introduction," in *The Use of LSD in Psychotherapy and Alcoholism*, ed. Harold A. Abramson (Indianapolis: Bobbs Merrill, 1967), ix; see also W. V. Caldwell, *LSD Psychotherapy: An Exploration of Psychedelic and Psycholytic Therapy* (New York: Grove Press, 1968).

50 Quoted in Lee and Shlain, *Acid Dreams*, 93.

51 Matthew Oram has recently claimed that the rise in prominence of the clinical trial with the biological revolution in psychiatry made it difficult to justify the context-dependent action of psychedelic-assisted psychotherapy; in other words, it wasn't all just countercultural backlash; see Matthew Oram, *The Trials of Psychedelic Therapy: LSD Psychotherapy in America* (Baltimore: Johns Hopkins University Press, 2018).

52 Torsten Passie, "The Early Use of MDMA ('Ecstasy') in Psychotherapy (1977–1985)," *Drug Science, Policy and Law*, 4 (2018): 1–19.

53 Peter Simek, "Playboy: Ecstasy Was Legal in 1984, and It Was Glorious," Multidisciplinary Association for Psychedelic Studies, maps.org; cf. Matthew Collin, *Altered State: The Story of Ecstasy Culture and Acid House* (London: Serpent's Tail, 1997).

54 Nicolas Rasmussen, *On Speed: The Many Lives of Amphetamine* (New York: New York University Press, 2008), 228; see Marsha Rosenbaum, "Ecstasy: America's New 'Reefer Madness,'" *Journal of Psychoactive Drugs* 34, no. 2 (2002): 137–42.

55 Jesse Noakes, "Psychedelic Renaissance: Could MDMA Help with PTSD, Depression and Anxiety?," theguardian.com, April 13, 2019.

56 Ryan Grim, *This Is Your Country on Drugs: The Secret History of Getting High in America* (Hoboken: John Wiley and Sons, 2009), 238.

57 Hannah Kuchler, "How Silicon Valley Rediscovered LSD," *Financial Times*, August 10, 2017.

58 Michael Pollan, *How to Change Your Mind: What the New Science of Psychedelics Teaches Us about Consciousness, Dying, Addiction, Depression, and Transcendence* (London: Penguin Books, 2019), 51.

59 Kuchler, "How Silicon Valley Rediscovered LSD."

60 Quoted in Stevens, *Storming Heaven*, 137; cf. Danielle Giffort, *Acid Revival: The Psychedelic Renaissance and the Quest for Medical Legitimacy* (Minneapolis: University of Minnesota Press, 2020).

61 Martin Torgoff, *Can't Find My Way Home: America in the Great Stoned Age, 1945–2000* (New York: Simon and Schuster, 2004), 416.

62 Ibid., 415.
63 Quoted in Pollan, *How to Change Your Mind*, 168.
64 Patrick Butler, "'Hidden' Drug Users Who Won't Be found Burgling Your Home to Fund Their Habit," theguardian.com, March 14, 2012.
65 Paul Stamets, "Paul Stamets on the Magic of Mushrooms," interview by Ethan Nadelmann, *Psychoactive*, February 24, 2022, iheart.com.
66 Christina Caron, "Can MDMA Save a Marriage?," nytimes.com, February 8, 2022.
67 Though someone already beat him to the punch: Charles Wininger, *Listening to Ecstasy: The Transformative Power of MDMA* (Rochester: Park Street Press, 2020).
68 Ross Ellenhorn and Dimitri Mugianis, "The Corporatization of Psychedelics Would Be a Disaster," *Jacobin*, February 18, 2022; Rustam Yulbarisov, "LSD Capitalism Promises a Bad Trip for Us All," *Jacobin*, April 2, 2022.
69 Luke Goldstein, "Rollups: The Emerging Magic Mushroom Monopoly," *The American Prospect*, January 10, 2022; *Global Psychedelic Drugs Market: Size and Forecast with Impact Analysis of COVID-19 (2021–2025)*, Research and Markets, March 2021, researchandmarkets.com.
70 Ellenhorn and Mugianis, "The Corporatization of Psychedelics."
71 Mike Jay, *Mescaline: A Global History of the First Psychedelic* (New Haven: Yale University Press, 2019), 57.
72 Alexander S. Dawson, *The Peyote Effect: From the Inquisition to the War on Drugs* (Berkeley: University of California Press, 2018), 2.
73 Marcus Boon, *The Road of Excess: A History of Writers on Drugs* (Cambridge, MA: Harvard University Press, 2002), 230.
74 Jay, *Mescaline*, 72.
75 Omer C. Stewart, *Peyote Religion: A History* (Norman: University of Oklahoma Press, 1987), 148.
76 Jay, *Mescaline*, 126.
77 Stewart, *Peyote Religion*, 232.
78 Ibid., 235.
79 Quoted in Boon, *The Road of Excess*, 251.
80 Aldous Huxley, *The Doors of Perception and Heaven and Hell* (New York: Harper, 2009), 72.
81 Jay, *Mescaline*, 172.
82 Ibid., 230.
83 Ibid., 252–3.
84 Quoted in ibid., 250.

85 Madison Margolin and Shelby Hartman, "Jews, Christians, and Muslims Are Reclaiming Ancient Psychedelic Practices, and That Could Help with Legalization," *Rolling Stone*, April 23, 2021; Shelby Hartman and Madison Margolin, "The Psychedelics Industry Could Offer a Whole New Approach to Work," *Rolling Stone*, October 2, 2021.

86 Peter Stafford identifies nine main families of psychedelics in *Psychedelics Encyclopedia*, but ketamine is not in any of them, Peter Stafford, *Psychedelics Encyclopedia* (Berkeley: Ronin Publishing, 1993).

87 Anna Silman, "Leave Your Body at the Door: How Ketamine Became the Drug of Choice for Our Dissociated Moment," *The Cut*, November 21, 2019, thecut.com.

88 Philip Jenkins, *Synthetic Panics: The Symbolic Politics of Designer Drugs* (New York: New York University Press, 1999), chap. 3.

89 Ibid., 64, 67.

90 Jim Newton, "Defense Says Use of Force on King Was Reasonable: Courts: A Motion in the Upcoming Civil Rights Case Refers to a 'PCP-Crazed Giant,' Suggesting That the Officers' Lawyers Will Aggressively Challenge King's Actions," latimes.com, January 20, 1993.

91 Jenkins, *Synthetic Panics*, 66.

92 Ibid., 59.

93 Ibid., 161; "The drug usually involved in date rape (at least 50%), car accidents, suicide, and murder is alcohol by a very wide margin," Karl Jansen, *Ketamine: Dreams and Realities* (Santa Cruz, CA: Multidisciplinary Association for Psychedelic Studies, 2004), 39.

94 Bita Moghaddam, *Ketamine* (Cambridge: MIT Press, 2021), 10.

95 Ibid., 17.

96 Karen Joe-Laidler and Geoffrey Hunt, "Sit Down to Float: The Cultural Meaning of Ketamine Use in Hong Kong," *Addiction Research and Theory* 16, no. 3 (June 2008): 259–71.

97 Charlie Williams, "On 'Modified Human Agents': John Lilly and the Paranoid Style in American Neuroscience," *History of the Human Sciences* 32, no. 5 (2019).

98 Jansen, *Ketamine*, 59.

99 Ibid., 60.

100 Moghaddam, *Ketamine*, 99.

101 Quoted in Kit Kelly, *The Little Book of Ketamine* (Berkeley: Ronin Publishing, 1999), 43.

102 Emily Witt, "Ketamine Therapy Is Going Mainstream. Are We Ready?," *New Yorker*, December 29, 2021.

8. Cocaine, or Hyperreality

1 Herman Knapp, *Cocaine and Its Use in Ophthalmic and General Surgery* (New York: G. P. Putnam's Sons, 1885), 15–16.

2 Dominic Streatfeild, *Cocaine* (London: Virgin Books, 2005), 72.

3 Ibid., 72; Mike Jay, *Emperors of Dreams: Drugs in the Nineteenth Century* (Sawtry: Dedalus, 2000), 164.

4 Joseph F. Spillane, "Making a Modern Drug: The Manufacture, Sale, and Control of Cocaine in the United States, 1880–1920," in *Cocaine: Global Histories*, ed. Paul Gootenberg (London: Routledge, 1999), 22; in W. Golden Mortimer's *History of Coca* from 1901, for instance, Köller is the one credited with suddenly concentrating "the attention of the scientific world ... on the remarkable possibilities of the Coca leaf," W. Golden Mortimer, *History of Coca: "The Divine Plant" of the Incas* (San Francisco: Fitz Hugh Ludlow Memorial Library Edition, 1974), 182.

5 Steven B. Karch, *A Brief History of Cocaine* (Boca Raton: CRC Press, 1998), 44.

6 Brigid Delaney, "It's Not Cocaine: What You Need to Know about the Pope's Coca Drink," theguardian.com, July 9, 2015.

7 Spillane, "Making a Modern Drug," 27, 32; cocaine and alcohol together produce a new compound (cocaethylene) that makes their combination much more potent than either substance by itself.

8 David T. Courtwright, "The Rise and Fall and Rise of Cocaine in the United States," in *Consuming Habits: Drugs in History and Anthropology*, ed. Jordan Goodman, Paul E. Lovejoy, and Andrew Sherratt (London: Routledge, 1995), 209; the first cocaine scare paled in comparison to the second; "At the height of the global panic in 1910, the total amount of cocaine produced worldwide was less than ten tons; in 1995 it was 740 tons and rising," Jay, *Emperors of Dreams*, 183.

9 Streatfeild, *Cocaine*, 140.

10 Paul Gootenberg, *Andean Cocaine: The Making of a Global Drug* (Chapel Hill: University of North Carolina Press, 2008), 199.

11 Ibid., 202.

12 Ibid., 198.

13 "The Cocain Habit," editorial, *Journal of the American Medical Association* 34, no. 25 (June 23, 1900): 1637; the next month, Dr. Frank Jones wrote a letter to the editor, adding that "the 'cocain sniffer' is found among the lowest and most ignorant class, both white and black," "Cocain Habit among the Negroes," *Journal of the American Medical Association* 35, no. 3 (July 21, 1900): 175.

14 Virginia Berridge, *Demons: Our Changing Attitudes to Alcohol, Tobacco, and Drugs* (Oxford: Oxford University Press, 2013), 87.

15 Carl L. Hart, "How the Myth of the 'Negro Cocaine Fiend' Helped Shape American Drug Policy," *The Nation*, January 29, 2014; Hamilton Wright also played to his audience: "It has been stated on very high authority that the use of cocaine by the negroes of the South is one of the most elusive and troublesome questions which confront the enforcement of the law in most of the Southern States," quoted in Doris Marie Provine, *Unequal under the Law: Race in the War on Drugs* (Chicago: University of Chicago Press, 2007), 75.

16 Tim Madge, *White Mischief: A Cultural History of Cocaine* (Edinburgh: Mainstream Publishing, 2001), 147; see Richard Ashley, *Cocaine: Its History, Uses, and Effects* (New York: Warner Books, 1975), 81.

17 Richard Davenport-Hines, *The Pursuit of Oblivion: A Global History of Narcotics* (New York: W. W. Norton, 2004), 359.

18 Madge, *White Mischief*, 148.

19 Courtwright, "The Rise and Fall and Rise of Cocaine in the United States," 216.

20 Streatfeild, *Cocaine*, 240–1.

21 Ibid., 241.

22 Gootenberg, *Andean Cocaine*, 311.

23 Quoted in David Farber, *Crack: Rock Cocaine, Street Capitalism, and the Decade of Greed* (Cambridge: Cambridge University Press, 2019), 32; cf. Peter Maguire, *Thai Stick: Surfers, Scammers, and the Untold Story of the Marijuana Trade* (New York: Columbia University Press, 2015), 107.

24 David Herzberg, *White Market Drugs: Big Pharma and the Hidden History of Addiction in America* (Chicago: University of Chicago Press, 2020), 236; there is historically an inverse relationship between the prevalences of cocaine and amphetamine use: when amphetamines became available in the '30s, cocaine was practically forgotten for a generation; see Farber, *Crack*, 27.

25 Quoted in Nicolas Rasmussen, *On Speed: The Many Lives of Amphetamine* (New York: New York University Press, 2008), 183.

26 Gootenberg, *Andean Cocaine*, 301.

27 Streatfeild, *Cocaine*, 245.

28 Matthew Brzezinski, "Re-engineering the Drug Business," in *Busted: Stone Cowboys, Narco-Lords, and Washington's War on Drugs*, ed. Mike Gray (New York: Thunder's Mouth Press/Nation Books, 2002), 101.

29 Streatfeild, *Cocaine*, 255.

30 Alexander Cockburn and Jeffrey St. Clair, *Whiteout: The CIA, Drugs and the Press* (London: Verso, 1999), chap. 7; Peter McFarren and Fadrique Iglesias, *The Devil's Agent: Life, Times, and Crimes of Nazi Klaus Barbie* (Bloomington, IN: Xlibris, 2013).

31 Farber, *Crack*, 82.
32 Craig Reinarman and Harry G. Levine, "The Crack Attack: Politics and Media in the Crack Scare," in *Crack in America: Demon Drugs and Social Justice*, ed. Craig Reinarman and Harry G. Levine (Berkeley: University of California Press, 1997), 34; "Historically, from the so-called 'gin epidemic' in the slums of eighteenth-century London to the 'heroin epidemic' of urban America in the 1970s, the worst drug problems have always been concentrated amid profound and preexisting human suffering," Craig Reinarman et al., "The Contingent Call of the Pipe: Bingeing and Addiction among Heavy Cocaine Smokers," in *Crack in America*, 90.
33 Quoted in Farber, *Crack*, 81.
34 Quoted in ibid., 46.
35 *Crack: Cocaine, Corruption, and Conspiracy*, directed by Stanley Nelson (Netflix, 2021).
36 Notorious B.I.G., "Ten Crack Commandments," *Life after Death*, Bad Boy, 1997; cf. Donald J. Trump with Kate Bohner, *Trump: The Art of the Comeback* (New York: Random House, 1997).
37 Farber, *Crack*, 133.
38 "New Drug Law: The Senate's Duty; The House Offers Only Empty Promises," nytimes.com, October 4, 1988.
39 Streatfeild, *Cocaine*, 310.
40 Dan Baum, *Smoke and Mirrors: The War on Drugs and the Politics of Failure* (Boston: Little, Brown, 1996), 218.
41 Farber, *Crack*, 4–5, 129; Farber believes "the mass media was by no means solely responsible for white Americans' widely shared fear that crack cocaine was coming for them and their children and that something had to be done to stop it," ibid., 132; but given the relentless and groundless media offensive, prepped for battle by the equally absurd PCP scare, it's difficult to separate natural inclinations in the populace from what's been absorbed from the news.
42 Quoted in ibid., 144.
43 Madge, *White Mischief*, 165; for the history of the phrase "Just say no," see Emily Dufton, *Grass Roots: The Rise and Fall and Rise of Marijuana in America* (New York: Basic Books, 2017), chap. 10.
44 Elizabeth Hinton, *From the War on Poverty to the War on Crime: The Making of Mass Incarceration in America* (Cambridge, MA: Harvard University Press, 2016), 316–17.
45 Courtwright, "The Rise and Fall and Rise of Cocaine," 219.
46 Ryan Grim, *This Is Your Country on Drugs: The Secret History of Getting High in America* (Hoboken: John Wiley and Sons, 2009), 174; see Gary Webb, *Dark Alliance: The CIA, the Contras, and the Crack Cocaine Explosion* (New York: Seven Stories Press, 1998).
47 Streatfeild, *Cocaine*, 353.

48 Peter Dale Scott and Jonathan Marshall, *Cocaine Politics: Drugs, Armies, and the CIA in Central America* (Berkeley: University of California Press, 1991), 172.

49 Jean Baudrillard, *Simulacra and Simulation*, trans. Sheila Faria Glaser (Ann Arbor: University of Michigan Press, 1994), 19.

50 Streatfeild, *Cocaine*, 310.

51 Cf. Farber, *Crack*, 4–5.

52 The *prevalence* of its use peaked but absolute demand did not fall until the mid-2000s (see appendix A). And today, global *production* is higher than it has ever been, it's just no longer Americans who are consuming the bulk of it.

53 Madge, *White Mischief*, 163.

54 Streatfeild, *Cocaine*, 247.

55 Davenport-Hines, *The Pursuit of Oblivion*, 433.

56 United Nations Office on Drugs and Crime, *World Drug Report 2010* (New York: United Nations, 2010), 65.

57 Davenport-Hines, *The Pursuit of Oblivion*, 433.

58 Madge, *White Mischief*, 167.

59 Peter Andreas, *Killer High: A History of War in Six Drugs* (Oxford: Oxford University Press, 2020), 255.

60 Streatfeild, *Cocaine*, 404.

61 Ibid., 414–15.

62 Ibid., 275.

63 Ibid., 472.

64 Paul Gootenberg, "Shifting South: Cocaine's Historical Present and the Changing Politics of Drug War, 1975–2015," in *Cocaine: From Coca Fields to the Streets*, ed. Enrique Desmond Arias and Thomas Grisaffi (Durham: Duke University Press, 2021), 290.

65 Andreas, *Killer High*, 238.

66 On the role of the American drug war in making Mexican drug trafficking more violent, see Benjamin T. Smith, *The Dope: The Real History of the Mexican Drug Trade* (New York: W. W. Norton, 2021).

67 Andreas, *Killer High*, 244; for the role of the US drug war in creating such paramilitary groups, through which "globalized capitalism can penetrate new territories and social worlds ... through the use of terror," see Dawn Paley, *Drug War Capitalism* (Oakland, CA: AK Press, 2014), 18.

68 Gootenberg, "Shifting South," 291.

69 Beau Kilmer, "Uncle Sam's Cocaine Nosedive: A Brief Exploration of a Dozen Hypotheses," in *After the Drug Wars: Report of the LSE Expert Group on the Economics of Drug Policy*, ed. John Collins (London: London School of Economics and Political Science, 2016), 67–75.

70 Hans W. Maier, *Maier's Cocaine Addiction*, trans. Oriana Josseau Kalant (Toronto: Addiction Research Foundation, 1987), 101.
71 Ibid., 101, 259.
72 Arthur Conan Doyle, *The Sign of the Four* (Racine, WI: Whitman Publishing, 1922), 9.
73 Arthur Conan Doyle, "Adventure 11: The Final Problem," *Memoirs of Sherlock Holmes*, etc.usf.edu.

9. Marijuana, or Profit Wins in the End

1 The Daily Dish, "Drugs and Toxicity," *Atlantic*, March 24, 2007; Oakley S. Ray, *Drugs, Society, and Human Behavior* (Saint Louis: C. V. Mosby, 1972), 261.
2 Terrence McCoy, "Even Casually Smoking Marijuana Can Change Your Brain, Study Says," washingtonpost.com, April 16, 2014; Carl L. Hart, *Drug Use for Grown-Ups: Chasing Liberty in the Land of Fear* (New York: Penguin Press, 2021), 100; the "gateway" theory was articulated early on by anti-marijuana evangelist Earle Albert Rowell. Anslinger himself denied this theory in hearings for the Marihuana Tax Act, but he would later adopt it, Larry Sloman, *Reefer Madness: The History of Marijuana in America* (Indianapolis: Bobbs Merrill, 1979), 108; Norman E. Zinberg and John A. Robertson, "Today's Drug Laws," in *Drugs in American Life*, ed. Morrow Wilson and Suzanne Wilson (New York: H. W. Wilson, 1975), 50–1.
3 These include the Indian Hemp Drugs Commission report (1894); the Panama Canal Zone studies (1925 and 1932); Walter Bromberg, "Marihuana Intoxication: A Clinical Study of Cannabis Sativa Intoxication," *American Journal of Psychiatry* 91, no. 2 (1934): 303–30; "Facts and Fancies About Marijuana," *Literary Digest* 122 (1936): 7–8; the LaGuardia Report (1944); President's Commission on Law Enforcement and Administration of Justice, *Task Force Report: Narcotics and Drug Abuse* (Washington, DC: US Government Printing Office, 1967); the Wootton Report (1968); Board of Health, *Drug Dependency and Drug Abuse in New Zealand* (Wellington: A. R. Shearer, 1970); "Interim Report of the Commission of Inquiry into the Non-medical Use of Drugs" (Ottawa: Queen's Printer for Canada, 1970); and the National Academy of Sciences study (1982). Mike Gray describes one of the studies used by anti-marijuana advocates, the "1975 study by Robert Heath of Tulane that proved marijuana smoke causes brain damage. Since rhesus monkeys don't normally smoke, Dr. Heath had to force it on them

through a gas mask, but he was unable to precisely measure the amount of dope that was pumped in. One fellow scientist claimed that Heath's doses were in the range of ninety joints a day, and he wondered whether the brain damage could have been caused by these large amounts," Mike Gray, *Drug Crazy: How We Got into This Mess and How We Can Get Out* (London: Routledge, 2000), 295; none of this is to say that cannabis cannot be harmful or addictive, simply that its harmfulness and addictiveness have routinely been blown way out of proportion.

4 Martin Booth, *Cannabis: A History* (London: Doubleday, 2003), 49.

5 Farhad Daftary, *The Assassin Legends: Myths of the Isma'ilis* (London: I. B. Tauris, 1995); Harry J. Anslinger, "Marijuana—Assassin of Youth," *Reader's Digest*, February 1938, druglibrary .org.

6 At the time opium and cocaine were coming up for prohibition, "the working classes had shown little or no interest in 'abusing' [marijuana]. Its limited vogue among bohemians, artists and aesthetes if anything reinforced the feeling that this was a foreign and frightening habit, an acquired taste only of interest to literary *poseurs* and perverts," Mike Jay, *Emperors of Dreams: Drugs in the Nineteenth Century* (Sawtry: Dedalus, 2000), 119.

7 David F. Musto, *The American Disease: Origins of Narcotic Control* (Oxford: Oxford University Press, 1999), 219; Richard J. Bonnie and Charles H. Whitebread II, *The Marihuana Conviction: A History of Marihuana Prohibition in the United States* (Charlottesville: University Press of Virginia, 1974), 47; Sarah Siff has found that there may have simply been confusion about what marijuana was, and that datura and astragalus were possibly mistaken for cannabis at the time, Sarah Siff, "The Name of the Weed: Marijuana Effects and Datura Alkaloid," (paper presented at Rethinking Alcohol and Drugs: Global Transformations / Local Practices in History, Mexico City, June 15–17, 2022).

8 Isaac Campos has recently argued that the associations around marijuana in Mexico were born in Mexico itself and drifted north to influence US policy, Isaac Campos, *Home Grown: Marijuana and the Origins of Mexico's War on Drugs* (Chapel Hill: University of North Carolina Press, 2012).

9 Sloman, *Reefer Madness*, 125.

10 Quoted in Booth, *Cannabis*, 151.

11 Ibid., 152.

12 Quoted in Richard Davenport-Hines, *The Pursuit of Oblivion: A Global History of Narcotics* (New York: W. W. Norton, 2004), 347–8.

13 Sloman, *Reefer Madness*, chap. 4.

14 Davenport-Hines, *The Pursuit of Oblivion*, 346–7.

15 Quoted in Alexander Cockburn and Jeffrey St. Clair, *Whiteout: The CIA, Drugs and the Press* (London: Verso, 1999), 72.

16 "Remarks Made by Honorable Alexander M. MacLeod, Judge of the Passaic County Court, Paterson, N.J., at the Time of Sentencing Charles Ervin, a Marihuana Peddler," in US Treasury Department, Bureau of Narcotics, *Traffic in Opium and Other Dangerous Drugs for the Year Ended December 31, 1951* (Washington, DC: United States Government Printing Office), 10–11.

17 Larry Sloman describes a similar about-face regarding sharks: In 1926, Anslinger wrote an article arguing that it was a myth that sharks attack humans. After receiving a good deal of hate mail, he then wrote a correction wherein he describes in gory detail various shark attacks that read much like his later descriptions of murderous addicts, Sloman, *Reefer Madness*, 33.

18 Bonnie and Whitebread, *The Marihuana Conviction*, 52.

19 Davenport-Hines, *The Pursuit of Oblivion*, 348; cf. Howard S. Becker, *Outsiders: Studies in the Sociology of Deviance* (New York: Free Press, 1963), 135–46.

20 Davenport-Hines, *The Pursuit of Oblivion*, 348; Jerome Himmelstein takes issue with what he calls the "Anslinger Hypothesis" that marijuana prohibition was the fruit of one man's effort to enforce his moral ideals and protect his bureau, Jerome L. Himmelstein, *The Strange Career of Marihuana: Politics and Ideology of Drug Control in America* (Westport, CT: Greenwood Press, 1983), 27; Himmelstein's point that the blame cannot be put *solely* on Anslinger alone is fair enough, but it is fact that his agency was at risk of being collapsed in the mid-1930s. Anslinger's sociopathy, and its destructive consequences, are also well documented. A scathing review of his writings concludes: "In the works of Mr. Anslinger, there are either no references or references to volumes which my assistants and I have checked and which, in our checking, we find to be based upon much hearsay and little or no experimentation. We found a mythology in which later writers cite the authority of earlier writers, who also had little evidence. We have found, by and large, what can most charitably be described as a pyramid of prejudice, with each level of the structure built upon the shaky foundations of earlier distortions," Linda Whitlock, "Marijuana," *Crime and Delinquency Literature* 2 (1970): 363–82.

21 Davenport-Hines, *The Pursuit of Oblivion*, 348.

22 Booth, *Cannabis*, 153.

23 Greg Campbell, *Pot, Inc.: Inside Medical Marijuana, America's Most Outlaw Industry* (New York: Sterling, 2012), 60.

24 Andrew Weil and Winifred Rosen, *From Chocolate to Morphine: Everything You Need to Know About Mind-Altering Drugs* (Boston: Mariner, 2004), 136.

25 Quoted in Bonnie and Whitebread, *The Marihuana Conviction*, 227.

26 Quoted in Paul Arras, *The Lonely Nineties: Visions of Community in Contemporary US Television* (Basingstoke: Palgrave Macmillan, 2018), 116.

27 Ernest L. Abel, *Marihuana: The First Twelve Thousand Years* (New York: Plenum Press, 1980), 172, 176, 178; Booth, *Cannabis*, 209.

28 Booth, *Cannabis*, 233.

29 Ibid., 239.

30 Ray, *Drugs, Society, and Human Behavior*, 260.

31 Dan Baum, *Smoke and Mirrors: The War on Drugs and the Politics of Failure* (Boston: Little, Brown, 1996), 110.

32 Ibid., 110.

33 Bonnie and Whitebread, *The Marihuana Conviction*, 238.

34 Ibid., 260.

35 Baum, *Smoke and Mirrors*, 87.

36 Bonnie and Whitebread, *The Marihuana Conviction*, 283.

37 Booth, *Cannabis*, 246.

38 Quoted in ibid., 253.

39 John P. Walters, "Illegal Drugs and Presidential Leadership," *Wall Street Journal*, September 24, 1996.

40 Baum, *Smoke and Mirrors*, 103.

41 Booth, *Cannabis*, 253–4; Baum, *Smoke and Mirrors*, 122.

42 Emily Dufton, *Grass Roots: The Rise and Fall and Rise of Marijuana in America* (New York: Basic Books, 2017), 151.

43 Ibid., 161.

44 Ibid., 196; as Dennis Rosenbaum concludes, "Across more than 30 studies, the collective evidence from evaluations with reasonably good scientific validity suggests that the core D.A.R.E. program does not prevent drug use in the short term, nor does it prevent drug use when students are ready to enter high school or college," quoted in Ryan Grim, *This Is Your Country on Drugs: The Secret History of Getting High in America* (Nashville: Turner Publishing, 2010), 101.

45 Grim, *This Is Your Country on Drugs*, 92.

46 Ray, *Drugs, Society, and Human Behavior*, 260.

47 Sloman, *Reefer Madness*, 26.

48 Abel, *Marihuana*, 184.

49 Booth, *Cannabis*, 293.

50 Campbell, *Pot, Inc.*, 184, 129.

51 Emily Swanson, "Here Are All the Drugs Americans Want to Legalize," *Huffington Post*, December 6, 2017.

52 Dom Roberjot, "Step inside Dosist's Wellness Experience, the First Self-Branded Stand-Alone Cannabis Boutique," *Natural Products*, March 17, 2020, naturalproductsglobal.com.

53 Quoted in Martin A. Lee, *Smoke Signals: A Social History of Marijuana—Medical, Recreational and Scientific* (New York: Scribner, 2013), 430.

54 Campbell, *Pot, Inc.*, xiv.

55 Ibid., 17.

56 Edward-Isaac Dovere, "The Marijuana Superweapon Biden Refuses to Use," *Atlantic*, July 6, 2020.

57 Dhrumil Mehta, "Americans from Both Parties Want Weed to Be Legal. Why Doesn't the Federal Government Agree?," *FiveThirtyEight*, April 23, 2021, fivethirtyeight.com; Big Pharma also has a vested interest in keeping marijuana on Schedule I and has funded anti-legalization lobbying groups, Dufton, *Grass Roots*, 253.

58 Rustam Yulbarisov, "LSD Capitalism Promises a Bad Trip for Us All," *Jacobin*, April 2, 2022.

59 Thomas Fuller, "No Longer the 'Devil's Lettuce': How the Town of Weed Embraced Weed," nytimes.com, May 18, 2021.

60 Robin Goldstein and Daniel Sumner, "Can Legal Weed Win?," New Books in Drugs, Addiction and Recovery, June 7, 2022, newbooks network.com.

61 Matt Stieb, "Who's Getting Rich from Weed Legalization in New York?," *New York Magazine*, April 10, 2021; June Thunderstorm, "Smoked Out," *The Baffler*, September 2017.

62 Kevin A. Sabet, *Smokescreen: What the Marijuana Industry Doesn't Want You to Know* (Nashville: Forefront Books, 2021), 35.

63 Rachel Sandler, "Cannabis King: Boris Jordan, Chairman of Curaleaf, Becomes the Only Pot Billionaire," *Forbes*, September 10, 2019.

64 Kojo Koram, "Cannabis and Capitalism: The Question of Ownership within Drug Policy Reform," *Common Wealth*, April 20, 2020, common-wealth.co.uk.

65 Stieb, "Who's Getting Rich?"

66 Quoted in Sabet, *Smokescreen*, 113.

67 Bonnie and Whitebread, *The Marihuana Conviction*, 299.

68 Patrick Anderson, *High in America: The True Story behind NORML and the Politics of Marijuana* (New York: Viking Press, 1981), 89; the organizational relationship fractured because the head of Amorphia slept with the head of NORML's wife.

69 Ibid., 89.

Conclusion

1 Benjamin Y. Fong and Melissa Naschek, "NGOism: The Politics of the Third Sector," *Catalyst* 5, no. 1 (Spring 2021).

2 Dominic Streatfeild, *Cocaine* (London: Virgin Books, 2005), 512; cf. Edward M. Brecher and the editors of *Consumer Reports, Licit and Illicit Drugs: The Consumers Union Report on Narcotics, Stimulants, Depressants, Inhalants, Hallucinogens, and Marijuana —Including Caffeine, Nicotine, and Alcohol* (Boston: Little, Brown, 1972), 522.

3 Martin Booth, *Opium: A History* (New York: St. Martin's Griffin, 1996), 342.

4 Mike Jay, *Emperors of Dreams: Drugs in the Nineteenth Century* (Sawtry: Dedalus, 2000), 240.

5 Arnold S. Trebach, *The Heroin Solution* (New Haven: Yale University Press, 1982), 236.

6 Mike Gray, *Drug Crazy: How We Got into This Mess and How We Can Get Out* (New York: Routledge, 2000), 256.

7 Jeremy Kuzmarov, *The Myth of the Addicted Army: Vietnam and the Modern War on Drugs* (Amherst: University of Massachusetts Press, 2009), 110; Jill Jonnes, *Hep-Cats, Narcs, and Pipe Dreams: A History of America's Romance with Illegal Drugs* (New York: Scribner, 1996), 293.

8 Carl L. Hart, *Drug Use for Grown-Ups: Chasing Liberty in the Land of Fear* (New York: Penguin Press, 2021), 19.

9 Dan Baum, *Smoke and Mirrors: The War on Drugs and the Politics of Failure* (Boston: Little, Brown, 1996), 256.

10 Christina Jacqueline Johns, *Power, Ideology, and the War on Drugs: Nothing Succeeds Like Failure* (New York: Praeger, 1992), 84.

11 *The Challenge of Crime in a Free Society: A Report by the President's Commission on Law Enforcement and Administration of Justice* (Washington, DC: US Government Printing Office, 1967), ojp.gov; quoted in Baum, *Smoke and Mirrors*, 5.

12 Baum, *Smoke and Mirrors*, 77; John Clegg and Adaner Usmani, "The Economic Origins of Mass Incarceration," *Catalyst* 3, no. 3 (Fall 2019).

13 Cf. Ross Coomber, "Social Fear, Drug-Related Beliefs, and Drug Policy," in *Drugs and Culture: Knowledge, Consumption, and Policy*, ed. Geoffrey Hunt et al. (Surrey, UK: Ashgate, 2011), chap. 1.

14 David E. Smith and George R. Gay, *"It's So Good, Don't Even Try It Once": Heroin in Perspective* (Hoboken: Prentice Hall, 1972).

15 Quoted in Oakley S. Ray, *Drugs, Society, and Human Behavior* (Saint Louis: C. V. Mosby, 1972), 270; for other science fiction on this theme, see Robert Silverberg, *Drug Themes in Science Fiction*

(Rockville, MD: National Institute on Drug Abuse, 1974); Francis Fukuyama argued in *Our Posthuman Future* that we were in the midst of massive changes in neuropharmacology and biotechnology (which he jarringly refers to as "the recommencement of history"), as evidenced (for him) in the astonishing effectiveness of drugs like Prozac and Ritalin (see chapter 6), Francis Fukuyama, *Our Posthuman Future: Consequences of the Biotechnology Revolution* (New York: Farrar, Straus and Giroux, 2002).

16 Laurence M. Vance, "Mises Explains the Drug War," Mises Institute, September 25, 2017, mises.org; Milton Friedman, "Why Drugs Should Be Legalized," YouTube video, uploaded June 6, 2008.

17 Robert J. MacCoun and Peter Reuter, *Drug War Heresies: Learning from Other Vices, Times, and Places* (Cambridge: Cambridge University Press, 2001), 181.

18 Matthew Collin, *Altered State: The Story of Ecstasy Culture and Acid House* (London: Serpent's Tail, 1997), 99–101.

19 Cameron Costa, "Peter Thiel–Backed Psychedelic Start-up's Shares Pop in Wall Street Debut," cnbc.com, June 18, 2021.

20 Cf. Mattha Busby, *Should All Drugs Be Legalized?* (London: Thames and Hudson, 2022), 133–4.

21 Andrew Weil and Winifred Rosen, *From Chocolate to Morphine: Everything You Need to Know About Mind-Altering Drugs* (Boston: Mariner, 2004), 29.

22 Hart, *Drug Use for Grown-Ups*.

23 Adaner Usmani and John Clegg, "The Economic Origins of Mass Incarceration," *Catalyst* 3, no. 3 (Fall 2019).

24 Quoted in Johns, *Power, Ideology, and the War on Drugs*, 176.

25 Gabriel G. Nahas, *Marihuana: Deceptive Weed* (New York: Raven Press, 1973), 319–20.

26 "91 Percent of Americans Support Criminal Justice Reform, ACLU Polling Finds," ACLU, November 16, 2017, aclu.org; Nick Sibilla, "Poll: Most Americans Want Congress to Abolish Civil Forfeiture," *Forbes*, November 12, 2020; cf. Baum, *Smoke and Mirrors*, 325; Kathleen J. Frydl, *The Drug Wars in America, 1940–1973* (Cambridge: Cambridge University Press, 2013), 430–6; in general, drug decriminalization (as accomplished in the example of Portugal) is a much sounder goal than drug legalization; see Jerrold Winter, *Our Love Affair with Drugs: The History, the Science, the Politics* (Oxford: Oxford University Press, 2020), 169; Thomas Dormandy, *Opium: Reality's Dark Dream* (New Haven: Yale University Press, 2012), 294; Gray, *Drug Crazy*, 323.

27 Johns, *Power, Ideology, and the War on Drugs*, 175.

28 Richard Davenport-Hines, *The Pursuit of Oblivion: A Global History of Narcotics* (New York: W. W. Norton, 2004), 452.

29 David F. Musto, "Opium, Cocaine and Marijuana in American History," *Scientific American* 265, no. 1 (July 1991): 40–7.

30 Hermann Schlüter, *The Brewing Industry and the Brewery Workers' Movement in America* (Cincinnati: International Union of the United Brewery Workmen of America, 1910), 306.

31 Brecher, *Licit and Illicit Drugs*, 514; cf. Edward Preble and John J. Casey, "Taking Care of Business—The Heroin User's Life on the Street," *International Journal of the Addictions* 4, no. 1 (1969): 1–24.

32 Eric C. Schneider, *Smack: Heroin and the American City* (Philadelphia: University of Pennsylvania Press, 2008), 204.

33 Michael Shiner, *Drug Use and Social Change: The Distortion of History* (Basingstoke: Palgrave Macmillan, 2009), 146, 142.

34 Elliott Currie, *Reckoning: Drugs, the Cities, and the American Future* (New York: Hill and Wang, 1993), 299.

35 Anne Case and Angus Deaton, *Deaths of Despair and the Future of Capitalism* (Princeton: Princeton University Press, 2020), 8.

36 Cf. ibid., chap. 13.

37 Philippe Bourgois, *In Search of Respect: Selling Crack in El Barrio* (Cambridge: Cambridge University Press, 2003), 319.

Appendix A

1 W. J. Rorabaugh, *The Alcoholic Republic: An American Tradition* (Oxford: Oxford University Press, 1979), table A1.2; "Alcohol Consumption per Capita from All Beverages in the U.S. from 1850 to 2019," Statista, May 11, 2021, statista.com.

2 David Herzberg, *White Market Drugs: Big Pharma and the Hidden History of Addiction in America* (Chicago: University of Chicago Press, 2020), 293; "Aggregate Production Quota History for Selected Substances," DEA, deadiversion.usdoj.gov.

3 *Medicine Use and Spending in the U.S.: A Review of 2017 and Outlook to 2022*, IQVIA Institute for Human Data Science, April 2018, iqvia.com, 19.

4 Ibid., 292.

5 "Per Capita Cigarette Consumption in the United States from 1900 to 2015," Statista, December 9, 2016, statista.com.

6 Susan S. Everingham and C. Peter Rydell, *Modeling the Demand for Cocaine*, RAND Drug Policy Research Center, 1994, rand.org, figure S.7, p. xvi; William Rhodes et al., *What America's Users Spend on Illegal Drugs: 1988–1998*, US Department of Justice Office of Justice Programs, December 2000, ojp.gov, table 7, p. 18;

What America's Users Spend on Illegal Drugs: 2000–2010, RAND Corporation, February 2014, obamawhitehouse.archives.gov, figure 4.1, p. 43; Gregory Midgette et al., *What America's Users Spend on Illegal Drugs, 2006–2016*, RAND Corporation, 2019, rand.org, figure 4.3, p. 37.

7 "Coffee, Tea, Cocoa: Per Capita Availability," US Department of Agriculture Economic Research Service, ers.usda.gov.

8 Rhodes et al., *What America's Users Spend on Illegal Drugs: 1988–1998*; Midgette et al., *What America's Users Spend on Illegal Drugs, 2006–2016*.

9 Andrew Golub and Bruce D. Johnson, "The Rise of Marijuana as the Drug of Choice among Youthful Adult Arrestees," *National Institute of Justice Research in Brief*, June 2001, ojp.gov; "National Survey on Drug Use and Health (NSDUH)," Substance Abuse and Mental Health Data Archive, datafiles.samhsa.gov.

10 "National Survey on Drug Use and Health (NSDUH)."

11 Herzberg, *White Market Drugs*, 291.

12 Ibid.

13 Bin Yu et al., "Marijuana Legalization and Historical Trends in Marijuana Use among US Residents Aged 12–25: Results from the 1979–2016 National Survey on Drug Use and Health," *BMC Public Health* 20 (2020).

Appendix B

1 Dan Baum, *Smoke and Mirrors: The War on Drugs and the Politics of Failure* (Boston: Little, Brown, 1996), 110; Ahmad A. Aref, "Cannabis and Glaucoma," *Glaucoma Today*, July/August 2020.